Population

The Dynamics of
Demographic Change

Population

The Dynamics of Demographic Change

Charles B. Nam
Florida State University

Susan O. Gustavus
University of Cincinnati

HOUGHTON MIFFLIN COMPANY   Boston
Atlanta   Dallas   Geneva, Illinois
Hopewell, New Jersey   Palo Alto   London

Printed in the USA

Library of Congress Catalog Card Number: 75-31031

ISBN: 0-395-20627-8

To Rebecca, Jessica, and David
Achievements of a small family norm

Contents

Preface

In recent years, public attention has increasingly been focused on the rapid changes in population taking place throughout the world and the impact which these changes have on ways of human life. The call for greater concern about population developments has come from many quarters — from government officials, lay leaders, environmentalists, and social scientists. Their approaches to the population question are varied. Some sound an alarm of impending doom without carefully assessing the facts; others express complete optimism based on faith in the human race to conquer its major problems; still others reserve normative judgment about the course of population and attempt instead to carefully study the causes and consequences of population change in a logical and systematic manner. The latter approach is that of the scientist and, especially, of the demographer — the specialist in population studies. It is the approach taken in this volume.

Every textbook is written with certain objectives in mind. Ours can be stated explicitly at the outset.

First, the book is written primarily for undergraduate college students taking a first course in population or demography. The book can also be used in departments of sociology, economics, political science, geography, or urban planning. This is not to say that it will not be of interest to others, for we have attempted to write it in such a way that a wide audience will find it both readable and informative.

Second, in contrast with lengthy volumes that often say more than the reader wants or has time to read, and with exceedingly short books which do not leave the reader with an adequate understanding of the subject matter, this treatise is designed to deal with the fundamentals of population study in an economical but complete manner. It should be possible for the student to cover the whole book in a reasonable amount of time, say in an academic quarter. If further reading of the subject is desired, guidance is given through suggested readings at the end of each chapter.

Third, the book gives a broad social orientation to demography. Any study of population must necessarily touch upon several academic fields since the subject has medical, biological, geographical, psychological, and economic, as well as sociological, aspects. But given our own limited training, and our belief that a general social approach is the single most useful approach to studying population, we have tried to stress this social approach. This means that we will be looking at population change mainly from the perspective of the sociologist, but we will not ignore other perspectives where they seem to be particularly relevant for comprehension of population trends.

Fourth, as the title suggests, the book perceives population in a dynamic framework. Too often the student of population is made to see it as a static phenomenon — people as almost lifeless objects making up a society or community and identified as statistics in a tabular presentation. Statistics are valuable as a tool for studying populations mainly because they enable us to give a needed quantitative dimension to demography; and censuses and vital records are critical to demographic analysis mainly because we can use them to provide a snapshot of the continuing process of population change. However, understanding the demographic process means not only counting and classifying people but also fully comprehending the mechanics of the process — what generates it, how it takes place, what conditions modify it.

Finally, we want to inform readers about both the determinants and consequences of demographic change. Population factors and social factors can be viewed as in continuous interaction, the second set affecting the first, and vice versa. If population change is to be understood by key decision-makers as well as by the public, its social determinants must be analyzed and those that are most critical identified. Once this is achieved, intelligent decisions can be made about how, if at all, the population process might be altered. At the same time, if an understanding of population change is needed to assess its impact on the quality of life, then the alternative ways demographic change affect social institutions and the behavior of individuals and groups in society must be traced out.

Achieving these objectives is a large order which cannot be solely the work of two persons. While some of the research reported here, the particular approach used, the organization of materials, and the form of expression are our own, the book is the result of efforts of many people. We are particularly grateful to our fellow social scientists who, over the years, have published the results of their studies and thus enabled us to integrate them into a more comprehensive framework. Phillips Cutright of Indiana University, Ross Purdy of the University of North Carolina, and Paul Williams of the University of Rochester read drafts of the manuscript and offered valuable suggestions for revision. Secretarial assistance was provided by Dorie Chesser and Betty Sue Kurth. Finally, thanks are due to the Houghton Mifflin staff for their faith that this book would eventually emerge.

Charles B. Nam

Susan O. Gustavus

Population

The Dynamics of
Demographic Change

*"But demographic projections
indicate that within twenty years, this town will be
big enough for both of us."*

© Handelsman cartoon reproduced by permission.

1

Overview of Population Trends

We have chosen to begin this book with a broad overview of population, looking at its development over history and its current status in the world and major regions. Our aim is to give the reader some notion of the dimensions of world population — the nature and pace of its evolution, the distinguishing characteristics of trends, and prospects for the future. We have concentrated in this first chapter of the book on a description of world demographic changes. Discussion of the basic components of population trends and explanatory variables have been reserved for later chapters. We hope that in this way the whole process of population development will unfold in a manner that will make it most perceptible and understandable.

The Status of World Population

Not long ago, it was calculated that if the current rate of world population growth were to continue for another 6,500 years, people would be accumulating so rapidly on earth that human bodies not only would cover the sphere but would be piling up away from the earth at a speed exceeding the velocity of light! This startling projection makes two points: first, that it is inconceivable that population on earth can grow to such dimensions, and second, that we have the inherent potential for very rapid population increase in the world.

The illustration is, of course, fantastic, since conditions of life in that far-distant year would be impossible. Some forces must operate to ultimately reduce the population growth rate. Later in this book we shall cover the reasons why world population has achieved its present level and what forces would be required to check its growth. It would benefit us at present, however, to examine the current conditions of world population growth — how many people there are in different parts of the world, how fast the population is growing in these areas, and what we can reasonably expect in the way of numbers of people in the near future.

The Numerical Picture

It is not yet possible to obtain a head count of all the humans on earth, but a good approximation would place the world's population in 1975 at close to four billion. Considering that there are roughly 135.8 million square kilometers of inhabitable land area and inland waters, this places the population density of the world at twenty-nine persons per square kilometer. This can hardly be regarded as overcrowding, but two factors must be considered. First, while much of the area on earth is technically inhabitable, either conditions for settlement are not at all ideal or the resources required to make the land habitable would be extremely costly. Second, even if we consider that there is far more land than is needed presently or in the near future to accommodate the population, the desire of most people for an adequate level of living and a gregarious social life requires them to congregate in particular places. If a given square kilometer contained twenty-nine persons, the chances are that all or nearly all of the people within it would be living together on a few acres rather than residing randomly throughout the area.

The nearly four billion people of the world in 1975 were distributed unevenly over the surface of the globe, as shown in Appendix B.[1] A majority (57 percent) were to be found on the Asian continent, with roughly one-fifth (21 percent) in the People's Republic of China and another one-seventh (15 percent) in India alone. Europe (excluding the USSR) contained 12 percent, Africa about 10 percent, and Latin America 8 percent. The USSR and North America together had only 12 percent of the world's population, and the remaining fraction of 1 percent were in Oceania. The United States, with 214 million people, had a population which was one-fourth the size of that of China, slightly smaller than that of the USSR, roughly four times as large as that of France or the United Kingdom, and about ten times the size of that of Canada.

Rates of Growth

Although the world's population in 1975 was growing at a rate of approximately 2 percent per year, the population in some parts of the world was growing more rapidly and in other parts less rapidly. Latin America's annual growth rate was 2.7 percent, while the rate was 2.6 in Africa, 2.1 in Asia, and 2.0 in Oceania. Below-average growth rates were found in North America (0.9), the USSR (1.0), and Europe (0.6). Within each of these broad regions of the world, population growth rates differed considerably. For example, within Africa the rate was as low as 1.0 in Gabon and as high as 3.4 in Rhodesia and 3.3 in Kenya; within Asia, it varied from 1.2 in Cyprus to a phenomenal 7.1 in Kuwait; within Latin America, the range was from 0.4 in Granada to 3.5 in Honduras; and within Europe there was a rate of only 0.2 in several countries as compared with a growth rate of 2.7 in Albania.

If the world growth rate of 2 percent per year were to continue into the future, it would take only thirty-five years for the population of the world to double its present size. That is, not long after the start of the new century the world's population would reach about eight billion. Whether we attain that figure or not will depend on the course of the population growth rate in the years ahead.

At present rates of growth, it would take Austria 347 years to double its population, the United States and the USSR about 70 to 80 years to double theirs, China 41 years to reach twice its present size,

India 29 years to double its population, and Kuwait only 10 years to increase from 1.1 to 2.2 million. It is quite clear, therefore, that some areas of the world are growing at a remarkable pace, while the rate of increase of others is rather moderate. None of these rates of growth is fixed, however, and it is reasonable to expect that most of them will be modified in years to come.

The Future Population and the Public's Perspective

Trying to determine the population of an area at a future date is at once a science and an art. It is a science in the sense that the analyst can use a systematic and carefully detailed procedure for estimating the population in subsequent years. For instance, the most widely used technique for estimating future population involves separating total population into its basic components of fertility, mortality, and migration (residential mobility), and estimating the probable trends in each component under various assumptions about developments in the components. It may be assumed, by way of illustration, that fertility will continue at its present rate, or, alternatively, that the rate may go up a certain amount, or, alternatively, that the rate may go down a certain amount. By putting together different combinations of estimated components, the analyst produces a set of population projections which are the consequence of the assumptions made. Determining future population is an art to the degree that the analyst must exercise sensitivity and sound judgment in deciding what the possible alternative assumptions are, which ones seem most reasonable, and which combinations of assumptions are most realistic.

The United Nations staff of demographers has combined the science and the art to produce the "medium" estimates of future population shown in Appendix B. Assuming a reduction of current fertility levels, world population in the year 2000 would be six and a quarter billion. The population of the Asian continent, over three and a half billion, would be close to the present world population. A more conservative projection, one that assumes a more modest decline in the fertility level, would result in over seven billion by the year 2000.

What size population might we, therefore, expect or plan for in the next few decades? Only crystal-ball gazers would attempt a precise estimate, and their record of accuracy is not encouraging. As fertility patterns develop in the years ahead, we shall be in a better position to choose the most reasonable assumptions about future trends. In the meantime, we can content ourselves with some notion about the range of possibilities and the high probability that world population will be between six and seven billion by the turn of the century. In any event, a substantial increase in the number of humans on earth can be anticipated in the next twenty-five years.

There is every reason to believe that the recent upsurge in public awareness of the dimension of population growth in the world and in most countries is due partly to the rate of growth itself and partly to improved education about population matters. Some segments of the society have formed interest groups concerned with the causes and consequences of population growth, and the mass media have been quick to respond to this growing concern by publicizing the facts about population change.

In 1965, the public in twenty-two countries was asked, "Is your impression that the number of people in (survey country) is increasing, decreasing, or remaining about the same?" About 86 percent believed their nation was growing, and in all the nations at least three-quarters of the respondents believed their population was increasing.[2] The respondents were then asked, "How about the number of people in the world as a whole? Do you think an increase in the world population would be a good thing or a bad thing?" and "All things considered, do you think having a larger population would be a good thing or a bad thing for this country?" An overwhelming proportion of Europeans, a substantial majority of Asians, and a bare majority of Latin Americans and Africans felt an increase in world population to be a bad thing. However, while a majority of the sampled populations believed world population increase to be a bad thing, most people believed a population increase would be a good thing for their own country.[3]

Recent studies in the United States revealed that a simple majority considered the population growth rate in the country to be a "serious problem"[4] and to pose one of the "greatest threats today to the future social and economic well-being of the country."[5] Many persons did not feel the "problem" or the "threat," however.

It is clear, therefore, that public perception of the population situation varies between and within societies. How much these different attitudes toward population are associated with knowledge about demographic facts is questionable, but recent research has established that attitudes about population growth and distribution vary to only a small extent among people with different characteristics (e.g., education, income, religion, age, and sex).[6] This suggests that differences in the perception of population problems arise from basic values that are not always indicated by general social and demographic characteristics.

Historical Development of World Population

A critical examination of the course of population from earliest times to the present seems in order, both because knowledge of history can heighten public awareness of population trends and because historical analysis of population provides a basis for understanding the current status and future prospects of population.

Population Trends in Prehistory

Estimates of when people first roamed the earth range from six hundred thousand to two million years ago, and new archaeological findings periodically give a basis for further speculation on the matter. Figure 1.1 crudely depicts the long history of the growth of population and suggests that from time immemorial until the modern era, world population was maintained at a precariously low level. It is likely that in those early periods people were congregated in a limited number of locations. Those in some locations were periodically decimated by waves of excess mortality, and those groups that survived withstood extinction by a combination of high fertility, development of natural

Figure 1.1   Long-range trend of world population growth

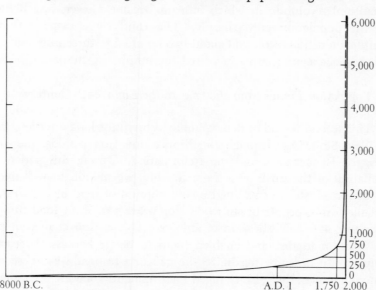

Source: John Durand, "The Modern Expansion of World Population," in *Proceedings of the American Philosophical Society*, Philadelphia, June 1967, p. 139.

immunity to certain diseases, and wandering to escape natural disasters. Increasing ability to cope with the environment enabled some settlements to increase their numbers and provide the base for further population gains.

Although the curve shown in the figure outlines a gradual and relatively smooth growth pattern until about the seventeenth or eighteenth century, Deevey proposes that an evolution of population took place in stages.[7] In the nearly one million years prior to 8000 B.C., the number of hominids (human-like primates, including human beings) was barely sufficient to guarantee survival of the species. Humans' intellectual superiority, claims Deevey, enabled them to maintain their numbers and compete favorably in a hunting and food-gathering era. A second population surge about ten thousand years ago heralded the agricultural revolution in which humans became plowers and herders, and the population grew sharply. The third surge came with the scientific-industrial revolution about two hundred to three hundred years ago and once again sharply increased the number of humans.[8]

Population Trends from 8000 B.C. to the Eighteenth Century

This second period of demographic history is of long duration, from the New Stone Age through the Bronze and Iron periods, the Dark Ages, the Renaissance, and the Reformation. During this period the population of the earth grew from roughly five million to well over a half billion. Instead of relying on consumption of food in its naturally available forms, people began to develop other sources of food through agriculture and domestication of animals. This critical change in people's relation to the land enabled them to better harness the earth's resources. In order to maximize the gains to be made by these new economic modes, they also changed their residential modes. Wandering gave way to settlement, and isolation of family and kinship groups was replaced by formation of communities, commercial towns, and then cities. Great empires and cultures developed, and the major religions came into being.

By about 4000 B.C. the number of people on the globe may well have reached eighty-six million. At the birth of Christ, it is believed that the figure stood between two hundred and four hundred million.[9] It must be understood, however, that no enumerations of population took place and that these estimates are the result of a piecing together of human history by anthropologists, paleontologists, and other scientists. The figures are approximate, but they do indicate very broad differences in order of magnitude between large epochs in past eras of history.

At the beginning of the Christian era, population size stabilized and in some periods even declined as devastating disease took a heavy toll of the populace. By the year 1000 the growth rate recovered, and from then until the middle of the fourteenth century population increase was rapid, especially in northern Europe. The bubonic plague, the Black Death of Europe, hit in 1348 and thwarted population growth for several decades. In fact, by the year 1400 the numbers on earth, and especially in Europe, were below what they had been fifty years earlier. Before another hundred years had passed, however, social, economic, and intellectual revolutions set the stage for the modern period of population expansion. By 1650, probably five hundred million or so people dotted the sphere, and the pace of demographic growth was augmented.

Population Trends Since the Eighteenth Century

What has come to be referred to as the world "population explosion" was a more or less gradual process which picked up momentum sometime during the late seventeenth and early eighteenth centuries. It is not possible to establish a critical turning point when the rate of population growth of the world began to accelerate markedly. For the sake of convenience, we have begun our statistical analysis of this modern period with the year 1750. "Medium" estimates of the population of the world and its major areas beginning at that time are shown in Table 1.1.

World population in the mid-eighteenth century had attained a level of nearly eight hundred million. The mark of one billion was first reached shortly after 1800, and one and two-thirds billion was topped by 1900. The 1975 population level thus was five times that in 1750 and more than twice that at the turn of the present century. In terms of growth rates, the population increased roughly 0.5 percent per year from 1750 to 1900, close to 1.0 percent per year in the first half of the twentieth century, and nearly 2.0 percent per year since 1950. On a relative basis, the real "population explosion" first occurred in the twentieth century.

Since the upsurge in population during the modern period is associated with the Industrial Revolution and the related social and eco-

Table 1.1 "Medium" estimates of population of the world
and major areas, 1750–1950

Areas	Population (millions)				
	1750	1800	1850	1900	1950
World total	791	978	1,262	1,650	2,515
Asia (exc. USSR)	498	630	801	925	1,381
China (Mainland)	200	323	430	436	560
India and Pakistan	190	195	233	285	434
Japan	30	30	31	44	83
Indonesia	12	13	23	42	77
Remainder of Asia (exc. USSR)	67	69	87	118	227
Africa	106	107	111	133	222
North Africa	10	11	15	27	53
Remainder of Africa	96	96	96	106	169
Europe (exc. USSR)	125	152	208	296	392
USSR	42	56	76	134	180
America	18	31	64	156	328
North America	2	7	26	82	166
Middle and South America	16	24	38	74	162
Oceania	2	2	2	6	13

Source: John Durand, "The Modern Expansion of World Population," in *Proceedings of the American Philosophical Society*, Philadelphia, June 1967, p. 137.

nomic development of the Western world, it has been commonly assumed that the contemporary population expansion began its rapid pace in Europe. Durand has demonstrated that, while European or European-origin peoples contributed more than their proportionate

Annual rate of increase (percent)			
1750–1800	1800–1850	1850–1900	1900–1950
0.4	0.5	0.5	0.8
0.5	0.5	0.3	0.8
1.0	0.6	0.0	0.5
0.1	0.3	0.4	0.8
0.0	0.1	0.7	1.3
0.2	1.2	1.2	1.2
0.1	0.5	0.7	1.3
0.0	0.1	0.4	1.0
0.2	0.5	1.2	1.4
0.0	0.0	0.2	0.9
0.4	0.6	0.7	0.6
0.6	0.6	1.1	0.6
1.1	1.5	1.8	1.5
—	2.7	2.3	1.4
0.8	0.9	1.3	1.6
—	—	—	1.6

share to the expansion of world population during the nineteenth century, accelerating population growth was common to many widely spaced parts of the earth throughout the modern period. Since the Industrial Revolution did not occur in many of these places, this raises questions about its role as a major source of the population upsurge.[10]

It has been pointed out that if one views total human existence on earth as lasting one day, then the modern era of population growth covers less than a minute. Yet probably a fourth of all human beings ever born have lived during this brief time span.[11] Estimates of all the persons who have ever lived on earth range from seventy to eighty billion.[12] On this basis, about one out of twenty-five persons ever on earth is now living. These numbers are, of course, only illustrative. An estimate of the number ever living on earth depends on a number of factors, including when the human race is assumed to have begun.

The conclusion to be reached from this overview of world population trends is that demographic growth in recent times has been more rapid than at any earlier period of human existence on earth. Furthermore, a continuation of these trends for an indefinite period of time will result in immensely larger numbers of humans on the globe.

Of particular concern are the factors leading to this course of population development, the human capacity for sustaining larger populations, and the prospects that the pace of population growth will diminish. These are amenable to scientific examination and will be discussed in subsequent chapters.

Typical Variations in Population Development

While all parts of the world have participated in the modern population expansion, it is still evident that the course of population development in different countries of the world has not been the same. A description of the trends in a few countries, therefore, will give some idea of these variations. Explanation of these varying trends will be attempted in later parts of this volume.

United States

For a century and a half prior to the establishment of this nation, it is estimated that the population growth rate was erratic but averaged about 3 percent per year. At the time of the first census in 1790, shortly after the country was founded, the population stood at 3.9 million. The 3 percent growth rate was maintained until about the Civil War period. Beginning in the 1860s, the rate began a progressive decline, falling below 2 percent per year just about the turn of the century. A low point was reached during the depression years of the 1930s. With the advent of World War II, population growth recovered, and the rate moved back up close to the 2 percent level by the mid-1950s.[13] The course of population shifted again, and the growth rate resumed its low level of less than 1 percent by 1972. The population pattern in the United States can thus be described as one of high growth in the early years, with the rate declining generally until the 1930s, rising again to a moderately high level by the 1950s, and then resuming its decline to the present.

Ireland

A number of European countries experienced population growth patterns not unlike those of the United States, although the trend toward stabilization of the growth rate began at an earlier period of history and developed over a longer period of time. Ireland is an example of a European country in which the growth pattern has been radically different. According to Connell's estimates, the Irish people numbered just over two million in 1687.[14] Despite erratic growth and some short periods of decline, the population grew steadily for the next one hundred years at an average of close to 1 percent per year. During the next half century the rate of growth quickened, with an annual average of over 1 percent reached by the 1830s. By the mid-1800s, the pattern reversed itself, and the population of Ireland began to decline. Even though the population of Ireland had risen from 3.7 million in 1777 to 6.5 million in 1841, by 1961 the population size had fallen to far below its 1777 level. Most of the decrease took place during the last half of the nineteenth century as a result of heavy emigration. The numbers stabilized after 1910 at nearly three million. Throughout the first half of the twentieth century the growth rate hovered close to

Table 1.2   Historical population trends for the United States,
Ireland, Japan, India, and Brazil

United States			Ireland			Japan		
Date	Population (000)	Average annual growth rate	Date	Population (000)	Average annual growth rate	Date	Population (000)	Average annual growth rate
1790	3,929	—	1687	2,167	—	1250	9,750	—
1800	5,308	3.01	1726	3,031	0.86	1575	18,000	0.19
1810	7,240	3.10	1777	3,740	0.41	1726	26,549	0.26
1820	9,638	2.86	1821	5,421	0.84	1792	24,891	−0.10
1830	12,866	2.89	1831	6,193	1.33	1852	27,201	0.15
1840	17,069	2.83	1841	6,529	0.53	1872	32,634	0.91
1850	23,192	3.07	1851	5,112	−2.45	1885	37,502	1.07
1860	31,443	3.04	1861	4,402	−1.50	1920	55,391	1.11
1870	39,818	2.36	1871	4,053	−0.83	1925	59,179	1.32
1880	50,156	2.31	1881	3,870	−0.46	1930	63,872	1.53
1890	62,948	2.27	1891	3,469	−1.09	1935	68,662	1.45
1900	75,995	1.88	1901	3,222	−0.74	1940	72,539	1.10
1910	91,972	1.91	1911	3,140	−0.26	1955	89,300	1.39
1920	105,711	1.39	1926	2,972	−0.37	1960	93,200	0.85
1930	122,775	1.50	1936	2,968	−0.01	1970	104,665	1.16
1940	131,669	0.70	1946	2,955	−0.04			
1950	151,326	1.39	1951	2,961	0.04			
1960	179,323	1.70	1956	2,898	−0.43			
1970	203,212	1.25	1961	2,818	−0.56			
			1966	2,884	0.46			
			1971	2,978	0.64			

[a] From 1891 onward, figures are adjusted to the present area of the country.

Sources: For the United States, U.S. Bureau of the Census, *Statistical Abstract of the United States, 1973*, U.S. Government Printing Office, Washington, 1973, p. 5. For Ireland, Robert E. Kennedy, Jr., *The Irish: Emigration, Marriage, and Fertility*, University of California Press, Berkeley, 1973, p. 212; United Nations, *Demographic Yearbook*, New York, 1972; and K. H. Connell, *The Population of Ireland, 1750–1845*, Clarendon Press, Oxford, 1950, p. 25. For Japan, Irene B. Taeuber, *The Population of Japan*, Princeton University Press, Princeton, N.J., 1958, pp. 20, 22, 46, 60, and 61; United Nations, *Demographic Yearbook*, New York, 1960, 1972. For India, Kingsley Davis, *The Population of India and Pakistan*, Princeton Univer-

	India[a]			Brazil	
Date	Population (000)	Average annual growth rate	Date	Population (000)	Average annual growth rate
1600	100,000	—	1808	2,419	—
1800	120,000	0.60	1823	3,961	2.82
1834	130,000	0.24	1830	5,340	4.27
1845	130,000	0.00	1854	7,678	1.51
1855	175,000	2.97	1872	9,930	1.43
1867	194,000	0.86	1890	14,334	2.04
1871	255,166	6.85	1900	17,319	1.89
1881	257,380	0.09	1920	30,636	5.70
1891	236,700	—	1940	41,565	1.53
1901	236,300	−0.02	1950	51,944	2.23
1911	252,100	0.65	1960	70,967	3.12
1921	251,400	−0.03	1970	93,204	2.73
1931	279,000	1.04			
1941	316,700	1.27			
1951	361,100	1.31			
1961	439,200	1.96			
1971	547,950	2.21			

sity Press, Princeton, N.J., 1951, pp. 25 and 27; S. Chandrasekhar, *India's Population*, Meenakshi Prakashan, Meerut, 1967, p. 4; and United Nations, *Demographic Yearbook*, New York, 1972. For Brazil, T. Lynn Smith, *Brazil: People and Institutions*, Louisiana State University Press, Baton Rouge, 1972, p. 44.

zero, but after 1950 the population again declined, and this change was sustained until the late 1960s, when a modest increase in the rate of growth was recorded. Ireland can thus be described as a nation whose population showed early moderate growth tendencies but which assumed a pattern of decline after the middle of the nineteenth century until the very recent past.

Japan

Population records in Japan cover more than a thousand years. Estimates suggest a population of less than four million in the early tenth century with an increase to nine or ten million by the thirteenth century. The population of the country seems to have grown at an irregular rate from the thirteenth to the sixteenth century. It is believed to have increased rapidly in the seventeenth century and to have changed little from the early eighteenth century until 1852.[15] Steady growth at a rate fluctuating narrowly at about 1 percent per year characterized the Japanese demographic picture between 1852 and 1920. For several decades after 1920 the population grew at about 1½ percent annually, and in recent years the rate has moved closer to 1 percent. Although demographic growth in Japan took place at a moderate rate through most of its modern history, the smallness of the land area created heavy population densities. In 1968, there were 273 persons per square kilometer in Japan, making it one of the more densely settled areas of the world. The population pattern in Japan can be summarized as one of fluctuating growth in early periods of history followed by moderate but steady growth through modern times.

India

More typical than Japan of Asian population development is India. During the 2,000 or so years prior to the modern period, India's population must have remained virtually stationary. The probable course was gradual growth for a short period followed by an abrupt decline, the long-term trend being one of virtually fixed numbers.[16] From 1600 until 1845 India's numbers may have increased from about 100 million to roughly 130 million. The average annual percentage growth during that time was infinitesimal. From 1845 to 1871, the date when the first Indian census was taken, there is reason to believe that the growth rate accelerated, but the data are of insufficient quality to document the trend. Beginning with 1871, however, ten-year censuses have been conducted, which provide a reasonable basis for reckoning demographic change. The average annual increase from the time of the first census until the eighth census in 1941 is calculated to be about 0.6 percent, close to the increase for the world as a whole. During the last two decades of that time span, though, the annual increase rose to 1.2 percent, and in subsequent years the rate has continued upward until it presently stands at 2.4 percent. What is particularly critical in the case of India is that such a growth rate will double its population in twenty-nine years, and its population in 1975 numbered over six hundred million, more than North America and Latin America combined. One can therefore describe the trend of India's demographic growth as one of general stability with a small margin of increase for a long sweep of its history, followed by rapidly rising rates of growth during the past half century. Allowing for variations in tempo and in population size, the Indian pattern is one shared by many countries in Asia, Africa, and Latin America.

Brazil

As is the case with many Latin American countries, reliable demographic data for Brazil are only available from about 1872, when the first census was taken. From that time until 1950, the growth of population in Brazil has been one of the most rapid in the larger countries of the world. The annual rate of increase averaged about 2 percent during this span of time. Since 1950 the growth rate has risen sharply and approaches 3 percent a year at the present time. Although Brazil's population size is only one-sixth that of India's, a continued annual growth rate of nearly 3 percent will double its population in less than twenty-five years.[17]

Summary of Variations

The population profiles of the countries just illustrated do not adequately define the range of trend patterns among nations throughout the world. Almost every country has some unique aspect to its population development. Many countries can be grouped, however, on the basis of general similarities in their population trends. There are countries that have never experienced rapid population expansion, others that are in the midst of such expansion, and still others that have encountered rapid expansion at some time in the past but that now have more moderate rates of demographic growth. Even within these types, there are variations in the regularity with which growth patterns evolve. In some nations, the transitions from slow to rapid increase and back again have been relatively smooth and gradual; in others, the changes have been irregular and sometimes quite dramatic. Moreover, population trends vary by areas within countries just as national patterns vary within the world.

We shall try in the next few chapters to throw light on these demographic changes, indicating the forces that apparently have been at work to produce them. Chapter 2 outlines the frameworks that have been used to organize our knowledge about population trends and identifies the key variables to be examined. More detailed examination of the operation of these variables is carried out in Chapters 3 to 6. By the end of Chapter 6, the reader should have developed an adequate perspective for understanding the historical development of population as already described.

Data on Population

As can be seen from the previous discussion, availability of useful data is a prerequisite for analysis of population trends. Satisfactory demographic information is likewise necessary for an accurate understanding of how population interrelates with other aspects of society. It is therefore appropriate at this point to ask: What are the sources of population data? What types of population data are we usually interested in? Which sources provide which types of data? What can we say about the quality of population data?

Sources of Population Data

Demographic information can be obtained from a variety of sources, among which are censuses, vital registration systems, population registers, sample household surveys, governmental and private records, and estimation techniques. Sources such as the census and vital registration are traditional, going back to early periods of history. Other sources, such as the sample survey, many governmental records, and estimation techniques, are fairly modern developments. Moreover, the latter are increasingly being used in population research.

Censuses are familiar to most people since they are taken in all regions of the world and are administered by countries that include about nine-tenths of the population of the globe.[18] Even if individuals have not been interviewed by census-takers or completed census forms, they are generally aware that census information about them was obtained from adult members of their households or from neighbors. Some may deny that they were counted in a census because they were unaware that the census-taker called, but the chances are exceedingly high that they were included because censuses are known to be substantially complete, particularly in modern nations. Some people are missed, however, and some are counted more than once.

A population census is a costly and time-consuming operation. The total process involves collecting, compiling, and publishing demographic, economic, and social data for a specified date covering all persons in a delimited territory. Reports of the population of the United States from the 1970 Census refer to the census date of April 1, 1970. What is probably scarcely known is that work on that census began about 1963, and work relative to that census may still be going on in 1977 or later. Decisions had to be made very early about how the census was to be carried out, what questions were to be asked, what segments of the population different questions would refer to, how the reported information was to be coded and tabulated, and how the resulting data would be disseminated to the public. Procedures were developed that were tested, revised, and retested in locations throughout the country. Census materials were subsequently prepared, the census field staff hired, and the count taken. A variety of publications, computer data tapes, and other unpublished materials were provided for public use.

As a consequence of census operations, a wealth of knowledge about the people of the United States is created, and governmental and private planning and program development can therefore take place on the basis of facts rather than speculation. The census data serve to meet a number of administrative needs, but they also are a mainstay of demographic research and analysis.

Vital registration entails systematically collecting and organizing records of critical or vital life events, namely, those relating to births, stillbirths, adoptions, marriages, annulments, separations, divorces, and deaths.[19] The records provide a validation of these events that is frequently useful for personal reasons. For example, proof of one's age can be established from a birth certificate. For demographic purposes, vital registration is an important adjunct to a census. Censuses are usually taken every five or ten years. Vital statistics, especially on births and deaths, permit an assessment of how the population is changing between censuses and what the components of population change are.

Although data from vital registration are published periodically, usually annually or biennially, the collection and processing of the data is a continuous operation. After the event occurs, a certificate is completed which describes the circumstances of the event, such as the names of the involved person or persons, their residence and characteristics; and the date, time, and place of occurrence of the event. The certificates are filed with a local agency, and copies or summaries of them are reported to successively higher administrative echelons, such as from county to state to national government.

Population registers are systems of continuous population accounting whereby local communities keep track of the population, recording additions to and subtractions from that population.[20] The register has features of both a census and vital registration. Like a census, total population coverage is attempted, and some characteristics of the people are identified. Like vital registration, births, deaths, and other vital events are recorded. Additionally, data are gathered on the movement of people into and out of the area.

In practice, population registers ordinarily consist of a personal card for each inhabitant or a book in which entries are made of critical events. When an infant is born in the community, a record is made of it. When someone in the community dies, that person's record is removed from the register. When a person changes residence, the record is removed from the collection and transferred to the community of destination. It would appear that population registers duplicate the functions of censuses and/or vital registration, but the countries (such as the Netherlands and Scandinavian nations) that maintain registers find them independently useful for both administrative and research purposes. They update censuses, and they go beyond vital statistics in the recording of events such as residential moves.

The *sample household survey* as a recurrent population data source is found in a limited, but increasing, number of countries. The idea of drawing a sample of the population from which to gather information that will be representative of the whole population is relatively new, having grown out of advances in statistical sampling techniques within the past few decades. Most censuses now employ this principle by asking some basic questions of everyone in the population and other questions of only a sample. The typical sample household survey is much like the sample part of a census, but it usually covers a much smaller sample, is conducted much more frequently (annually or monthly), and has greater flexibility in terms of including untested questions and items that may not be appropriate for, or be difficult to collect in, a census. Furthermore, sample surveys can be conducted by private agencies and university organizations as well as by governments, thus increasing their potential as a data source.

A number of *public and private records* other than vital registration are used to supplement the population sources already described. These include immigration and naturalization records, Social Security records, unemployment insurance records, hospital and other health agency records, life insurance records, and armed forces and military conscription records, as well as genealogies and city directories.

Finally, it is sometimes the case that none of the aforementioned sources offers the kind of data needed for population analysis, or that the available data are of extremely poor quality. Here, the methodological ingenuity of demographers has led to a number of *estimation techniques* which enable one to approximate the needed data. It has been possible, for example, to estimate the size, composition, distribution, and characteristics of a population by making use of what little demographic data may be available in combination with known trends and relationships among demographic variables as they exist for other similar populations. In this way, we can estimate population information for periods of time before systematic record-keeping, for dates between censuses, and for the future. We can also estimate information for categories of the population not separately identified in a regular data-collecting system.

Types of Population Data

There are basically seven categories of information that are of interest in studying population — population size, mortality, fertility, residential mobility, population composition, population distribution, and population characteristics. Within several of these categories a number of subcategories can be specified. For instance, residential mobility may be differentiated by whether the movement was across national boundaries or within those boundaries and, if the latter, within or between communities, and by distance moved. Population composition refers to age, sex, and racial or ethnic status; population distribution to the location of people classified by type of area, ranging from regions and countries of the world to small subdivisions of cities and towns; and population characteristics to marital and family status, education, occupation, income, and the like.

In our previous review of world population status and trends, we dealt primarily with total population. In our subsequent discussion of the components of population change, we will be concerned with mortality, fertility, and residential mobility. In order to study employment patterns among teenage boys, we must have data that combine two items of population composition (age and sex) with one population characteristic (employment status). If we want to know further how these patterns differ among various areas, we need to have the data by categories of population distribution.

Which Sources Provide Which Types of Data?

By relating the several types and sources of data, we can discover where the different types of data are ordinarily found. Total population figures can be obtained from a census count, by a count of cards in a population register, or by some estimation technique. Vital registration and other administrative records deal with only certain events or with limited populations, and sample surveys, while they may be representative of total populations, do not provide reliable figures on the size of the populations themselves. Mortality data are obtained principally from death registration statistics. They can also be gotten from population registers and from life insurance records, although the latter do not cover all deaths. When all other sources are lacking or the data are regarded as poor, mortality data can be estimated. At times, death statistics are compiled from retrospective questions in censuses or surveys (e.g., "Has anyone in this household died within the past twelve months?"), but this procedure sometimes suffers from problems of recollection and the absence in the household of persons familiar with the event. It can serve, however, as an interim source of mortality data pending development of a reliable death registration system.[21]

Fertility information is obtained both from birth records in the vital registration system and population registers and from questions in censuses or surveys. In the former sources, births are counted one at a time as they occur; in the latter sources, a woman can be asked about all the children she has had up to that time. Fertility data can also be generated by estimation.

Population registers are the only source of information on each and every move that takes place in a population. Since censuses and surveys are taken at particular points in time and are usually limited in scope, questions on mobility in these sources deal with whether or not a person has moved in, say, the previous five years. Although residential mobility is not generally recorded as are births and deaths, except in population registers, statistics on immigration and emigration (movement into and out of a country) are usually compiled by governments. Since direct data on mobility are often not available, such data are calculated indirectly through various estimation techniques.

The items encompassed by population composition, distribution, and characteristics are traditionally covered in censuses and surveys, and to some extent in registers. A number of population characteristics are recorded in various administrative sources. For example, education data can be drawn from school records, income data from tax records, and health data from medical records.

The Quality of Population Data

It is one thing to have data available, and another thing to have usable data. How reliable is the demographic information at our disposal? Questions can be raised about both the completeness and the accuracy of the data. On both scores, it is necessary to point out the variations that occur among countries and according to the particular type or source of data.

Consider the report of the United Nations on fertility statistics for the world as a whole:

> The exact number of births cannot be ascertained owing to the wide range in the degree of accuracy of the supporting statistics for different countries. . . . Substantially accurate vital statistics are kept in virtually all of Europe, the Union of Soviet Socialist Republics, Japan, countries of predominantly European settlement in North and South America and Oceania, and also

in some other countries, most of them small. . . . For the most part, the birth rates prevailing in other parts of the world . . . are less adequately documented. . . . Countries lacking all quantitative data for an estimate of the birth rate are now very few and comprise only a small proportion of the world's population, but there are still large areas in which the birth rate can at best be estimated within rather wide limits of possible error.[22]

In the United States, birth registration is now considered to be about 99 percent complete. Census information on children ever born to a woman is subject to some error, the sources of which include nonresponse to the question on the part of some women, misreported information, sampling errors, and errors introduced in the processing and tabulation of the data. Evaluation studies done after recent censuses in the United States indicate that, despite the existence of errors of these kinds, the fertility data are reasonably accurate and can be used with some confidence. In countries having less advanced census operations, the quality of the statistics may not be as high.

Even in a census judged to be reasonably accurate, there are some notable deficiencies. The last few censuses of the United States undercounted the population of the country by some 3 percent, according to independent estimates. For some segments of the population, the percentage undercount was much higher. Young adult nonwhite males, for example, tend to be difficult to enumerate because many of them are exceptionally mobile and do not live in typical household situations. It was estimated that nearly one-fifth of this group was missed in the 1970 census.[23] The impact of this undercount could be severe in some cases, such as when the published census data are being used to reckon the number of young adult nonwhite males who are in need of employment.

We should, therefore, not blindly accept the population statistics that are obtained from various sources. Demographers have generally become attuned to the deficiencies in demographic data and take account of them in their analysis. If precise data are not required for a particular study, then data subject to some error may be regarded by them as adequate. If, on the other hand, a study necessitates accurate figures, as when the uses to which the study will be put are of substantial consequence, then the analyst will have to incorporate knowledge about data deficiencies into the interpretations.

Notes

1. This World Population Data Sheet, produced by the Population Reference Bureau, is the source of most of the following figures and will be referred to at several points throughout this volume.
2. J. Mayone Stycos, "Public and Private Opinion on Population and Family Planning," in *Studies in Family Planning*, The Population Council, No. 51 (March 1970), pp. 10–17.
3. Stycos, pp. 11–13.
4. John F. Kantner, "American Attitudes on Population Policy: Recent Trends" in *Studies in Family Planning*, The Population Council, No. 30 (May 1968), pp. 1–7.
5. Larry D. Barnett, "U. S. Population Growth as an Abstractly Perceived Problem," *Demography*, 7 (February 1970), 53.
6. Larry D. Barnett, "Education and Religion as Factors Influencing Attitudes Toward Population Growth in the United States," *Social Biology*, 17 (March 1970), 26–36; Carl C. Hetrick, A. E. Keir Nash, and Alan J. Wyner, "Population and Politics: Information, Concern, and Policy Support Among the American Public," in *Governance and Population: The Governmental Implications of Population Change*, Vol. IV of research reports of the U. S. Commission on Population Growth and the American Future, U. S. Government Printing Office, Washington, 1972, pp. 301–331.
7. Edward S. Deevey, Jr., "The Human Population," *Scientific American*, 203 (September 1960), pp. 194–204; Annabelle Desmond, "How Many People Have Ever Lived on Earth?" *Population Bulletin*, 18 (February 1962), pp. 1–19.
8. Deevey, pp. 196–197.

9. John Durand, "The Modern Expansion of World Population," *Proceedings of the American Philosophical Society*, 111 (June 22, 1967), 137.

10. Durand, 140.

11. Desmond, 12.

12. Desmond, 1; Nathan Keyfitz, "How Many People Have Lived on Earth?", *Demography*, 3, No. 2 (1966), 581–582.

13. For a general discussion of American population history, see Conrad Taeuber and Irene B. Taeuber, *The Changing Population of the United States*, Wiley, New York, 1958, chap. 1; and Donald J. Bogue, *Principles of Demography*, Wiley, New York, 1969, chap. 6.

14. K. H. Connell, *The Population of Ireland, 1750–1845*, Clarendon Press, Oxford, 1950, pp. 24–25; Robert E. Kennedy, Jr., *The Irish: Emigration, Marriage, and Fertility*, University of California Press, Berkeley, 1973, pp. 212–213.

15. Irene B. Taeuber, *The Population of Japan*, Princeton University Press, Princeton, N.J., 1958, p. 16.

16. Kingsley Davis, *The Population of India and Pakistan*, Princeton University Press, Princeton, N.J., 1951, chap. 4.

17. T. Lynn Smith, *Brazil: People and Institutions*, Louisiana State University Press, Baton Rouge, 1972, chap. 3.

18. Statistical Office of the United Nations, *Handbook of Population Census Methods*, I, *General Aspects of a Population Census*, United Nations, New York, 1958.

19. Statistical Office of the United Nations, *Principles and Recommendations for a Vital Statistics System*, United Nations, New York, 1973.

20. Statistical Office of the United Nations, *Methodology and Evaluation of Population Registers and Similar Systems*, United Nations, New York, 1969.

21. Georges Sabagh and Christopher Scott, A *Comparison of Different Survey Techniques for Obtaining Vital Data in a Developing Country*, Laboratories for Population Statistics, Reprint Series No. 10, The University of North Carolina, Chapel Hill, 1973.

22. United Nations, *Demographic Yearbook*, 1965, p. 1.
23. Jacob S. Siegel, "Estimates of Coverage of the Population by Sex, Race, and Age in the 1970 Census," *Demography*, 11 (February 1974), p. 17.

Suggested Additional Readings

Useful references on world population growth are the United Nations publications:

A Concise Summary of the World Population Situation in 1970. United Nations, New York, 1971.

Demographic Yearbook (an annual compilation of population statistics).

Other population textbooks which give some attention to the topic of world population growth are:

Bogue, Donald J. *Principles of Demography.* Wiley, New York, 1969, chaps. 3 and 6.

Goldscheider, Calvin. *Population, Modernization, and Social Structure.* Little, Brown, Boston, 1971, chap. 4.

Matras, Judah. *Populations and Societies.* Prentice-Hall, Englewood Cliffs, N.J., 1973, chap. 1.

Petersen, William. *Population.* Macmillan, New York, 1969, chap. 9 and parts of chaps. 10 to 12.

Thomlinson, Ralph. *Population Dynamics.* Random House, New York, 1965, chaps. 2 and 21.

Thompson, Warren S., and David T. Lewis. *Population Problems.* McGraw-Hill, New York, 1965, chaps. 14 to 16.

Books of readings that include selections on world population growth are:

Heer, David M., ed. *Readings on Population*. Prentice-Hall, Englewood Cliffs, N.J., 1968.

Nam, Charles B., ed. *Population and Society*. Houghton Mifflin, Boston, 1968.

Other general books on population that give some treatment of world growth patterns are:

Freedman, Ronald, ed. *The Vital Revolution*. Doubleday Anchor, Garden City, N.Y., 1964.

Frejka, Tomas. *The Future of Population Growth*. Wiley, New York, 1973.

Kammeyer, Kenneth C. W. *An Introduction to Population*. Chandler, San Francisco, 1971.

Stockwell, Edward G. *Population and People*. Quadrangle, Chicago, 1968.

Thomlinson, Ralph. *Demographic Problems*. Dickenson, Belmont, Calif., 1967.

Wrong, Dennis H. *Population and Society*. Random House, New York, 1967.

Volumes dealing with sources, types, and quality of population data are:

Barclay, George. *Techniques of Population Analysis*. Wiley, New York, 1958.

Benjamin, Bernard. *Demographic Analysis*. George Allen and Unwin, London, 1968.

Shryock, Henry S., and Jacob S. Siegel and Associates. *The Methods and Materials of Demography*. 2 vols. U. S. Government Printing Office, Washington, 1971.

Spiegelman, Mortimer. *Introduction to Demography*. Harvard University Press, Cambridge, Mass., 1968.

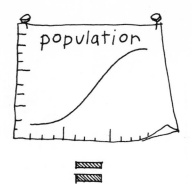

population

=

=

IN
MEMORY
OF
. . .

+

TALLANT
TRANSFER CO.

2

The Variables in Population Change

Systematic inquiry into what factors produce population change and the nature of their effects has been carried out on a large scale only in recent times. Writings about population, as both cause and effect in society, are not new, however. In this chapter we will review some of the theoretical approaches to population patterns from earliest times to the present. Through such a review, it should become apparent that these theories have become increasingly more sophisticated in their view of population processes. In addition, however, some of the earliest ideas about how populations change still serve as cornerstones of modern-day explanations.

Early Approaches to Population

One of the characteristics of early writing on population is that population is frequently discussed as a unitary phenomenon; that is, population is not generally broken down into components or parts, and the size of the population is the major concern. Much early writing on population was value-oriented, in that it stated that certain population sizes were good or preferred, while others were undesirable or even evil. The Biblical injunction to "be fruitful and multiply" is an example of this kind of writing about population. But religious scripture is not the only value-oriented work on population from early times.

A body of early literature can be identified which addresses itself to the issue of the optimum or best population. Of course, a decision about what is the optimum population depends on the chosen goals. In the case of the Romans, the optimum population was that which enabled them to maintain a large empire,[1] while for Plato and other Greek philosophers, optimum population was that which allowed constitutional government and yet adequate division of labor (5,040 citizens per city, to be exact).[2] For Chinese writers, optimum population was that which provided an adequate balance between land and people for the type of agricultural economy then prevailing.[3] Other examples of writing on optimum population could be cited,[4] but let it suffice to say that this value-oriented literature does not try to explain how population changes. Rather, most of it discusses a population goal, with little guidance as to how this optimum might be reached.

Population writing in much later periods did deal with how populations change. Quetelet, for example, postulated that resistance to population growth tends to increase in proportion to the square of the velocity of increase in population growth.[5] Thus, population tends to grow more and more slowly as time goes on. This was a picture of what Quetelet believed population change to be like; however, he lacked documentation of this hypothesis, and he did not elaborate the mechanisms that would produce such changes.

Pearl and Reed proposed that population tends to grow in the form of a logistic or S-shaped curve.[6] They were not the first to suggest such a pattern but were the first to refine it to any great extent.[7] Population at first increases in a geometric progression but is later hindered in growth, so that it attains a level where it remains in stationary equilibrium. This idea was developed by Pearl and Reed in the course of working with populations of fruit flies confined in a small living space. While generalizing this finding from insect to human populations might be questioned, Pearl and Reed did postulate some explanations for this logistic behavior of population. The causes of change they cited were primarily biological rather than social in origin.

Other writers proposed biological explanations for the change in population. Prominent among them was Corrado Gini, who stated that population grew in a series of cycles.[8] He believed that population followed a course of growth like that of individual human beings, passing through stages of growth and undergoing death or extinction. Gini suggested "demographic metabolism," a sort of biological deterministic factor, to explain this behavior of population. By and large, this factor influences populations through its impact on fecundity, or the ability to have children.

Most of these views of population change are limited in one or more ways. First, they may not be proposed explanations of population change at all, but injunctions to change or value statements about what population sizes would be "good" for a society. Second, some of these writers stated laws of population change which were not explanations of the changes, but only descriptions. Finally, those that did offer explanations for population change typically offered simplistic explanations. Not only was population viewed as a unitary phenomenon, but just one or two factors affecting population change were seen as adequate for understanding that change.

It is worth noting that not all writers in early periods viewed population as simply the effect of other processes in society. Some felt that population change caused other changes in society as well. Probably most prominent in this group of writers were various economists who saw population sizes as related to the division of labor, the cost increase or decrease in production, the level of agricultural production, the level of unemployment, and other economic conditions.[9] This set of writings, while quite useful for other types of analyses, was not primarily concerned with what produces population change of a given kind, but instead dealt with how population change affects various aspects of the economy. While this direction of relationship is important (Chapters 7 and 8 are devoted to it), it did not improve early knowledge of the dynamics of population change.

Components of Population Change

Probably the first theories or explanations for population change came when students of the subject began to think of population in terms of its basic components: births, deaths, and residential mobility.

To begin to think in this way is a first step in providing an explanation for population change, since it emphasizes the primary set of variables through which all population change occurs.

Considering population change between two points in time, population at any point in time is equal to population at an earlier point in time, plus the births, minus the deaths, plus the movement of persons into the area, and minus the movement of persons out of the area. The effect of these last two may be combined into a positive or negative net effect. In symbols, this basic population equation appears as follows:

$$P_2 = P_1 + B - D \pm M$$

For example, if we use data (expressed in thousands) for the United States between 1960 and 1970, the equation becomes[10]:

$$
\frac{\text{1970}}{\underset{203,849}{\text{population}}} = \frac{\text{1960}}{\underset{179,067}{\text{population}}} + \frac{\text{1960–1970}}{\underset{39,185}{\text{births}}} - \frac{\text{1960–1970}}{\underset{18,225}{\text{deaths}}} + \frac{\text{1960–1970}}{\underset{3,822}{\text{net migration}}}
$$

This equation assumes a constant land area under consideration, although population in a given political unit (e.g., a city) may also increase or decrease by boundary changes resulting from annexation or cession of territory.

The net effect of the first two components of the population equation (births and deaths) constitutes *natural increase or decrease*. This term arises from the observation that births and deaths are "natural" phenomena and are the boundary points in the human life cycle. The term natural is perhaps unfortunate, however, in that it may seem to imply that mobility is unnatural in some way.

Models of Natural Increase

Perhaps because of this emphasis on births and deaths being natural, or perhaps because people may only migrate within a finite space — our planet at present — some explanations of population change have ignored residential mobility and concentrated on natural components. One such formulation is the theory of the *demographic transition*.

Demographic transition originally began as a classification of types of population, each with different combinations of birth- and death-rate levels.[11] Later these types of populations were regarded as stages of growth that one population may pass through. This process is illustrated in Figure 2.1.

Basically, classical demographic transition theory posits three types of populations. In the first, the population has both high fertility and high mortality. Obviously, since growth is determined by the balance

Figure 2.1   The demographic transition

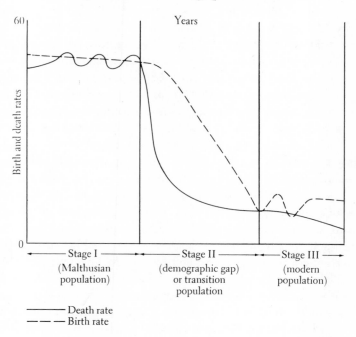

between fertility and mortality, such a population has a low rate of growth, or may occasionally decline in numbers. Such a society is generally characterized by a preindustrial economy and is not urbanized.

This first type of population was dealt with at great length by Thomas Malthus in his much-discussed essay on population.[12] Malthus maintained that population growth was basically controlled by a variable death rate. Left to its own devices, population growth would approach the limit of the food supply, according to Malthus, and the only preventatives for this catastrophe were certain natural checks. The natural checks Malthus deemed important were of three main kinds: moral restraint, vice, and misery. Included here were war, disease, famine, pestilence, want, and delayed marriage.

Malthus's theory was based on two assumptions: (1) that people would always need food, and (2) that passion between the sexes was necessary and would continue in the same state. The first assumption made by Malthus can hardly be argued, but it can at least be said of Malthus that he was short-sighted where agriculture was concerned. He failed to see the revolutions in agriculture that increased immeasurably the amount of food per acre of land that people were able to produce. As to his second assumption, Malthus probably had a point in observing that passion between the sexes was likely to continue. What he did not foresee was the possibility of venting that passion without the risk of conception. Malthus was opposed to any form of birth control, and certainly did not foresee the technological improvements made in that field since his time.

While not applicable to all populations at all times, then, Malthus's picture of population processes is applicable to the type of population described in the first stage of the demographic transition. Such a population has high birth and death rates and a low rate of growth, and that growth is largely controlled by a rising and falling death rate.

The second type of population described by the demographic transition is one which has high fertility and declining or low mortality. This stage of the transition is sometimes referred to as the *demographic gap*, since the levels of the birth and death rates are quite different. Such a population obviously experiences a very high growth rate. The economy in such a society is generally an industrializing one, so that some control over death has been achieved, but little regulation of births is yet occurring.

Finally, the third type of population included in the demographic transition is one with generally low fertility and mortality. This type of population is generally characteristic of industrialized countries where there is a fairly low rate of growth. Here the major factor in growth is a variable birth rate, since death rates have become low and stable.

These three types of populations seem to describe stages in a process occurring in Western Europe and the United States during the last few centuries. In fact, there was a transition from high birth and death rates to a period of falling death rates, with birth rates falling more slowly, and finally to a period with low birth and death rates. Pushing the formulation even further, some demographers began to speculate that the transition would occur in less-developed countries of the world as they began to industrialize.[13]

But here the transition idea began to run into challenges. Some writers questioned whether the transition happened at all in the way described by the three types of population. Joseph Davis cautioned against the assumption that "the demographic world is one world," and enjoined demographers to avoid any form of "globaloney."[14] Transition may have occurred in some areas at some times, according to Davis, but certainly transition is not an ever-present phenomenon which inevitably occurs in all developing nations.

William Petersen, in his study in the Netherlands, found that the demographic gap, or the period of rapid growth, was caused not only by a falling death rate, but by a rising birth rate as well.[15] As Petersen explains it, the nuclear family became more widespread as industrialization took place. When more people who were normally tied to the land and to the extended family were free to marry, the birth rate went up somewhat, helping to increase the gap between birth and death rates. Thus, it is false to postulate that all the growth in the gap period was caused by falling death rates.

Another serious criticism of the demographic transition idea is that while the transition framework may offer a partial picture of what happened to some countries during the last few centuries, it does not qualify as a true theory, since its predictive power for the future is very low. This criticism has been made in various ways. For example, as early as 1929, Thompson pointed out that the time required for lowering birth rates could be subject to great variability between nations.[16] He suggested that this time depends on some weighted combination of the rate of spread of birth control and the rurality of the population — a time which he was unable to predict.

Other variables may also enter in. Taeuber pointed out that the initial levels of fertility and mortality in a country will affect the time it takes the vital rates to come down.[17] She included the variability in the means available for reduction of these rates as a further complication in determining just how long transition takes. Taeuber was quite skeptical of the ability of transition theory to predict future population growth patterns:

> A reappraisal of the Western demographic transition in terms of its resource base and its economic, social, and intellectual aspects indicates that its precise repetition anywhere in the world is so improbable as to approach the inconceivable.[18]

It has been noted by many demographers that even the time required for the decline in the death rate, which has been occurring in many nations of the world, is subject to great variability.[19] While the countries of Western Europe had to wait for the slow development of medical technology in order to bring death rates down, the countries of Asia, Latin America, and Africa today can "borrow" death-control technology from more-developed countries and speed the reduction of their death rates greatly. The desire to control death is, after all, a cultural universal, whereas the desire to control birth is not. A country may eagerly adopt methods of saving lives, but hesitate or refuse to control births. The period of the demographic gap may thus be lengthened, making for high and sustained population growth. Will the death rate go back up in such countries before births are controlled?

This possibility has led some writers, Cowgill notable among them, to suggest that demographic transition, while useful, does not cover all the possible ways in which natural increase or decrease may occur.[20] Cowgill assumes that populations change in such a way as to ultimately produce an S-curve of growth. Exploring the logical possibilities which such an assumption would produce, Cowgill came up with four cycles of growth. These are illustrated in Figure 2.2.

Cycle I is called the *primitive cycle* and is typical of underdeveloped areas. In these areas, the birth rate remains stationary while the death rate declines. The death rate then eventually rises again to terminate the cycle. This pattern is reminiscent of the Malthusian or first-stage transition population.

Cycle II is the *modern cycle* and is characterized by falling birth

Figure 2.2 Cowgill's population growth cycles

The mechanics of Cycle I
(the primitive cycle).

The mechanics of Cycle II
(the modern cycle).

The mechanics of Cycle III
(the future cycle).

The mechanics of Cycle IV

- - - - - Birth rate
———— Death rate

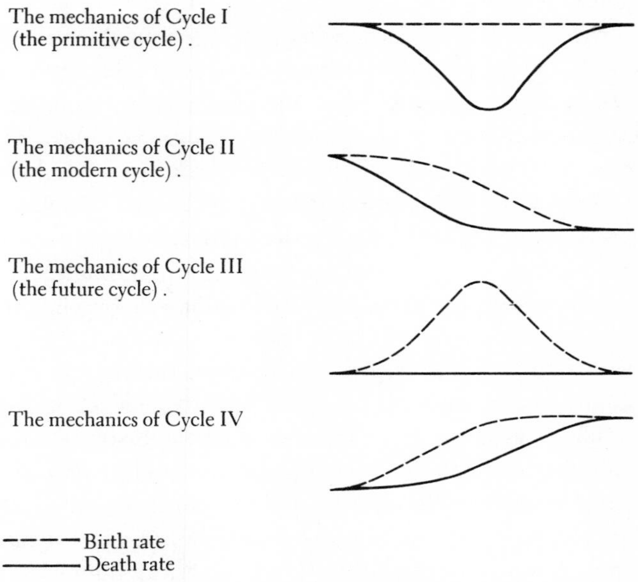

Source: Donald Olen Cowgill, "The Theory of Population Growth Cycles," AJS 55:2 (Sept. 1949): 163–170, Figs. 2–5, pp. 165–166 redrawn as one figure.

and death rates, with the death rate falling more rapidly than the birth rate. The cycle is closed when the birth rate overtakes the death rate. This is much like the traditional model of the demographic transition.

Cycle III, which Cowgill called the *future cycle,* is characterized by a rising birth rate while the death rate remains constant. To close the cycle the birth rate falls. Such a pattern characteristically occurs for short periods of time in countries that have completed the transition and may have occurred for short periods of time in nations in the first stage of the transition.

Finally, Cycle IV opens with a rising birth rate and closes with the death rate also rising to overtake the birth rate. While this cycle has little precedent in history, it does constitute the other mathematical possibility in an S-shaped model. Some writers have offered this fourth cycle as the possible outcome in some countries where death rates have come down rapidly and birth rates have remained stable for some time or increased somewhat.

One other possibility exists with regard to birth- and death-rate combinations. Some populations may have lower fertility rates than mortality rates. Such a population would not be growing, but decreasing in numbers. This pattern was originally predicted as the last stage of the demographic transition and called *incipient decline.* Certainly some primitive societies have become extinct under such a condition, but modern examples of higher mortality than fertility are short-term.[21]

Incorporating the Residential Mobility Component

As an explanation for population change, demographic transition theory has also been soundly criticized for its neglect of residential mobility. This neglect has arisen for several reasons. First, cross-cultural data on migration are not plentiful. Second, most authors have assumed that migration has no long-term effect on the population growth of a nation.[22] These writers claim that internal migration only serves to redistribute population within a political boundary, whereas international migration has only been heavy for short periods of time.

But a look at population growth rates with the migration component included has shown that the assumptions about the importance of migration are not altogether true.

For example, in 1955 the growth-per-thousand population for Israel was 39.[23] The natural increase per thousand in Israel during this same time period was only 23.1. In Puerto Rico, the growth rate was 10 per thousand during 1955, while the natural increase was 27.2 per thousand — a difference accounted for by a net out-migration of 17.2 persons per thousand. George Wilber presents sufficient data to illustrate that were the amount of migration added to the natural increase in population in many countries, the original three-type categorization of these countries which demographic transition offers might be changed drastically in the future.

Other examples of migration as an important variable in population growth or decline are readily available. Certainly in early times, when many cultures were based on a hunting and/or gathering economy, the wanderings of people made a difference in the population size of an area they abandoned or invaded. Irish history shows a steady loss in population in that country for many years, in spite of a high birth rate and a lower death rate. This loss in population was almost entirely due to emigration from Ireland (as discussed in Chapter 1).

Modern examples of the importance of migration in explaining patterns of population growth or decline include the large-scale movement of people during times of war. Refugees and displaced persons, as well as temporary movements of armies and citizens evacuating cities, cannot be ignored in calculations of population growth and decline. Further, in countries where natural increase or decrease is zero — that is, births and deaths are equal — migration accounts for 100 percent of the change in population size.

Internal migrations are also relevant for certain types of population growth and decline. The westward movement in the United States accounted for the tremendous growth of the West Coast population in this country. This growth could not have been predicted by looking at the natural increase of this area alone.

Another way in which migration can be important is in its effects on natural increase or decrease. Friedlander, for example, has posited that the rate of natural increase in a community may be directly related to the ease with which the number of excess persons can be reduced by out-migration.[24]

In spite of its importance, little work has been done to include migration in models like the demographic transition that deal with the natural components. Certainly any theory which purports to explain population change will have to reckon with this basic component of demographic change.

Other Variables in Population Change

To say that population change is caused by changes in fertility, mortality, and migration, however, is only the beginning of an explanatory scheme. Certainly, analyzing change in terms of components of population is a worthwhile improvement over viewing population as a unitary phenomenon. But many questions about population change are still left unanswered. What causes fertility to increase or decrease? Why do some societies have higher mortality than others? Why do people migrate? These are only a few of the questions that a complete theory of population change might need to answer in order to be useful in explaining and predicting population growth or decline. The models discussed above are therefore weak in another way, in that they do not deal, except in a limited way, with the question of what factors in society cause the components of population to change.

The task of answering some of these questions is well underway. Cowgill has worked on the problem of extending and improving demographic transition theory. He includes such variables as resources of the environment in which populations grow, industrialization, urbanization, socioeconomic status, and changes in the economic structure of societies in order to provide more complete explanations for the changes in birth and death rates evident in the transition stages.[25]

Explaining Population Components

In regard to each of the components of population, frameworks have already been constructed using factors which may explain changes in fertility, mortality, or migration. Illustrative of this type of work is the list of intermediate variables affecting fertility offered by Davis and Blake.[26] These authors postulate that the three sets of intermediate variables affecting fertility are those influencing exposure to intercourse, conception, and gestation and parturition. Such variables include the amount of time spent between stable marital unions, voluntary and involuntary fecundity, use of contraception, voluntary and involuntary fetal mortality, and many others. Extending the notions of Davis and Blake, Freedman has pointed out that each of these intermediate variables is influenced by the norms prevailing in the society relative to that area.[27]

The Davis-Blake work and Freedman's elaboration are extremely important for the development of population theory since they focus on a limited number of variables immediately preceding fertility and connect these to more general societal influences.

While there is no comparable formulation in the area of mortality, much has been written about factors in a society which may affect mortality. Work by the United Nations includes a listing of factors that are related to the level of mortality throughout the world, such as level of living, level of education, number of medical and health facilities, and occupations of males.[28]

There are no comprehensive theories of migration, but there is a variety of approaches to listing variables which influence this population component. There are classifications of migration, wherein authors try to distinguish, say, "forced" migrations from "free" migrations and discuss the factors associated with each.[29] There are "laws" of migration, which amount to catalogues of empirical generalizations about migrant characteristics.[30] There are even conceptual frameworks that look at the decision to migrate in orderly stages.[31] Each of these approaches to explaining population components will be given more attention in later chapters dealing with the components individually.

The greatest emphasis in demographic literature has been on empirical research. Demographic journals abound with studies testing relationships of societal, group, and individual factors to fertility, mortality, and migration. This work, too, can be a great contribution to the attempt to explain population growth, since it tests theoretical propositions, elucidates conceptual frameworks, and suggests new relationships for future testing.

A Suggested Framework

In an attempt to provide some orderly framework for the discussion of these research findings and their relationship to existing theory, we shall adopt a classification of influences on population components. In future chapters, when we discuss the influences on fertility, mortality, and mobility, we shall deal with these effects on three levels: societal influences, normative or group influences, and individual influences.

Societal influences are those institutional, organizational, or other society-level factors which may change or condition fertility, mortality, or mobility in some way. An example of such an influence on fertility might be changing business cycles, which show a consistent relationship to the birth rate. Breakthroughs in medical technology are society-level factors which affect mortality. Economic change and the consequent need for mobility of labor is such a factor influencing migration within or between societies.

We have loosely termed another group of factors *normative* or *group influences*. These are the mores, laws, and folkways of a society that may influence each of these components and are usually connected with some institutional framework in the society, such as the family or religion. The government may influence mortality in a society by supporting war or health measures. The family may influence fertility by endorsing a given role for women in the society, or religion may influence migration by decreeing that a son must be born in the birthplace of his mother, and so on. These are the kinds of normative influences that may affect population components and, in turn, population change.

Finally, the *individual* mediates and affects all such societal and normative influences. As individuals live in society, they learn some norms and are not exposed to others. While nearly all individuals are affected by the class of influences we are calling societal, certainly the degree to which individuals are affected varies. Besides decision-making ability, each individual also brings to the process a personal biological makeup. A man or woman may be physiologically unable to produce children, an invalid may be incapable of migration, or a person with a genetic deficiency may be subject to the risk of early mortality. Any complete explanation of population change would have to take into account these individual factors, as they mediate societal and normative influences.

As even this brief discussion should indicate, explaining population change is a complex task. Certainly the magnitude of the task is perceived quite differently now than it was by the early writers discussed at the beginning of this chapter. From consideration of population as a unitary phenomenon, demographic explanations progressed to consideration of population components, and then to both empirical and theoretical consideration of what factors influence these population components.

This task can proceed on several different levels. It is one thing to explain why one society has a high rate of growth and another society a low rate of growth, and quite another to explain why one family has three children and another four. The factors to be considered in each problem, while related, are really quite different. Furthermore, if we were to try to explain why populations differ in their rates of growth, we might begin by saying that they have different fertility rates. But that first level of explanation is only a beginning. Next, an investigation of why their fertility rates differ would be in order. That task might lead us to societal, group, or individual variables.

The complexity of the explanatory task should not lead the reader to think that it cannot be accomplished — or at least approximated.

While demography has discarded most of what posed as comprehensive theory in an earlier day, it is hard at work on what might better be called *propositions,* or smaller theories, to explain and elucidate population phenomena. Such theories might only explain how socioeconomic status and fertility are related, or how occupational change and migration are related, but this work represents the emergence of theoretical propositions from empirical research. It is our hope that the following chapters will provide some contribution by organizing these empirical findings and theoretical frameworks in such a way that they will help the reader understand the dynamics of demographic change.

Notes

1. For a general discussion of these theories, see Population Division, United Nations, *The Determinants and Consequences of Population Trends,* New York, 1953, pp. 21–44.
2. Plato, *The Laws,* translated with introduction by A. E. Taylor, Dent, London, Dutton, New York, 1960; Plato, *The Republic,* translated into English by B. Jowett, Modern Library, New York, 1941; Aristotle, *The Politics,* translated with introduction by T. A. Sinclair, Penguin Books, Baltimore, 1962.
3. For example, see Chen Huan-Chang, *The Economic Principles of Confucius and His School,* Longmans Green, New York, 1911.
4. For a brief general discussion of optimum theory see Warren C. Robinson, "The Development of Modern Population Theory," in *American Journal of Economics and Sociology,* 23 (October 1964), 375–392.
5. Lambert Adolphe Jacques Quetelet, *A Treatise on Man and the Development of His Faculties,* a facsimile reproduction of the English translation of 1842, with an introduction by Solomon Diamond, Scholars' Facsimiles and Reprints, Gainesville, Florida, 1969.
6. Raymond Pearl and Lowell Reed, "On the Rate of Growth of the

Population of the United States Since 1790 and Its Mathematical Representation," *Proceedings of the National Academy of Science,* 6 (1920), pp. 275–288.

7. P. F. Verhulst also postulated such a growth pattern in "Recherches mathmatiques sur la loi d'accroissement de la population," *Nouveaux Memoires de l'Academie Royale des Sciences et Belle-Lettres de Bruxelles,* 18:1 (1845).

8. See Corrado Gini, *Population,* University of Chicago Press, Chicago, 1930.

9. See Edwin Cannan, *A Review of Economic Theory.* P. S. King, London, 1929.

10. These estimates are from "Estimates of the Population of the U. S. and Components of Change: 1972," in *Current Population Reports,* U. S. Bureau of the Census, Series P-25, No. 499, May 1973. (The data have been adjusted for "errors of closure" and rounding errors to make the equation balance exactly.)

11. The earliest formulation of this idea was apparently Warren S. Thompson, "Population," *American Journal of Sociology,* 34 (May 1929), 959–975; later expansions of it include Frank W. Notestein, "Population — The Long View," in *Food for the World,* ed. Theodore W. Schultz, University of Chicago Press, Chicago, 1945, pp. 36–57.

12. Thomas R. Malthus, *An Essay on the Principle of Population.* London, 1709.

13. See Kingsley Davis, "The World Demographic Transition," *Annals of the American Academy of Political and Social Science,* 237 (1945), 1–11.

14. Joseph S. Davis, "Population & Resources: Discussion of Papers by Frank W. Notestein and P. U. Cardon," *Journal of the American Statistical Association,* 45 (1950), 346–349.

15. William Petersen, "The Demographic Transition in the Netherlands," *American Sociological Review,* 25 (June 1960), 334–347.

16. Thompson, p. 969.

17. Irene B. Taeuber, "The Future of Transitional Areas," in Paul K.

Hatt (ed.), *World Population and Future Resources,* American Book Company, New York, 1952, pp. 25–38. See also Irene B. Taeuber, "Japan's Demographic Transition Re-examined," *Population Studies,* 14 (July 1960), 28–39.

18. Taeuber, *World Population,* p. 28.

19. For example, see George J. Stolnitz, "The Demographic Transition: From High to Low Birth Rates and Death Rates," in *Population: The Vital Revolution* ed. Ronald Freedman, Doubleday, Garden City, N.Y., 1964, pp. 30–46.

20. Donald O. Cowgill, "The Theory of Population Growth Cycles," *American Journal of Sociology,* 55 (September 1949), 163–170.

21. For an example of such a country, see Joseph Spengler, *France Faces Depopulation,* Duke University Press, Durham, N.C., 1938.

22. George L. Wilber, "Demographic Transition: An Analytic Framework," a paper prepared for annual meeting, Population Association of America, April 28–29, 1967, Cincinnati, Ohio, pp. 3–4.

23. Wilber, Table 1.

24. Dov Friedlander, "Demographic Responses and Population Change," *Demography,* 6 (November 1969), 359–381.

25. Donald O. Cowgill, "Transition Theory as General Population Theory," *Social Forces,* 41 (March 1963), 270–274.

26. Kingsley Davis and Judith Blake, "Social Structure and Fertility: An Analytic Framework," *Economic Development and Cultural Change,* 4 (April 1956), 211–235.

27. Ronald Freedman, "Norms for Family Size in Underdeveloped Areas," *Proceedings of the Royal Society,* 159 (1963), 220–234.

28. United Nations, *Determinants and Consequences.*

29. For example, William Petersen, "A General Typology of Migration," *American Sociological Review,* 23 (June 1958), 256–266.

30. See, for example, E. G. Ravenstein, "On the Laws of Migration," *Journal of the American Statistical Society,* 48 (June 1885), 167–235.

31. See, for example, Lawrence A. Brown and Eric G. Moore, "The Intra-Urban Migration Process: A Perspective," *Geografista Annaler* (Stockholm), Series B (1970), 1–13.

Suggested Additional Readings

Useful summaries of population thought in history include:

Bonar, James. *Theories of Population from Raleigh to Arthur Young*. A. M. Kelley, New York, 1966.

Glass, D. V., and D. E. C. Eversley (eds.). *Population in History*. E. Arnold, London, 1965.

Hutchinson, E. P. *The Population Debate*. Houghton Mifflin, Boston, 1967.

Population Division, United Nations. *The Determinants and Consequences of Population Trends*. New York, 1953, pp. 21–44.

Spengler, J. J., and O. D. Duncan (eds.). *Population Theory and Policy*. Free Press, Glencoe, Ill., 1956.

Discussions of the general role of demographic theory are contained in:

Robinson, Warren C. "The Development of Modern Population Theory." *American Journal of Economics and Sociology*, 23 (October 1964), 375–392.

Vance, Rupert. "Is Theory for Demographers?" *Social Forces*, 31 (October 1952), 9–13.

Van Nort, Leighton. "On Values in Population Theory." *Milbank Memorial Fund Quarterly*, 38 (October 1960), 387–395.

Useful classical writings on demographic theory and present-day discussions of them include:

Malthus, Thomas Robert. *An Essay on the Principle of Population*. Ward, Lock, and Co., London, 1890.

Petersen, William. "The Malthus-Godwin Debate, Then and Now." *Demography* 8 (February 1971), 13–26.

Spengler, Joseph J. "Malthus on Godwin's *Of Population*." *Demography*, 8 (February 1971), 1–12.

3

Mortality: Trends and Determinants

It is clear from the preceding chapter that mortality is not only one of the basic components of population change but also one of the most critical in terms of the history of modern population expansion. Declines in the death rate preceding any major declines in the birth rate account for a considerable part of the "population explosion" which has occurred in many countries. At the same time, the trend of mortality has not always been downward, nor has it ordinarily been smooth. In different parts of the world at different points in time death rates have risen, and there have typically been annual and seasonal fluctuations in mortality patterns.

The aim of this chapter is to analyze mortality as a component of population change. In so doing, we shall first examine long-term trends of mortality in the world and its major regions, then look at short-term variations in the death rate, and finally deal with the way mortality is related to age. Using the explanatory framework outlined in Chapter 2, attention is given to societal, group, and individual factors which influence mortality. Finally, a view of the future trend of mortality is taken.

51

Long-Term Mortality Trends[1]

The World as a Whole

Accurate measures of the mortality of a population have come about only in comparatively recent times. Yet some information has been developed which shows the mortality experience of people in early history. There is no evidence that *life span* (the ultimate age to which people can live) has changed at all over time. Some humans are believed to live to about age 120 today, and no reliable record suggests a greater life span in previous eras. There are occasional reports of those who are celebrating their 150th birthday or whose parents had lived to that age, but one might suspect such reports since it has been shown that a high proportion of people assumed to be even centenarians have misreported their age and are, in fact, somewhat short of a hundred years old.[2] At least, such longevity would be exceedingly rare.

One may be confident, however, that *life expectancy* (the average number of years of life remaining to a group of people) has been changing over time. Even though life span has remained constant, the greater survival of infants and reductions in mortality at middle and older ages mean that more persons today live beyond infancy and to more advanced ages than was true previously. Archaeologists have determined that Neanderthal man lived, on the average, to age twenty-nine, with a rather small chance of surviving to forty years of age. The average length of life increased slightly during the Upper Paleolithic and Mesolithic periods, reaching approximately thirty-two years.[3] Slow but continued increases are estimated to have occurred during the Neolithic and Bronze Age eras, but more reliable records for classical Greece and Rome put life expectancy in the thirty-two to thirty-five age range.[4]

While these early estimates of life expectancy are questionable, the evidence indicates that no ancient or medieval population boasted a mean longevity greater than about thirty-five years. Moreover, no sharp changes in average length of life took place until about the eighteenth or nineteenth century. Beginning about that time, various means of death control produced profound alterations in mortality patterns. Average life expectancy for the world population in 1975 probably stood at fifty-five years, despite the fact that the figures for some of the least-developed countries of the earth were not much above those of the world as a whole in medieval times.

Because the data required to calculate life expectancy are not available for many countries, it is often necessary to use less refined measures of mortality in comparing areas throughout the world. The population table in Appendix B provides two frequently used measures, the *crude death rate* (number of deaths per thousand population) and the *infant mortality rate* (deaths before one year of age per thousand live births). The latter measure is a particularly important one, since a substantial part of the total death rate in countries with high mortality is due to the death of infants, yet the statistics are lacking for many of the nations. It should be noted that comparisons of the crude death rate are very much affected by the age composition of the populations compared. Older populations will tend to have higher proportions of their people subject to the risks of death.

Developed Regions of the World

The estimated crude death rate for the world in 1975 was about thirteen per thousand. The death rates of all nations in North America, Europe, and the USSR are relatively low by worldwide standards. The highest rate for any of these countries in 1975 was in the Democratic Republic of Germany (12.4), and it was still below the world average. The lowest rate was in Albania (6.5), and the other countries were bunched between these rates. Infant mortality rates for these countries were more disparate, being as low as 10 in Sweden and Finland and as high as 87 in Albania. Almost all these countries had infant mortality rates between 15 and 40, far below the world level of 98 in 1975.

It is only within the past few decades that this uniformly low level of mortality has been attained in these modernized nations. In Europe, for example, the only countries in 1906–1910 with crude death rates

Figure 3.1   World mortality pattern, 1972

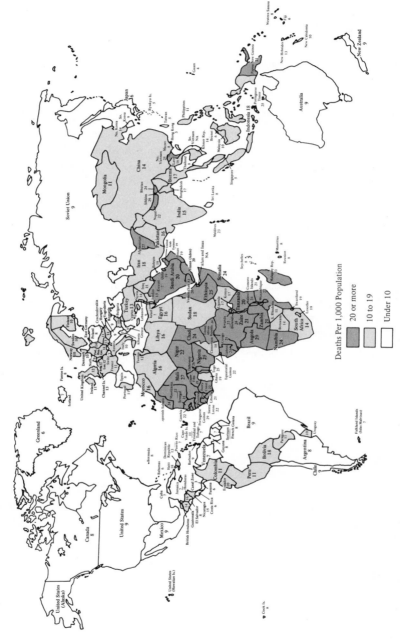

Source: International Statistical Programs Center, U. S. Bureau of the Census.   Prepared under a participating agency service agreement with the Office of Population, Agency for International Development, April 1974.

below fifteen per thousand were Denmark, England and Wales, the Netherlands, Norway, and Sweden. In other parts of Western Europe the rates were in the range of fifteen to twenty per thousand, and in Southern and Eastern Europe rates higher than twenty prevailed. By 1935–1938 the crude death rates for most European countries were below fifteen or approaching it. The decline in mortality leveled off for Western Europe by 1955–1958, and further reductions for other European countries brought them all to a comparably low level.

Patterns of mortality decline in North America and Oceania were not unlike those in Western Europe. In the United States, for instance, a crude death rate of 16.2 in 1900–1904 was progressively reduced, falling below 10 in about 1950 and stabilizing between 9 and 10 since that time. The downward trend was even more pronounced in the Soviet Union, where a death rate of 32.4 in 1896–1897 fell to 17.6 by 1938–1940 and to below 10 by 1950–1954.

Declines in infant mortality played a major role in raising life expectancy in modernized nations. Whereas infant mortality rates of one hundred or more per thousand were common in Europe in 1935–1938, by 1955–1958 no country on the continent had a rate at that level. Between 1900–1904 and 1973 the infant mortality rate declined from 100.8 to 17.3 for Australia and from 142.9 to 17.6 for the United States. The Soviet Union's infant mortality rate was recorded as 273 in 1913 and fell to 22.6 by 1973.

As a result of these mortality improvements, life expectancy at birth rose dramatically in developed countries. In some countries, it doubled (as indicated in Table 3.1).

Although the mortality levels of the developed countries were already moderately low when death statistics were first compiled, substantial gains in survival were made in the ensuing years. It is impossible, without the benefit of adequate data, to trace the long course of mortality in these nations as they underwent the demographic transition. It is reasonable to expect, however, that death rates were considerably higher before than after death records became available, and that the long-term history of mortality in developed countries was

Table 3.1   Trends in expectation of life at birth for selected developed
nations since the turn of the century

Country	Period	Expectation of life at birth (years)	Percentage increase since first period cited
Austria	1901–1905	40.1	—
	1930–1933	56.5	41
	1949–1951	64.4	61
	1971	70.5	76
Belgium	1891–1900	47.1	—
	1928–1932	57.9	23
	1946–1947	64.7	37
	1959–1963	70.7	50
Hungary	1900–1901	37.5	—
	1930–1931	49.8	33
	1955	66.9	78
	1970	69.4	85
Italy	1901–1911	44.5	—
	1930–1932	54.9	23
	1954–1957	67.9	53
	1964–1967	70.7	59
Spain	1900	34.8	—
	1930–1931	50.3	45
	1950	61.1	76
	1960	69.7	100
Australia	1901–1910	57.0	—
	1920–1922	61.2	7
	1946–1948	68.4	20
	1956–1958	70.5	24
	1960–1962	71.2	25
USSR	1896–1897[a]	32	—
	1926–1927[a]	44	38
	1957–1958	68	113
	1968–1969	70	119

Country	Period	Expectation of life at birth (years)	Percentage increase since first period cited
United States	1900–1902	47.3	—
	1929–1931	59.7	26
	1949–1951	68.2	44
	1971	71.1	50

a For European Russia.

Sources: United Nations, *Population Bulletin*, No. 6, 1962, New York, 1963, pp. 22–23, 28, and 31; and United Nations, *Demographic Yearbook*, 1972, Table 27.

one of a slow but continual transition from high to low death rates. Once low mortality levels were achieved, they were subject to periodic fluctuations that sometimes resulted in higher rates. In recent years, some crude death rates have risen as a consequence of increasing proportions of older persons in the population.

Developing Regions of the World

It is characteristic of the bulk of countries in Latin America, Asia, and Africa that their mortality rates remained at a high level for a longer period of time than those in modernized nations. When death control became more widespread, death rates in these countries fell more precipitously than they ever did in the developed countries. It is still the case, however, that important variations can be noted among the broad regions and individual countries.

Latin American mortality trends have been similar to those of developed nations, with some time lag. This would be especially true of countries such as Argentina and Uruguay, whose death rates at the turn of the century were already quite low, and to a lesser extent of Costa Rica, Puerto Rico, and Venezuela. With the exception of Haiti and Bolivia, other Latin American nations have experienced significant reductions in the death rate, and the prevailing rate in many of these lands is now below the death rates for the majority of modernized countries, partly because of mortality declines and partly because of favorable age distributions.

The downward course of mortality can also be documented for the major areas of Asia. Reductions have been observed since shortly after the turn of the century, with the steepest declines taking place in recent decades. In Japan, the death rate dropped from 21.8 in 1921–1925 to 7.8 in 1958 and has stayed at that low level. But decreases of the same order of magnitude are also shown by official data for most other Asian countries. Some of the sharpest reductions in mortality were recorded for Ceylon (now Sri Lanka), Malaysia, and Hong Kong. However, in 1975 death rates of at least twenty per thousand were estimated for Yemen, Nepal, Saudi Arabia, Afghanistan, Bangladesh, Bhutan, Laos, and the Republic of Vietnam.

The death rate for Africa as a continent stood at twenty per thousand in 1975, and virtually every country of Western and Middle Africa, as well as some in Eastern and Southern Africa, had death rates at that level or above. Where death rates were at least moderately low, they could be attributed partly to the presence of European settlers.

The overall picture in the developing countries is one of declining mortality, but with the decline at different stages of development. Latin American countries, by and large, have effected the mortality transition. Death control has been rapidly achieved in most parts of Asia. Only in Africa is such control lagging. Crude death rates there remain generally high, infant mortality rates tend likewise to be sustained at levels far above those in most other parts of the world, and life expectancies for some countries are reminiscent of those in the medieval world.

Short-Term Mortality Patterns

We have been discussing the long sweep of mortality trends without paying attention to variations in death rates that take place in the short run. Closer examination of the trends, when death rates are plotted on a month-to-month basis, reveal fluctuations throughout the year. Rosenberg has broken down mortality patterns for the United States in the 1957–1960 period into three components.[5] As depicted in Figure 3.2, the seasonal component, which consists of intrayear variations which are repeated more or less regularly each year, accounts for more than half of the month-to-month mortality variations. Year

Figure 3.2 United States death rates by month, raw data, and seasonal, cyclical, and irregular components, 1957–1960

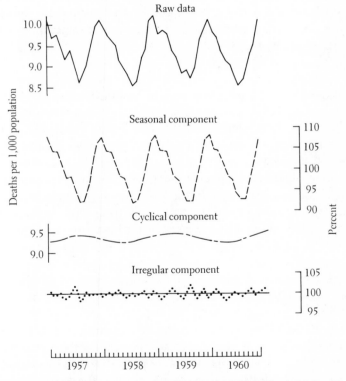

Source: Harry M. Rosenberg, "Seasonal Adjustment of Vital Statistics by Electronic Computer," *Public Health Reports*, Vol. 80, No. 3 (March 1965), 206.

after year, one can observe peaks in the winter months and troughs during the autumn months. The seasonal patterns in countries other than the United States may vary, depending on their location and the climatic conditions in the area. (Severe weather may occur in other calendar months.) The cyclical component, which incorporates the continuing long-term trend and shorter-run cyclical movements made up of continual alternating periods of increase or decrease spaced a few years apart, is relatively smooth and declining. The irregular component, residual fluctuations which exhibit no recurrent pattern, accounts for about one-fourth of the total variation in the death rate. On balance, then, the level of the death rate at any point in time is composed of a quite predictable seasonal pattern, a somewhat predictable cyclical pattern, and a most unpredictable irregular pattern, all superimposed on the long-term mortality trend.

The Age Curve of Mortality

The element of predictability found in the mortality trend can also be discovered in age patterns of mortality. The human organism develops from creation until shortly after puberty, at which time a steady state of body cell population exists. From that point onward, growth becomes negative, cells are lost, and the process of aging continues.[6] The risks of mortality correspond, to a great degree, with this human growth process, being greatest at birth and during old age, when cells are first forming or becoming depleted, and least during the later childhood years.

This pattern of biological development, noted in all types of peoples, results in a standard age curve of mortality. As shown in Figure 3.3, the death rate starts at a high peak immediately after birth, falls to a minimum in the early teens, and then rises, gradually at first, then more and more rapidly as age advances, until the last survivors of the generation are gone.[7] Six curves are presented in the figure, showing for each sex the death rate according to age for three hypothetical populations. These three populations have mortality levels indicative of high, intermediate, and low life expectancies at birth in the world in modern times. In the case of Model I, a life expectancy of thirty years for persons of both sexes would be typical. Model II is characteristic of countries with a life expectancy of the population of 52.5 years, while the average longevity of persons in Model III is 70.2 years. The most impressive feature of the figure is that the general shape of all the curves is the same. Regardless of the level of mortality in the population, death rates decline from infancy to teen ages, and increase thereafter. What does differ among the model populations is the level of death rates reached at the various ages. Those countries with more favorable life expectancies have considerably lower death rates at the younger ages and somewhat lower rates at middle and older ages.

A country undergoing the mortality transition from a life expectancy at birth of fifty-two years to one of seventy years, as was the case for the United States between about 1915 and 1960 and as is represented by a shift from the mortality curve of Model II to that of Model III, would experience reductions in the death rate of roughly 40 to 50 percent at ages up to forty, and even 20 to 25 percent after the age of seventy-five. These are approximately the magnitudes of reduction in age-specific mortality that will be necessary to bring the overall mortality picture in many of the developing countries of the world in line with what is now observed for many of the developed nations.

Not all countries that have made the transition in mortality from Model II to Model III have had the same pattern of reductions in the death rate at each age. In Europe, North America, Australia, and New Zealand, the decline of mortality in its early stages affected mainly the death rate of infants and children, and that of young adults to a lesser extent. In the developing countries of Africa, Asia, and Latin America, adults up to age forty or fifty appear to have shared with children the benefit of recent mortality reduction.[8] Even within these groups of countries, the magnitudes of declines varied somewhat, and during short periods of time, some mortality increases have been noted.

It is clear from available historical data that general improvements

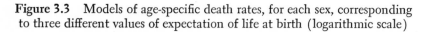

Figure 3.3   Models of age-specific death rates, for each sex, corresponding to three different values of expectation of life at birth (logarithmic scale)

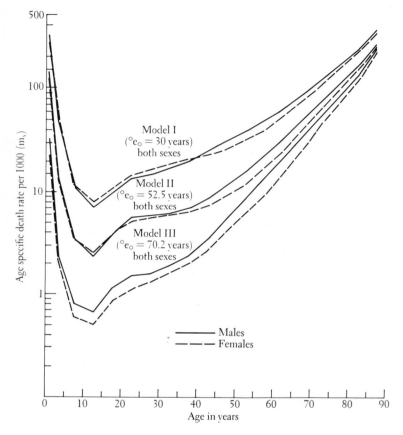

Source: United Nations, *Population Bulletin of the United Nations*, No. 6, 1962, p. 52.

in mortality have had no impact on life span and little effect on the life expectancy of those reaching older ages. In the first half of the twentieth century in Sweden, percentage decreases in death rates amounted to between 64 and 81 percent at ages under forty-five, 27 percent at ages forty-five to sixty-four, and only 7 percent at ages sixty-five and over.⁹ Thus, for example, a male Swedish baby born in 1950 could have expected about sixteen more years of life than one born in 1900, yet a Swedish male who had reached the age of sixty-five in 1950 could have looked forward to barely one more year of life than his counterpart in 1900.

Factors Affecting Mortality

Now that we have surveyed the course of mortality as it has developed in all parts of the world, to what can we attribute the changes that have taken place? Which factors seem to have been most important, and how differently have the several factors operated to bring about alterations in death rates in various countries? In providing the answers to these questions, we shall use the analytical framework outlined in Chapter 2. First, the effects of societal factors are examined; second, attention is given to the role of group influences; third, the importance of individual decisions and practices is assessed.

Societal-Level Variables

Although a great number of global factors could be cited as affecting mortality, four are of particular relevance in understanding trends in the death rate. These are *natural environmental factors, economic development and technological change, advances in public health and medical science,* and *changing causes of death.*

NATURAL ENVIRONMENTAL FACTORS

Little research has been done to determine the effect of these factors on mortality. It is difficult to disentangle such effects from others with which they are closely related, but it is probable that they have operated in many places to affect the death rate. *Climate* is one such factor. People in areas of high average temperature, low humidity, and low levels of rainfall may experience greater risks of certain types of ailments, such as malaria. On the other hand, residents in areas of low average temperature, high humidity, and excessive precipitation may be more subject to other mortal risks, such as those from pneumonia and influenza. It would seem that it is extreme or changing climatic conditions which present the greatest hazards to health and thus to life. *Terrain* is another environmental factor of importance. Very mountainous areas may limit transportation and communication, which are often crucial to the distribution and availability of food and medical services. *Bodies of water* may be hindrances or aids for similar reasons. *Quality of the soil* and *mineral resources* may determine the fruitfulness of the land and hence its ability to provide food, other material goods, and shelter. *Altitude* may have an impact on the ability of the body to function effectively.

ECONOMIC DEVELOPMENT AND TECHNOLOGICAL CHANGE

A considerable amount of evidence points to these factors as contributing substantially to the reduction of mortality in Western countries. Various authors have recognized the importance of *industrialization, commercial development,* and the increasing *efficiency of agriculture* in providing the economic basis for a more abundant and more healthful life and for advances in public health and medicine which made the present low mortality rates possible.[10] The theoretical statement of the demographic transition hypothesized the important role of economic change in reducing deaths, and this relationship can be used to describe the history of mortality trends in industrialized nations. The theory proposes, according to Coale and Hoover, that:

> . . . an agrarian peasant economy (characterized by a high degree of self-sufficiency within each community and even each family, by relatively slow change in technique, and by the relatively unimportant role of market exchange) typically has high average death rates. Moreover, these death rates usually fluctuate in consequence of variations in crops, the varying incidence of epidemics, etc. In such an economy birth rates are nearly

stable at a high level. Death rates are high as a consequence of poor diets, primitive sanitation, and the absence of effective preventive and curative medical practices. . . .

Economic development, according to the theory of the demographic transition, has the effect of bringing about a reduction in death rates. Economic development involves evolution from a predominantly agrarian economy to an economy with a greater division of labor, using more elaborate tools and equipment, more urbanized, more oriented to the market sale of its products, and characterized by rapid and pervasive changes in technique. It also involves improvements in transportation, communications, and productivity, and these improvements have had the effect (notably in Europe, the United States, Canada, Australia, and New Zealand, and later in Japan) of bringing a striking reduction in death rates. The reduction in death rates may be ascribed partly to greater regularity in food supplies, to the establishment of greater law and order, and to other fairly direct consequences of economic change. Other factors contributing to the decline — improvements in sanitation, the development of vaccines and other means of preventive medicine, and great and rapid strides in the treatment of disease — can themselves be considered as somewhat indirect consequences of economic change.[11]

Economic change can be said to have contributed both directly and indirectly to long-term mortality reductions in what are now the industrialized portions of the world. But it is clear that economic factors have had less direct effect on declines in the death rates of developing countries. Many low-income countries, such as Sri Lanka, Malaysia, some of the Caribbean islands, and parts of Latin America, have attained low death rates without any major transformation in their resources.[12] Most of these countries have borrowed death-saving technology and materials already developed in modernized nations and have benefited, to some extent, from economic aid from those countries.

ADVANCES IN PUBLIC HEALTH AND MEDICAL SCIENCE

It is increasingly being recognized that better health and medical improvements have been major factors in the decline of mortality in both developed and developing countries. High levels of mortality had been maintained, in large part, as a result of epidemic disease and poor community health conditions. The plague, smallpox, cholera, and typhus took a heavy toll of the population, primarily in the earlier periods, and smallpox, tetanus, dysentery, typhoid, scarlet fever, tuberculosis, and pneumonia posed great threats in later periods. Inadequate provisions for sanitary facilities, water, and sewerage systems contributed substantially to the existence of these diseases and the difficulty of controlling their spread throughout the population. Accordingly, control of these diseases was achieved by the introduction of vaccines and techniques of mass immunization; the development of bacteriology and the consequent prevention and cure of infections through asepsis (protection against bacteria) and antisepsis (inhibition or destruction of bacteria); vector control (the elimination of disease-carrying pests at points where they breed); improved standards of public sanitation; creation of more extensive water and sewerage systems; and expansion of health services, including the proliferation of hospitals, training of more physicians and auxiliary medical personnel, and growth of health education programs.

The relative importance of health and medical advances as compared with economic development in accounting for the long-term decline in mortality is a matter of dispute among students of the topic. History has shown that many diseases, such as scarlet fever, diphtheria, and measles, substantially diminished without human control because of natural immunity developed in a society.[13] It may be, therefore, that medical science was greatly aided by tendencies inherent in the population to overcome certain diseases. It is also true that a strong case can be made for the early improvement in standards of living which were generated by economic change. Thus McKeown has argued that gains in health in England and Wales since the eighteenth century were due to a rising standard of living since about 1770, to sanitary measures since 1878, and to treatment, both preventive and curative, from the second quarter of the twentieth century.[14] This explanation probably serves well for understanding modern mortality declines in industrialized countries. Developing countries, on the other hand, have reduced their previously high mortality rates primarily by borrowing the techniques of vector control and mass immunization already used in the Western world, and only secondarily through progress in classical medical services, sanitation, education, and level of living.

CHANGING CAUSES OF DEATH

Long-term improvements in survival resulting from the diminution of many fatal diseases have led to sharp changes in the distribution of causes of death in the population. Historical mortality declines were achieved mainly by controlling communicable diseases. As a result, such causes of death as cardiovascular-renal diseases and cancer became more prominent. This was partly because control over these causes of death could not be achieved, and partly because avoidance of the communicable diseases permitted many people to live to older ages, when the risk of cardiovascular-renal diseases and cancer were greater.

Figure 3.4 illustrates what typically happens to cause-of-death patterns in a population as life expectancy is increased from forty to seventy-five years. Causes of death are grouped into five categories, each of which includes causes which have reacted similarly to health improvements. As life expectancy at birth rises from forty to sixty years, a sharp decline is observed in Group I diseases (infectious and parasitic diseases, influenza, and pneumonia); a slight increase is noted for causes in Group IV (violence) and Group V (other causes, such as diseases of the digestive system, children's diseases, and senility); while somewhat greater relative increases are recorded for Group II diseases (cancer) and Group III diseases (cardiovascular diseases and bronchitis after the age of five). An increase in life expectancy from sixty to seventy-five years accentuates the decline of communicable diseases and increases the importance of cardiovascular-renal diseases and cancer. Extension of the average life expectancy at birth beyond seventy is associated with

Figure 3.4   Distribution, in a standard population, of deaths (all ages and both sexes) by cause-of-death groups for different levels of expectation of life at birth ranging from 40 to 76 years

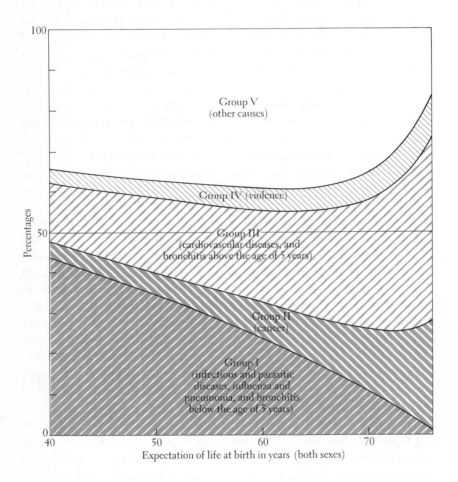

Source: United Nations, *Population Bulletin of the United Nations*, No. 6, 1962, p. 110.

continued reductions in the first set of causes, further prominence of the second and third sets, a higher rate of death by violence, and a rapid contraction of other causes.[15]

Group Membership and Normative Influences

Just as societal-level variables act to establish or change conditions affecting mortality, the group memberships that individuals have help to determine their life chances. By group memberships we mean the social categories of the society with which persons are associated — type of family, social class, religious denomination, etc. These memberships are important to mortality expectations both because opportunities for maintaining life are characteristic of each group and because individuals derive norms of behavior, including those affecting mortality, from the groups.

THE FAMILY AND THE SEXES

Examination of the family as a factor affecting mortality is crucial, because the formative years of life are a critical stage in the age curve of mortality, and the family is the principal institution determining behavior in these early years. From the time we are born, members of our family influence, sometimes explicitly and often subtly, the attitudes and behavior that partly determine our life expectancy. In nearly all families the infant and child is *socialized to standards of health and avoidance of death*. Parents and other family members instruct children in how to behave, and themselves exhibit behavior which the child may copy or use as a model. Some areas in which family behavior provides a guide for the child's own current and later behavior affecting mortality include toilet training, cleanliness, diet, dress, and knowledge about hazards, such as those in water, on roads, from poisons, and from smoking.

Cussler and De Give have reported an example of how distinctive family patterns in food consumption emerge and shape the behavior of the child. In their study of Southern rural families in the United

States, they examined the role of mothers in imparting eating habits to their children:

> The mother's direct control of the eating habits of her children — her technique of control — is of great importance. Whether or not she displays her own food dislikes to her children, for them to imitate, or forces herself to eat foods she doesn't like in order to set a good example; whether or not she commands or entices or fools her family into eating what she thinks is good for them, or caters to their prejudices and cajoles their appetites; whether or not she insists on discipline at table; whether or not she uses food as reward or punishment — all of these are significant in the development of food habits. The process of socialization — the initiation into "the standard of expected performance" — both in regard to eating behavior and general behavior, which the child undergoes when growing up in a society, thus affect the child's experience with certain foods.[16]

This family socialization pattern undoubtedly varies among socioeconomic strata as well as among other groupings in the population.

Family factors are also important in determining the extent of the *health care* received by individuals. A survey of American families in 1962 found that the annual amount of money spent for all types of health care in a family increased as the size of the family rose, but that the rise in expense was not constant with increased family size.[17] Health expenses per family member decreased as the size of the family increased. The amount spent on health is, of course, related to the ages of family members, and expenses for children other than infants may be relatively small, while those for older persons may be comparatively large. But smaller families tend also, on the average, to have higher incomes, and this permits them to afford more health services. A similar survey in 1968 showed that more than four-fifths of all members of families had some hospital insurance coverage, but that smaller proportions of those that lived with other relatives or nonrelatives were covered. Likewise, a smaller but significant fraction of individuals living alone had health insurance coverage.[18]

Research has also shown that there are differences in the extent to which the sexes avail themselves of medical services. Females have reported more illnesses in surveys than males, have reported seeing physicians more often, and have made more use of hospitals for reasons other than childbearing, despite similar levels of morbidity.[19] It may seem surprising, therefore, that data indicate a greater life expectancy for women than for men. This differential can be observed in most countries of the world for long periods of time. Exceptions are noted in some areas of Asia, Africa, and Latin America and among some cultural subgroups within countries that have higher female life expectancy. There are also variations by age, with instances of higher female death rates reported at younger ages, but the *sex differential in mortality* can be generalized across all age groups. What is especially impressive about this phenomenon is that the advantage females have over males in life expectancy has been widening in virtually all countries, particularly in populations experiencing substantial mortality declines. Moreover, the female advantage obtains for death rates from each major cause.

Studying mortality trends by sex in the United States between 1900 and 1958, Enterline discovered that death rates for males and females diverged most notably after 1922 and most significantly at ages fifteen to twenty-four and forty-five to sixty-four. Changing patterns in three causes of death accounted for most of the divergence at the younger ages. Deaths from tuberculosis, of which there had been relatively more among girls than among boys, were considerably reduced. Deaths from deliveries and complications of pregnancy and childbirth were reduced sharply. Finally, the more widespread use of automobiles, especially by young men, contributed to a significant increase in the incidence of mortality among males.

At ages forty-five to sixty-four, the causes of death that contributed most to diverging sex mortality trends were different from those that contributed at the younger ages. The increasing incidence of heart disease accounted for a sizable proportion of the increasing difference in death rates of men and women at these ages. Deaths from various types of cancer also contributed substantially. These are causes which have affected both sexes but have afflicted men more than women.[20]

In order to examine this phenomenon in cross-cultural perspective and test the worldwide generalizability of Enterline's findings, Geis compared sex mortality patterns in various countries at different stages of their socioeconomic development and demographic transition, paying special attention to changing causes of death. He found that death rates for females declined faster than death rates for males as societies developed socioeconomically and, further, that a considerable part of the higher mortality for males could be ascribed to the shifts in causes of death that occurred over time.[21]

Since mortality is a result of both biological and socioenvironmental forces, a debate has developed among students of sex mortality patterns as to which set of causes provides a better explanation. Enterline interpreted his findings to give more weight to environmental causes of death and to the generation by society of an increasing incidence of other causes (for example, automobile accidents). Research on the Hutterites, a small religious sect in the United States which has a very low death rate and a very high birth rate, supports the socioenvironmental argument. Contrary to the traditional sex differences in mortality observed in the wider population, death rates among Hutterite females are higher than those among males in the fifteen-to-sixty age bracket. The explanation for this unusual pattern can be found in the high birth rate among Hutterite women, which generally lowers their resistance to illnesses during the childbearing period and for a decade or so afterwards.[22] In countries where males have had a more favorable life expectancy, a similar explanation involving high fertility performance among women, with its consequent weakening of the body (and often higher maternal mortality), can be given.

Additional support for the socioenvironmental explanation of diverging sex mortality trends comes from several large-scale surveys of the effects of social and psychological stress on the occurrence of several different diseases. Surveys of mental illness, heart disease, tuberculosis, arthritis, ulcers, alcoholism, diabetes, and many other diseases have all indicated that such diseases as these occur more often under stressful conditions.[23]

Differences in the use of tobacco have been identified as a critical factor in the sex mortality differential. Almost half of the sex difference in deaths at adult ages in the United States in 1962 could be accounted for by differences in smoking, and three-fourths of the widening gap between 1910 and 1962 was attributable to smoking patterns. The use of tobacco is apparently associated with the greater incidence among men of cardiovascular diseases and cancer.[24]

On the other hand, support for the biological explanation comes from several sources. First, there is the information that the sex mortality differentials are also found among species other than humans. These species range from the mealworm to the rat. Second, sex differences in the death rate have been recorded not only at all ages of life but even during the prenatal period, when a much weaker case for the effect of socioenvironmental effects can be made.[25] Third, a case for the biological position was made as a result of Madigan's study of the mortality patterns of religious teaching orders of brothers and sisters.[26] By selecting groups of men and women with similar styles of life, he was able to control for a considerable part of the sociocultural differences between men and women in the general population. The men did not serve in the armed forces, nor were they apt to engage in illicit behavior. The women were not subject to the rigors of childbearing, nor were their occupations less stressful than those of the men. Diet, housing, and medical care were the same for the two groups, as was time allotted for sleep, work, study, and recreation. Of course, not all sociocultural differences between the sexes were eliminated, but they were at least diminished, and one would expect more similar mortality experience if sociocultural conditions were an important explanatory factor. A sample was drawn from 20 brothers' communities and 41 sisters' communities, and life records since 1900 were accumulated. Madigan found that both sexes in the religious orders enjoyed a greater life expectancy than their counterparts in the general population, but that the gap in life expectancy between the sexes was as apparent in the religious orders as in the general population.

The similarity of lifestyles of these men and women, which was greater than that of men and women in the general population, did not result in comparably similar mortality patterns.

It is clear that both biological and social forces affect one's chances of dying, and that mortality differences between the sexes are the result of a combination of the two. Since there is little reason to suppose that the physiological makeup of males and females has been undergoing any significant change in modern times, the explanation for the widening gap between mortality trends of the sexes must be found primarily in the changing pattern of causes of death and environmental forces that increase the life expectancy of women more than men.

SOCIOECONOMIC GROUPS

Socioeconomic differences in mortality have been known for some time. Villerme reported on their existence as far back as 1828.[27] Data on the subject from the Registrar-General's Office of England and Wales go back at least to 1851. In the United States, the first census records showing mortality by occupation appeared in 1890.[28]

Of all the studies linking mortality with socioeconomic status, the most prominent are those relating occupational categories to death rates. Nearly all the early studies were of this type, and the greater availability of occupational data than of other socioeconomic data in connection with death records makes such studies typical even today. In general, this research has found an inverse relationship between occupational status and mortality — the lower the status, the higher the death rate at a given age or the lower the life expectancy. Such a finding was made for the French population by Huber in 1907–1908. He discovered that mortality for managers and officials in industry was lower than for wage earners, either clerks or craftsmen. The mortality of craftsmen varied from one occupation to another, apparently because of different occupational risks. In the professions of law and teaching, mortality was much lower than for the total population. Statistics published by the French government for 1923–1928 confirmed Huber's observations.[29]

Beginning in 1851, the government of England and Wales issued data on the deaths in several hundred occupations related to the number of people in each occupation as determined by the census. Similar studies have been made at ten-year intervals since, in conjunction with the British census. The death rates calculated by comparing deaths and population in each occupational category have traditionally been adjusted to take account of differences in the age structure of different occupations. Since 1911, the various occupations have been grouped together into social classes. Analysis of these data over time shows that the classical inverse relationship between socioeconomic status and mortality has been modified. For example, in 1921–1923 and 1930–1932 there was an uninterrupted upward gradient of mortality from social class I (professional) to social class V (unskilled), but at the later date the differences between classes were much less. By 1950, the inverse pattern was disturbed, the lowest mortality being in intermediate classes II and IV. At that time, however, the highest mortality was still in the lowest class.[30] More recent studies in the United States provide evidence of a continuing but narrowing occupational differential in mortality.[31]

One question that often arises in interpreting data on occupational differences in the death rate concerns whether the variations are primarily due to the differing risks of death associated with occupations or mainly a function of the socioeconomic levels of the occupations. This question has been answered using statistics for England and Wales at several dates that compare the mortality of men by occupation with the mortality of married women by their husband's occupation (Table 3.2). The mortality rates by occupation are largely ranked in the same order for men and their wives, suggesting that mortality for the male population is affected to a greater extent by the standard of living associated with an occupation than by the occupational risk itself.[32] However, for

Table 3.2 Standardized mortality ratios for all causes, for age group
20–64 years: England and Wales, 1921–1923 and 1930–1932

Social class	1921–1923 Males (excluding noncivilians)	1930–1932 Males (including noncivilians)	Married women (by class of husband)	Employed single women
All groups	*100*	*100*	*100*	*100*
Class I (high)	82	90	81	—
Class II	93	94	89	—
Class III	94	97	99	95
Class IV	99	102	103	102
Class V (low)	121	111	113	112

Source: *The Registrar-General's Decennial Supplement,* England and Wales, 1931,
Part IIa, Occupational Mortality, p. 20, table E.

a number of occupations the inherent risks are clearly important factors.
Included would be such occupations as miner, steel foundry furnace-
man, "sandhog," and police officer.

These overall patterns relating mortality to socioeconomic status
vary for different causes of death. The typical inverse relationship can
be found, for example, for respiratory ailments, cancer of the stomach,
and myocardial degeneration among both sexes; for cancer of the lung
among men; and for cancer of the cervix and diabetes among women.
On the other hand, a direct relationship (higher rates among the upper
strata) can be observed for leukemia among both sexes; for coronary
heart disease and diabetes among men, and for cancer of the breast
among women.[33] Although very little research has been done to explain
these variations, it can be hypothesized that they are a function of the
lifestyles of the social strata. For example, respiratory ailments take a
greater toll of the lower strata because persons in these strata have less
adequate health and medical care and are more likely to live in environ-

ments that subject them to the risks of such ailments. Higher rates of coronary heart disease among upper-status men might be explained by their more excessive dietary habits and the physical and mental stress related to their lifestyles.

Further evidence that socioeconomic factors are associated with mortality is presented in a study conducted in the United States in 1960 in which death certificates were matched with earlier census records for the decedents and analysis of mortality patterns by a variety of census socioeconomic indicators was performed.[34] Not only occupational differentials but education and income differentials were discovered. In general, inverse relationships between these variables and death rates existed, but the relationships were not strong, and there were some exceptions for particular segments of the population or for certain causes of death. On the whole, one can presume that socioeconomic variations in mortality will diminish as nations undergo social and economic development and death control becomes more equally accessible to all strata of societies.

ETHNIC GROUPS

Among the several differentials in mortality observed in various societies, ethnic status (race, nationality, and other cultural characteristics) appears to be an important variable. In the United States, racial differences in death rates have been noted for some time in official statistics. In 1900, the crude death rate stood at 17.0 for whites and 25.0 for nonwhites; by 1969, it had declined to 9.5 and 9.6, respectively.[35] Part of the reason for the reduction of the difference was the changing age composition of the two groups, with the age distribution of the nonwhite population favoring a lower death rate more as time passed. At most ages, the death rates are considerably higher for nonwhites. Even allowing for this fact, however, the overall mortality differential has narrowed since the turn of the century.

Despite a continuing differential in the crude death rate, the age curves of mortality for whites and nonwhites have been remarkably similar. Death rates for both groups have been lowest in the early teens and thereafter increase with age. There has been a tendency for non-whites to have somewhat higher rates at most ages up to the very old ages. From about age seventy-five onward, death rates are recorded as higher for whites. The "crossing" of the age curves of mortality cannot be attributed to limitations of the statistics even though mortality and population data tend to be more poorly reported for older non-whites.[36] The logical explanation for the crossing of curves is the selection that takes place with regard to who survives. The higher death rate of nonwhites at the earlier ages presumably reflects their relatively unfavorable socioeconomic circumstances. With advancing age, the fact that the "heartiest" are most likely to survive probably becomes more important and socioeconomic factors relatively less important. By older ages, the physiological selection has become so much more pronounced for nonwhites than whites, the latter including many "weaker" persons who have survived because of socioeconomic advantage, that death rates begin to favor nonwhites.[37] Future research will help establish the validity of these propositions.

Mortality rates also differ among groups distinguished by nationality or other cultural traits. Typical of such differences are those found some years ago between traditional Spanish-origin populations in the southwestern part of the United States and the indigenous white Americans of that area. Death rates of the former were found to be appreciably higher. The Spanish-origin people were generally distinguished from other groups by their physical appearance, their cultural background, their socioeconomic level, and their psychological identification with their distinct origins.[38] People from this subculture drew their knowledge of illness and its treatment from a combination of contemporary scientific medical sources and Spanish, American Indian, and Anglo folk medicine. When they were ill, any combination of these sources might have been used, and although older people were more likely to resort to folk medicine, this practice was followed by people of all ages.[39] It is clear that the use of folk medicine related to the traditions passed down from generation to generation within the Spanish-origin community, but it also came about because conventional modern-day medicine was far more expensive, not as readily accessible, and dispensed by practitioners with whom the individual was often not culturally compatible.[40] In short, the traditional Spanish-origin population relied on folk medicine to a considerable extent for a combination of socio-economic and cultural reasons. While such practices did afford some measure of medical relief, they were not as beneficial as modern medical and health practices.

RELIGION

Cultural factors associated with mortality include those based on religious affiliation. Although it is often difficult to separate the religious influence from ethnic and socioeconomic influences, distinctive religious practices relating to health and survival frequently have the effect of positively or negatively modifying the death rate.

An example can be found in the once-traditional practice of *suttee* in ancient India, in which a widow was expected, on the basis of religious tenets, to sacrifice herself on the funeral pyre of her husband.[41] This practice, begun in the pre-Christian era, was abolished and then reinstituted periodically. At times, it took the form of mass suicide as the harems of deceased sultans followed the practice. Although no estimates of the mortality rate generated by this tradition are available and the practice was officially abolished in India in the nineteenth century, it is an illustration of how religion-based customs can have an impact on mortality trends.

Some modern-day religions are very explicit about matters affecting health and longevity. The writings of Christian Science suggest that through mental health the life expectancy of followers of the religion will be increased. Christian Scientists shun most forms of medical aid, but they are required to avoid smoking and drinking of alcohol and beverages containing caffeine. Analysis of causes of death among Christian Scientists, as compared with the general population, indicates that they have a higher incidence of many forms of heart disease and malignancies but maintain a life expectancy similar to that of the general population.[42] How much of the mortality difference between

Christian Scientists and other religious groups depends on the social class, age, and marital status composition of the groups and how much on the distinctive religious practices of the groups cannot be determined from available data, yet it seems clear that some practices modify the probability of death, perhaps increasing it in the case of shunning medical service and decreasing it in the case of avoidance of smoking and drinking.

Many contemporary religious denominations and sects support extensive medical and health work. They establish hospitals, clinics, and sanitariums; schools of medicine, nursing, dentistry, and medical technology; and health and medical publications. These activities are usually justified in terms of health as one aspect of the Gospel message and of Christian living. Seventh-Day Adventists, for example, believe that Christians should have a concern for health for the practical reason that only in a sound body can they render the most effective service to God and to others.[43] They cite Biblical verses on which they base their belief that each person is accountable to God for the preservation of health, and that the person who knowingly violates simple health principles, thereby bringing on ill health, disease, or disability, is living in violation of the laws of God.[44]

GOVERNMENT

Mortality control has been achieved substantially through national and community effort; it is understandable, therefore, that governments have played a vital role. Although some form of organization for public health was known in ancient times, it was not until the modern era that what we now know as public health developed. At the turn of the nineteenth century in England, community sanitation programs were introduced, first through voluntary popular participation and later through compulsory appointment and activity of local Boards of Health.[45] A number of European countries began to build state hospital systems in the early 1800s. The American public health organization followed that of the English, giving emphasis to administration by local authorities with the assistance, supervision, and support of state and national agencies.

Public health flourished after World War I as several countries modeled their systems after the existing ones, and it became almost universal after World War II.[46] The extent of the health needs of countries adopting systems during the latter period was much greater than that of countries which adopted them earlier, and the means to meet the burden of sickness and suffering were as limited as needs were great. In the postwar period, the World Health Organization and other United Nations agencies emerged as supporters and facilitators of public health.

The origins of international collaboration in public health, like those of national public health, are found in the fear of epidemic spread.[47] Many nations adopted quarantine regulations in order to keep certain health hazards away from their shores. Although quarantine is still practiced selectively today, the emphasis in international public health has shifted to disease prevention and control. Technical commissions under the League of Nations studied the major causes of death and made recommendations for programs to contain them. It was not, however, until the World Health Organization was formed following the establishment of the Charter of the United Nations that international cooperation took place on a worldwide scale. The agency was designed to assist governments in strengthening health services, promote improved health and medical standards and environmental hygiene, promote and coordinate health research, and generally advance knowledge concerning various aspects of health and medicine.

Although national and international efforts to improve health and longevity through general public health programs have succeeded in reducing the death rate, their effects would have been limited without the inclusion of mass immunization campaigns. Moreover, it is inconceivable that such campaigns could have succeeded without the involvement of governmental organizations. Vaccination for smallpox was required of everyone in the United States until quite recently, and immunizations for yellow fever and cholera are required for travelers to countries where these diseases are prevalent.[48] Immunizations may be recommended for typhoid, tetanus, typhus, diphtheria, influenza, plague, and poliomyelitis, depending on location and circumstances. Through such health practices, and through health programs such as Medicare, the government has contributed to increased life expectancy in a way that could not have brought similar results had it been left to private groups or associations.

Not all government action serves to depress mortality. A glance at Figure 3.5 will show that the American white male population experienced a considerable increase in deaths during periods of war. The groups born in 1896–1900 and 1916–1920, who reached military age during periods of war, show excessive mortality. A nation's military involvement increases the death rate both of its own military population and of the general population against which it wages war. For instance, the German population during World War II lost heavily among its fighting men but also lost substantial numbers of women and children, who were victims of bombings.

Governments have also affected mortality rates through sanitation programs, police and other protective services, labor laws, social security and social welfare legislation, food and drug laws, regulations regarding sewage disposal, provision and purification of water supplies, and laws concerning capital punishment. Depending on the direction of the action, the effect may be either an increase or a reduction in mortality.

The Individual as an Element in Mortality Trends

In addition to the social factors which help determine the chances of life and death, both biological and physical factors peculiar to the individual have an impact. Moreover, the individual can be seen as a focal point in a decision-making process on which both psychological and social forces are brought to bear to affect life chances.

BIOLOGICAL AND PHYSICAL MAKEUP OF INDIVIDUALS

The individual at birth is endowed with a genetic and physical makeup which partly determines life expectancy. Much fetal loss (deaths prior to birth) occurs because the fetus is not properly formed or is genetically unequipped for life. Likewise, many early infant deaths

Figure 3.5 Mortality rates for cohorts born 1896–1900, 1906–1910, and 1916–1920 for white males: death-registration states, 1900–1968

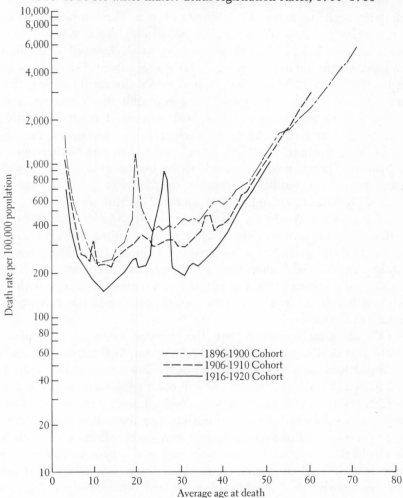

Source: U. S. Public Health Service, *Cohort Mortality and Survivorship: United States Death-Registration States, 1900–1968*, Vital and Health Statistics, Series 3, No. 16, p. 6.

(those taking place soon after birth, called *neonatal deaths*) are caused by the same conditions. One of the most important factors in neonatal mortality is the maturity of the infant at birth. Those infants with low birth weight, a critical measure of immaturity, have a much lower probability of survival than those weighing more. In the United States in 1950, among infants weighing 2,500 grams (about 5½ lbs.) or less at birth, 174 per 1,000 died within four weeks after birth; among those weighing more than 2,500 grams, the comparable death rate was 8 per 1,000. Although children with low birth weights accounted for only 7 percent of live births, deaths of these children accounted for two-thirds of all neonatal deaths.[49] Closely related to low birth weight is prematurity (birth before the end of the typical nine-month term of pregnancy of the mother). Statistics on mortality of infants on the basis of prematurity are similar to those based on birth weight.

Some infant deaths are also traceable to physical difficulties experienced by the mother shortly before birth or during delivery. Causes of death that can be classified here are hypoxia (insufficient oxygen intake), intracranial hemorrhage, and congenital malformations. Blood conditions, particularly those resulting from matings of women with the Rh negative factor and men with the Rh positive factor, can lead to disease of the newborn.

Physiological limitations are the primary cause of a significant number of deaths beyond infancy. At age one to fourteen, congenital malformations and malignancies combined were exceeded only by accidents as a cause of death.[50] At still older ages, such factors as overweight, being crippled, high or low blood pressure, weak heart, urinary impairments, blindness, and deafness increase the risk of mortality.[51]

While societal and group factors may exert influence on each individual's life expectancy, and biological and physical makeup may provide additional constraints, individuals themselves affect their own chances of living or dying through their own behavior — the extent to which they take account of these other factors in their daily living and their own idiosyncratic actions.

Individuals may avail themselves of health and medical care or not, they may take mortal risks or not, and they may enjoy nutritional diets and optimum physical activity or not. Life expectancy will be determined partly by these choices, which are somewhat independent of societal and group forces.

Future Mortality Trends

Further gains in life expectancy are bound to occur in nearly all parts of the world. The greatest gains should be expected in less-developed countries, where death rates are now the highest and where infectious, parasitic, and respiratory diseases and related ailments still result in substantial loss of life.[52] In more advanced countries, where mortality rates are now lower, further improvements in life expectancy will be slight unless medical discoveries and their implementation provide control over chronic diseases.

According to recent mortality projections made by the United Nations staff,[53] the crude death rate for more-developed regions will increase slightly between now and the year 1990 because of the aging of their populations and the unlikely prospect of major new forms of mortality control. The rate for the less-developed regions of the world, on the other hand, is expected to reach the level of the more developed regions by 1990 and fall below that level by the year 2000, due to both a continuing youthful population and considerable control over infectious and parasitic diseases.

The future picture of mortality in the world is thus partly determinable by the obvious policies and events of recent years. There is still, however, an indeterminable part, that associated with new medical discoveries, the relative rate at which governments support public health activities, and the course of fertility with its attendant consequences for population pressures and unhealthful life in some parts of the world.

Notes

1. Much of the material in this section is drawn from *Population Bulletin of the United Nations*, No. 6, 1962, chap. 3.
2. Robert J. Myers, "Validity of Centenarian Data in the 1960 Census," *Demography*, 3 (1966), 470–476.
3. Edward S. Deevey, Jr., "The Probability of Death," *Scientific American*, 182 (April 1950), 58–60; Louis I. Dublin, Alfred J. Lotka, and Mortimer Spiegelman, *Length of Life*, Ronald Press, New York, 1949, pp. 28–29; G. Acsadi and J. Nemeskeri, *History of Human Life Span and Mortality*, Akademiai Kiado, Budapest, 1970.
4. Deevey; Dublin et al.
5. Harry M. Rosenberg, "Seasonal Adjustment of Vital Statistics by Electronic Computer," *Public Health Reports*, 80 (March 1965), 201–210.
6. Donald B. Cheek, *Human Growth*, Lea & Febiger, Philadelphia, 1968, p. 3.
7. *Population Bulletin*, No. 6, p. 51.
8. *Population Bulletin*, No. 6, p. 53.
9. *Population Bulletin*, No. 6, p. 54.
10. United Nations, Population Division, *The Determinants and Consequences of Population Trends*, New York, 1953, p. 56.
11. Ansley J. Coale and Edgar M. Hoover, *Population Growth and Economic Development in Low-Income Countries*, Princeton University Press, Princeton, N.J., 1958, pp. 9–10.
12. Coale and Hoover, p. 14.
13. Hans Zinnser, *Rats, Lice, and History*, Little, Brown, Boston, 1935, p. 67.
14. Thomas McKeown, "Medicine and World Population," *Public Health and Population Change*, ed. Mindel C. Sheps and Jeanne Clare Ridley, University of Pittsburgh Press, Pittsburgh, 1965, p. 39.
15. *Population Bulletin*, No. 6, p. 111.
16. Margaret Cussler and Mary L. De Give, *Twixt the Cup and the Lip*, Twayne Publishers, New York, 1952, pp. 56–57.
17. U. S. Department of Health, Education, and Welfare, "Family

Health Expenses," *Vital and Health Statistics*, Series 10, No. 41 (November 1967), pp. 4–6.

18. U. S. Department of Health, Education, and Welfare, "Hospital and Surgical Insurance Coverage, United States, 1968," *Vital and Health Statistics*, Series 10, No. 66 (January 1972), p. 22.

19. Monroe Lerner and Odin W. Anderson, *Health Progress in the United States, 1900–1960*, University of Chicago Press, Chicago, 1963, p. 102.

20. Philip E. Enterline, "Causes of Death Responsible for Recent Increases in Sex Mortality Differentials in the United States," *Milbank Memorial Fund Quarterly*, 39 (April 1961), 312–325.

21. Thomas S. Geis, *The Effects of Socio-Economic Development upon Sex Differences in Mortality*, unpublished thesis, Florida State University, 1966.

22. Joseph W. Eaton and Albert J. Mayer, "Man's Capacity to Reproduce: The Demography of a Unique Population," *Human Biology*, 25, No. 3 (1954), 34–35.

23. Edward A. Suchman, "Public Health and Medicine," in *Survey Research in the Social Sciences*, ed. Charles Y. Glock, Russell Sage, New York, 1967, p. 458.

24. Robert D. Retherford, "Tobacco Smoking and the Sex Mortality Differential," *Demography*, 9 (May 1972), 203–216.

25. Dublin, Lotka, and Spiegelman, pp. 129–130.

26. Francis C. Madigan, "Are Sex Mortality Differences Biologically Caused?" *Milbank Memorial Fund Quarterly*, 35 (April 1957), No. 2, pp. 202–223.

27. Jean Daric, "Mortality, Occupation, and Socio-Economic Status," *Vital Statistics — Special Reports*, 33 (September 21, 1951), p. 177.

28. Edward G. Stockwell, "Socioeconomic Status and Mortality in the United States," *Public Health Reports*, 76 (December 1961), 1081–1082.

29. Daric, p. 179.

30. W. P. D. Logan, "Social Class Variations in Mortality," *Public Health Reports*, 69 (December 1954), 1219.

31. Stockwell.

32. Daric, p. 181.
33. Logan, p. 1220.
34. Evelyn M. Kitagawa and Philip M. Hauser, *Differential Mortality in the United States*, Harvard University Press, Cambridge, 1973, pp. 151–180.
35. Helen C. Chase, "White–Nonwhite Mortality Differentials in the United States," *Health, Education and Welfare Indicators* (June 1965), p. 28; and A. Joan Klebba, Jeffry D. Maurer, and Evelyn J. Glass, "Mortality Trends: Age, Color, and Sex, United States, 1950–69," *Vital and Health Statistics*, Series 20, No. 15 (November 1973), pp. 26, 28.
36. Thea Zelman Hambright, "Comparison of Information on Death Certificates and Matching 1960 Census Records: Age, Marital Status, Race, Nativity, and Country of Origin," *Demography*, 6 (November 1969), 413–423.
37. Russell G. Thornton and Charles B. Nam, "The Lower Mortality Rates of Nonwhites at the Older Ages: An Enigma in Demographic Analysis," *Research Reports in the Social Sciences* (February 1968), pp. 1–8.
38. Lyle Saunders, *Cultural Difference and Medical Care*, Russell Sage, New York, 1954, pp. 42–43.
39. Saunders, p. 141.
40. Saunders, pp. 164–168.
41. H. G. Rawlinson, *India: A Short Cultural History*, Praeger, New York, 1952, pp. 58, 214, 407.
42. Gale E. Wilson, "Christian Science and Longevity," *Journal of Forensic Sciences*, 1 (1956), 43–60.
43. Don F. Neufeld, ed., *Seventh-Day Adventist Encyclopedia*, Review and Herald Publishing Association, Washington, 1966, p. 512.
44. Neufeld, p. 512.
45. Fraser Brockington, *World Health*, Little, Brown, Boston, 1968, pp. 133–134.
46. Brockington, pp. 149–160.
47. Brockington, p. 169.
48. Hugh Rodman Leavell and E. Gurney Clark, *Preventive Medicine*

for the Doctor in His Community, McGraw-Hill, New York, 1965, p. 151.

49. Sam Shapiro, Edward R. Schlesinger, and Robert E. L. Nesbitt, Jr., *Infant, Perinatal, Maternal, and Childhood Mortality in the United States*, Harvard University Press, Cambridge, 1968, p. 51.
50. Shapiro et al., pp. 175, 177.
51. Dublin, Lotka, and Spiegelman, pp. 193–202.
52. *Population Bulletin*, No. 6, p. 11.
53. United Nations, *A Concise Summary of the World Population Situation in 1970*, New York, 1971, p. 3.

Suggested Additional Readings

In addition to the United Nations *Population Bulletin*, No. 6, useful readings concerning mortality include the following:

Dodge, David L., and Walter T. Martin. *Social Stress and Chronic Illness*. University of Notre Dame Press, Notre Dame, Ind., 1970. Valuable for its theoretical insights into social structural and social psychological factors that account for differential morbidity and mortality, particularly from chronic diseases.

Dublin, Louis I., Alfred J. Lotka, and Mortimer Spiegelman. *Length of Life*. Ronald Press, New York, 1949. This is an historical and analytical treatise of progress in health and longevity.

Dubos, Rene. *Man Adapting*. Yale University Press, New Haven, 1965. A microbiologist's view of the human animal which analyzes biological, social, and environmental forces that impinge upon physical survival and population growth.

Preston, Samuel H. *Older Male Mortality and Cigarette Smoking*. University of California Institute of International Studies, Berkeley, 1970. An evaluation of smoking as a cause of death that is based on a demographic analysis of a number of countries. This book supplements public health studies of smoking as a cause of death derived from clinical evidence.

"Madam, I should have thought one of those would have been more than enough."

4

Fertility: Trends and Determinants

During the last twenty years, a substantial amount of demographic research and writing has been focused on fertility. In the developed countries, attention to fertility has been encouraged by the need to sharpen population projections and by the feeling that fertility is the most unpredictable of the population components. With death rates fairly low and stable and with international migration regulated, fertility has been the most variable of the components. In addition, motivation to avoid death is rather constant, while fertility desires can fluctuate. In the developing countries, attention has been focused on fertility in an attempt to understand the reasons for its high level and how it might be reduced. Even in developing countries where mortality is low or decreasing, fertility remains high. Great concern over the resulting high rate of growth of population has fostered attempts to understand what affects fertility.

In studying fertility patterns in any nation, two major perspectives are employed: the period approach and the cohort approach. In the period approach to fertility, birth rates at any one period in time are calculated. The crude birth rate is an example of a measure computed in this way, since it is the number of births occurring per thousand population in one year. Conversely, the cohort approach to fertility examines the total fertility of a group with a similar birth date throughout its childbearing years. In this way, measures of completed fertility or final family sizes can be computed. The gross reproduction rate is a measure calculated in this way. It represents the average number of daughters that would be born per woman in a cohort of women if they all survived to the end of their reproductive periods and bore children at the prevailing rate.

Understanding the relationship of cohort and period fertility is crucial to an informed approach to fertility. For example, during any given time, period fertility may be falling even though cohort fertility does not change. This can occur, for example, when couples are postponing births because of wars or economic adversity. Even though the current birth rate or period fertility may be low, these births will be made up later, and the number of children these couples will eventually have may be no different from that of their parents' generation, making cohort fertility constant. Likewise, though period fertility measures may indicate higher birth rates in one year than another, this fluctuation may only reflect changing age patterns of childbearing, and not signal a change in cohort fertility levels. Both of these ways of examining fertility patterns will be employed in this chapter.

Since the proliferation of literature on fertility has been so great, it would be impossible to be comprehensive in our review of it here. Rather, we shall attempt to illustrate the factors that affect fertility. As was the case with mortality, we shall first discuss trends in fertility in the world as a whole, and then in the developed and developing countries.

Long-Term Trends in Fertility

It is really quite pretentious to claim to be able to trace fertility rates in the world over a "long term." In light of the data available to accomplish that task, any conclusions drawn must be tentative. As late as 1965, for example, 35 percent of the areas in Africa had incomplete birth registration data.[1] In South America, 50 percent of areas lacked birth data. This is compared with 19 percent of areas in North

America and 3 percent of areas in Europe lacking birth registration systems in 1965. If this was the situation in the mid-sixties, data were even more incomplete at earlier dates. In Africa, 78 percent of areas had no data on births before 1935. The comparable figure in South America is 38 percent, and in Asia, 61 percent. By contrast, only 17 percent of North American areas and 15 percent of European areas lacked data on births before 1935. While demographers have techniques for estimating statistics on births without registration data, the uneven amount of direct information available on world fertility should be noted.

Early Fertility Trends

Given the inadequacy of birth data, the reader must already perceive the insecurity with which demographers discuss fertility rates in preindustrial or primitive times. In order to talk about the birth rate of primitive people, we must rely on archaeological evidence, any drawings or writings located from those times, and a good bit of surmising. Most demographers are willing to say only that the birth rate must have been high in those days. It is fairly certain that the death rate was high, so that human beings must have had a high birth rate or they would have become extinct.

Such reasoning, while logical, is less satisfying than a census or vital registration system. We might also look at relatively primitive peoples of today and draw some parallels with living conditions and their effect on fertility in earlier times. In such studies, fertility has been shown to be quite high, in the neighborhood of fifty-five or more births per thousand population.[2]

One interesting aspect of these findings is that fertility, even among primitive peoples, is often far below the biologically possible maximum. Techniques of contraception, abortion, and infanticide were known to such societies. The techniques used, while seeming crude today, were nevertheless effective. In many primitive societies, lactation continued for several years after a child was born, reducing pregnancy risk. These factors combined with various cultural practices, such as sexual abstinence on certain special days, marriage and mating restrictions, and other taboos, to reduce the birth rate.

When looking at the fertility of societies prior to industrialization, we can also rely on church and government records. Church records of baptisms, burials, and marriages have been particularly useful in demographic research.[3] But the limitations of these records are numerous, since not all persons in a community are likely to be registered with a church, and we have very little information about how thorough the record keepers of those times were.

In spite of these data limitations, it appears that most countries had high fertility prior to about 1650. Around 1650, and there is some dispute about the date, a tremendous growth in population began occurring in countries that were undergoing industrialization. This growth was apparently due to a large decrease in mortality, although more recently there has been some evidence that birth rates rose slightly during the early stages of industrialization.

Following this period of rapid population growth, birth rates began to decline. This decline began in the seventeenth century in some nations, and not until the eighteenth or nineteenth century in others. Several reasons are postulated for this decline in the birth rate. It would appear that with industrialization replacing agricultural economies, children were not the asset they had been when they were needed to work the land. The decline in mortality meant that it was no longer necessary to have several extra children to ensure that a sufficient number survived to adulthood. Still other hypotheses include the greater use of coitus interruptus, the condom, and possibly abortion as methods of birth control. In any case, it seems that smaller families came to be more popular — at least in the countries that are now called developed. We turn now to an examination of twentieth-century trends in fertility rates in these countries and in the developing countries.

Fertility in the Developed Countries

As the United Nations has noted, no other single characteristic distinguishes developed areas from developing ones as clearly as does the birth rate. In the more-developed regions of the world, primarily Europe and North America, about two-thirds of the countries have birth rates between seventeen and twenty-three per thousand population.[4] Still, there are no strict continent boundaries for developed and developing countries, and examples of countries with low birth rates can be found in nearly every region of the world.

In developed countries where birth rates have declined throughout this century, much variation in the pattern of decline is evident. Figure 4.1 shows crude birth rates for selected nations of the world from 1920 to 1973. Four countries on the graph are usually considered developed: Sweden, the United States, Japan, and the USSR. Guatemala and India are developing countries, while Taiwan is a transition country with urbanization and economic growth under way but relatively recent.

Close examination of the patterns in Figure 4.1 will illustrate the variations in birth rate decline evident in these nations. In the United States, the birth rate was 22.8 in 1920–1924, and then dropped to 17.2 during the Depression years of the early 1930s. Then, following World War II, the birth rate rose to 24.6. Another birth rate decline began in the late 1950s and continued until 1968. While this is not shown in Figure 4.1, the birth rate rose slightly in 1969 and 1970 but began declining rather sharply again in 1971.

While the general shape of the birth rate curve is the same for Sweden, some interesting differences from the United States pattern can be noted. Sweden, too, had declining birth rates in the 1930s, with a return to slightly higher rates following the war. However, this rise in the birth rate after World War II was less prolonged in Sweden than in the United States. In addition, for every year from 1920 to 1973, Sweden's birth rates have been below those in the United States. This has been the common European pattern in these years.

Figure 4.1   Crude birth rates, selected countries, 1920–1973

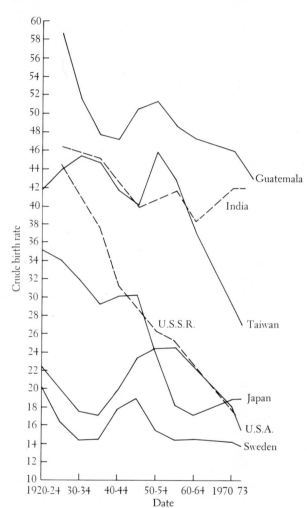

Source: Figures for these graphs are from *United Nations Demographic Yearbook 1965*, New York, 1966, Table 12, pp. 276–299, and from Population Reference Bureau, *World Population Data Sheet*, 1969, 1970, and 1973.

Still a third pattern of birth rate decline in a developed country is shown by Japan. Japan's birth rate was much higher than that of either the United States or Sweden in the early part of the century. Decline in the birth rate during the Depression years is evident, as is a slight rise in the birth rate during the early 1940s. Following World War II, however, Japan experienced a marked decline in the birth rate, a pattern widely different from the postwar baby boom noted in the United States and Sweden. After 1960, Japan's birth rate rose slightly, and is currently higher than rates in the United States and Sweden.

Figure 4.1 also includes the birth rates for the USSR during this same time period. Relative to the other developed countries represented here, the USSR is quite deviant. None of the dramatic rises and falls evident in the birth rates of Japan, the United States, and Sweden are displayed in the USSR. Rather, the birth rate has steadily declined throughout this century.

Each of these nations shows a different birth rate pattern, but there are also common factors. All these countries currently have low birth·rates, and, except for the USSR, each of them has apparently shown responsiveness to economic conditions and wars. Reasons for these differences and similarities will be explored later in the chapter.

Fertility in the Developing Countries

The remaining countries in Figure 4.1 are generally called less-developed or developing areas of the world. In such areas the United Nations has noted that about two-thirds of the countries have birth rates between thirty-nine and fifty per thousand population.[5]

The pattern of the birth rate in Guatemala is illustrative of birth rates in much of Central and South America, as well as the majority of African countries. While the Guatemalan birth rate shows increases and decreases at about the same time periods as the United States and Swedish birth rates, in every period shown in Figure 4.1, the birth rate in Guatemala was more than twice that in the United States. Declining from 62.6 in 1920–1924, the crude birth rate was 47.2 in 1940–

1944. During the postwar period, the Guatemalan birth rate rose to 51.3 in 1950–1954 and has been declining since that time.

In India, the birth rate has also been high throughout the fifty years covered in Figure 4.1. While fluctuations are evident, the Indian birth rate does not fall below thirty-eight or rise above forty-seven per thousand during this entire period. Further, the rises and declines in the Indian birth rate do not occur at the same time as those in Guatemala, the United States, or Sweden, indicating that different factors are influential. Nevertheless, the Indian and Guatemalan birth rates, while somewhat different from each other, illustrate the common high level of fertility in developing nations.

Taiwan might be considered a transition country, both demographically and economically. From forty-two in 1920–1924, the Taiwanese birth rate showed rises and declines until 1950–1954, when a period of steady and rather steep decline began. That decline has clearly placed the Taiwanese birth rate in a middle-ground position between the rather extreme highs of India and Guatemala and the lows of the United States, Sweden, Japan, and the USSR.

The trend of the birth rate in Taiwan and a good many other countries has led some authors to speculate that the previous sharp division between high- and low-fertility countries is disappearing as new countries enter the demographic transition.[6] Most of these countries have not shown declining birth rates for long enough periods to determine whether permanent declines in birth rates are under way. However, there is reason to believe that the birth rate patterns of more and more countries will begin to look like the pattern evident in Taiwan.

While we have not included it in Figure 4.1, a special word needs to be said about birth rates in the People's Republic of China. Since estimates of China's population ranged from 753 to 871 million people in 1970,[7] it is true that nearly every fifth child born in the world is Chinese. The wide range of that estimate reflects the lack of data on the Chinese population. The Chinese government has simply not made such information available. However, the Population Reference Bureau estimates the current Chinese birth rate at twenty-seven per thousand, very close to the birth rate in Taiwan. In addition, scattered information indicates that the crude birth rate in China has declined in the last ten years, also paralleling the Taiwanese pattern. There is much speculation about the future course of China's birth rate, but it appears that a concerted effort is being made toward further reductions.[8]

Seasonal Variation in Fertility

One of the most interesting short-term variations in fertility is that by season. It has long been a source of curiosity that births, like deaths, show a seasonal fluctuation.[9] To illustrate this trend for the United States, Figure 4.2 shows seasonal indexes of live births, by color, for 1933, 1943, and 1963.[10] Two peak periods of birth are apparent: the period centering around February and the period centering around September. From 1933 to 1963, the September peak became even more pronounced, while the February peak declined.

For nonwhites, the peaks are even sharper, but the lessening of the February peak and the increase in the September peak is also evident for this group. Regional data on seasonality of birth have shown that the South exhibits the most pronounced seasonality, while the Northeast exhibits the least. This is not due to the concentration of nonwhites in the South, since whites in the South have a season-of-birth curve much like that of nonwhites in the area.

Other countries of the world have seasonal patterns of birth, but those patterns may differ greatly from those in the United States.[11] For example, European countries have more births in the late winter months, while the South Pacific and Gulf of Mexico areas of Mexico show birth peaks in December.[12]

No definitive answer to why births occur with greater frequency in some months than in others has been found. Writers have looked at seasonality of sexual relations, social customs such as religious holidays, climate, season of marriage, socioeconomic status and even data registration error in an attempt to explain this phenomenon.[13] No one of

Figure 4.2   Seasonal indexes of live births, by color:
United States, 1933, 1943, and 1963

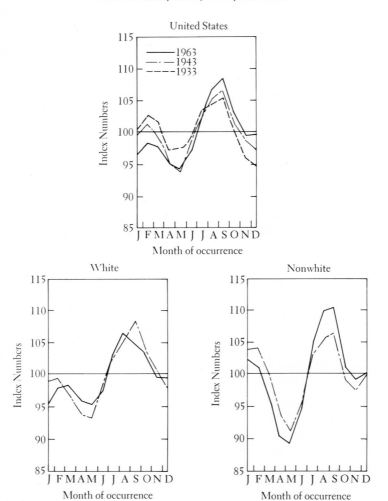

Source: National Center for Health Statistics, *Seasonal Variation of Births: United States, 1933–1963*, Series 21, No. 9, U. S. Government Printing Office, Washington, 1966.

these factors seems to be a total explanation. It may be that the causes of seasonality of birth are different for each society and that, within societies, influences on the birth curve vary in importance over time.[14]

The Age Curve of Fertility

For several measures of fertility the assumption is made that ages fifteen to forty-four are the reproductive ages for women. For men, the period of fecundity is generally longer. While there are, of course, exceptions to this general assumption (that is, women who have children after age forty-four or before fifteen), these exceptions are rare.

Between fifteen and forty-four years of age, childbearing is not likely to be evenly distributed. In fact, fertility is usually concentrated quite heavily between ages twenty and twenty-nine. Figure 4.3 illustrates the differences between a hypothetical age curve of fertility, were women to distribute their childbearing throughout the fecund years, and an actual age curve of fertility, produced by using data from seventy-two countries of the world. This figure demonstrates the uneven distribution of births within the years of potential fecundity.

Among these seventy-two countries, the United Nations has identified three different age patterns of fertility that describe nearly every country for which there is data.[15] These three are early-peak countries, in which maximum fertility occurs between twenty and twenty-four years of age; late-peak countries, in which maximum fertility occurs between twenty-five and twenty-nine years of age; and broad-peak countries, in which fertility between twenty and twenty-four years of age differs only slightly from fertility between twenty-five and twenty-nine years of age, with little fertility occurring at younger or older ages.

In low-fertility countries births seem to be concentrated in a much narrower range of ages than is the case in high-fertility countries. The contribution to the total fertility of the country from women below age twenty and above age thirty-five is much higher in countries of high fertility than in countries of low fertility. The age curves of fertility for the United States and Mexico, shown in Figure 4.4, illustrate this

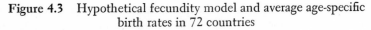

Figure 4.3   Hypothetical fecundity model and average age-specific
birth rates in 72 countries

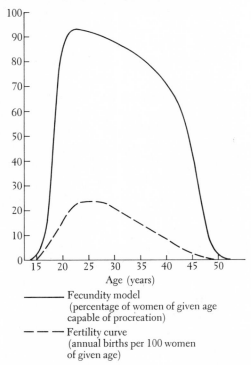

Source: *Population Bulletin of the United Nations*, No. 7, 1963, Figure 7.1, p. 101.

difference between early-peak, or low fertility, and broad-peak, or higher
fertility, countries. The fertility of women in the United States is
highly concentrated between the ages of twenty and twenty-nine, while
Mexican women are more likely to bear children at later ages. This is
not to say that fertility rates are higher among women in the United
States than among those in Mexico at these ages, but only that a
greater proportion of United States childbearing occurs between the
ages of twenty and twenty-nine.

Figure 4.4 Mean percent of total fertility contributed by women in each age group, United States and Mexico, 1960

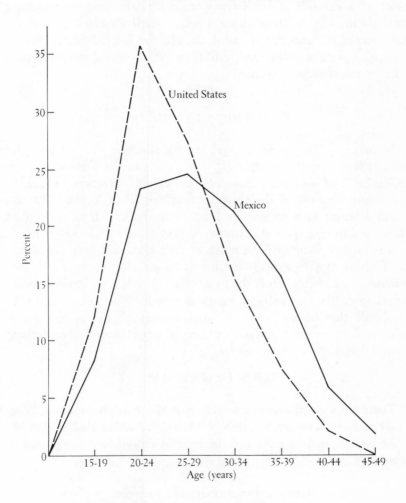

Source: Data for these graphs obtained from *Population Bulletin of the United Nations*, No. 7, 1963, Table 7.2.

Earlier marriages in the high-fertility countries and less control over fertility in general account for these differences. It would seem that women in low-fertility countries can or do regulate their fertility more effectively in order to concentrate it into a relatively small part of the total number of fecund years available. In the United States, for example, 62.5 percent of the total fertility in 1960 occurred among women twenty to twenty-nine years old.

Factors Affecting Fertility

In order to discuss the myriad factors affecting the patterns and trends of fertility just described, we shall return to the framework given in Chapter 2 of societal, group, and individual influences. Certainly we will not mention all the variables that can affect fertility. Rather, we will attempt to mention the kinds of variables which may affect fertility and to give specific examples of how these variables operate.

Any factors discussed here must, of course, constitute a provisional list. The attempt to explain fertility is an ongoing effort which produces new and contradictory data each day. Further, as fertility trends change, so do the explanations for these trends. The following discussion should thus be read with the usual caution about the source and quality of data involved, and with a sense of expectation that something new and different may soon emerge.

Societal-Level Variables

There are some things in a society that affect nearly everyone living in that society. Two such variables which also are related to fertility are the natural environment and the level of economic development of the country.

NATURAL ENVIRONMENTAL FACTORS

A considerable number of writers have been willing to maintain that the natural environment is the primary, if not the sole, cause of human behavior. The location of cities, religion, economic development, and even reproductive behavior have been ascribed wholly or in part to the climate, resources, and topography available.

In the realm of fertility, there has even been a popular fiction that peoples from warm climates are more sexually active, and hence more fertile, than those from colder climates. While the picture of a naked savage surviving on tropical fruits and warmed by the sun may conjure up ideas of virility to some, no reliable data are available to make this picture more than fantasy. In fact, there has been almost no research on the relationship of climate and fertility per se.[16]

The relationship of altitude to fertility has been explored in some depth by several authors, and an interesting debate has emerged. Some authors have found differences in the fertility of populations living at high and low altitudes in Peru.[17] These differences were first interpreted as due to cultural variations in mating practices or to conscious attempts to control births.[18] Later analysis of these same populations suggested that the different altitudes at which they lived was the most important variable accounting for their fertility differences.[19] Some writers have now proposed collaborative research of biologists and social scientists to explore the role of high altitude in fertility rates as well as in other demographic phenomena.[20] Such collaboration may help decide whether high-altitude populations indeed have different demographic patterns not accounted for by social variables.

Other aspects of the natural environment have been examined as possible sources of influence on fertility. Adequate food and water to support life are obviously essential. In addition, popular notions about what kinds of foods produce fecundity or increase sexual activity and, in turn, fertility have been abroad for some time. The food supply and its impact on fertility have been receiving more serious attention in developing countries in recent years as part of the general examination of what factors influence high fertility rates in these countries.

In nations with little food, the infant death rate is likely to be high. Maternal health is weakened by nutritional deficiencies, affecting the child even before birth. Then, lacking resistance to disease because of vitamin or protein deficiencies, the child is vulnerable to death from even minor illnesses. Families in these countries are particularly interested in having children survive to adulthood, since that is the main form of social security for elderly parents. High infant mortality then encourages high birth rates to ensure old age security. In India, for example, it has been estimated that a family must have 6.3 children to be 95 percent certain that one son, an especially valuable commodity, will survive until the father's sixty-fifth birthday.[21] If more food and more nourishing diets were available in these countries, lower mortality rates would produce higher population growth, at least in the short run. However, it is often argued that improved diets in the developing countries would be an important factor in lowering births over a long period of time.

It has been argued that the amount of vitamins and protein in the diet have a direct impact on fertility as well. De Castro has maintained that the birth rate is inversely related to the daily consumption of protein in societies.[22] He presents very convincing data to show that, statistically speaking, fertility and protein intake are related in this way. De Castro explains this relationship by hypothesizing that in countries where hunger is chronic but starvation not eminent, this hunger stimulates sexual appetites and speeds up the production of female hormones.

Critics of De Castro have noted that the birth rate is also negatively correlated with the number of motor vehicles, level of literacy, and telephones per thousand population in society. Karl Sax writes, "It would be just as logical to assume that people who spend much of their time riding, talking, or reading have low birth rates because they have so little time for reproduction."[23] Sax goes on to present data to show that the relationship De Castro cites does not always hold. Other authors have cited experimental studies of hunger and its apparent depressant effect on sexual activity in order to refute De Castro.[24]

Taken together, the literature on natural environmental factors and their relationship to fertility does not seem to provide a substantial explanation of observed fertility trends. Indirect effects of climate, food, water, and other resources on fertility may be felt as these factors change the health of the population concerned. But the general level of health in the population seems to be most greatly affected by the economic development of the society, and so it will be discussed under that heading.

ECONOMIC DEVELOPMENT

It is hard to live amid the current avalanche of materials on population and not know that fertility is related to the economic development of a society. Most people are aware that the poorer countries of the world have higher fertility rates than the more wealthy ones.

Even the terminology of the United Nations, which would like to avoid such implications, implies that "developed" nations are rich nations, while "underdeveloped" or, more gently, "developing" nations are poor ones. Indeed, the evidence that economically poorer nations have higher fertility rates is overwhelming.

Figure 4.5 graphically portrays this inverse relationship between economic well-being and the level of the birth rate. Gross national product per capita has been used as the measure of economic development in this figure. The crude birth rate used does not take account of age differences in these nations, a factor which may make fertility appear somewhat distorted. Nevertheless, these two measures were chosen because they are virtually the only economic and fertility indicators available for this number of countries.

The inverse relationship between economic development and fertility is clear. Figure 4.5 also indicates that some countries might be considered middle-range on both economic development and fertility, a reminder of the notion that some countries are now in a demographic and economic development transition.

That this inverse relationship between economic development and fertility generally holds is well documented, but that this relationship always holds or has held in the past can be questioned. First, within the low-fertility countries, it is not those with the highest gross national product per capita that have the lowest fertility. As Figure 4.5 illustrates, the United States, Sweden, and Canada, although highly developed economically, do not have the lowest crude birth rates. Even more startling exceptions can be seen in the cases of Kuwait or the

Figure 4.5   Crude birth rates and per capita gross national product
for countries of the world, 1973

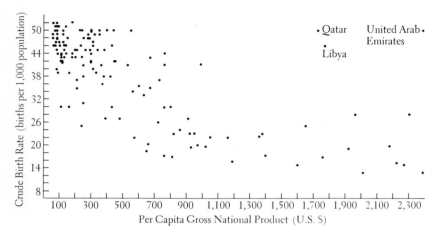

Source: Courtesy of Population Reference Bureau Inc., 1973 *World Population Data Sheet*, Washington, D.C.

United Arab Emirates. These countries have very high GNPs per capita, owing to oil wealth, while maintaining crude birth rates of forty-three and fifty, respectively. While the general inverse relation between economic development and fertility may hold, then, other factors within a nation may cause deviation from this pattern. We will discuss what some of these factors may be below.

In some Latin American countries, for example, Heer and Turner found fertility inversely related to the proportion of the population engaged in agriculture, positively related to the proportion literate, and positively related to the proportion living in urban areas.[25] In trying to sort out the causation involved in these variables, Heer and Turner hypothesized:

> An increase in the level of economic development leads to an
> increase in fertility as married couples become more optimistic

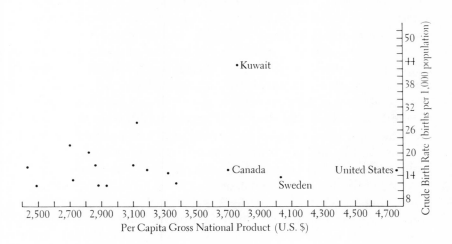

concerning their future economic status. On the other hand, the increase in the level of economic development then sets in motion other forces, such as increased knowledge and use of birth control and increases in net economic cost of children, which tend to reduce fertility. In the long run, the forces depressing fertility tend to be stronger than the forces increasing fertility unless the increase in income per head continues at a high rate. Thus, many, if not most, nations exhibit the classic pattern of fertility decline with advancing industrialization.[26]

In a later article, Heer expanded on this hypothesis and found the health and education levels of the population to be determinative of fertility levels, holding economic development of the nation constant.[27] Economic development per se will not necessarily reduce fertility, according to Heer, but must be accompanied by other social changes in order to do so. Highest priority among these social changes would seem to go to the development of extensive educational programs and public health services, both of which facilitate the spread of birth-control information and improve lifestyles and life chances.

It is apparent that the general health level of the population is related to its fertility rate. We have already noted that parents in very poor societies, where the infant mortality rate is high, may wish to have large numbers of children in order to ensure that at least a few survive to adulthood. Conversely, raising the general health education level of the society can further reduce the fertility rate, both by affecting infant mortality and by making family planning programs part of the public health services that are already trusted and used by the people.[28]

Poor health levels in a population can have a negative as well as a positive impact on fertility. Farley has discussed the role of three diseases known to produce subfecundity — pellagra, gonorrhea, and syphilis — in explaining rising and falling birth rates among blacks in the United States.[29] Farley maintains that increases in the prevalence of these diseases accounted for a decline in black fertility from the end of the nineteenth century until about 1930. After this period, many blacks moved to urban areas and experienced improvements in their economic well-being. While these factors would seem to predict continued low fertility for blacks, fertility rates rose, beginning in about 1940 and continuing for about twenty years. It is Farley's contention that this fertility increase resulted primarily from improved health conditions. While other authors have disagreed with Farley's judgment about the amount of subfecundity caused by venereal disease,[30] there is no argument that general health conditions among this population have influenced birth rates.

The factors we have been discussing are primarily associated with long-term trends in economic development. The growth of urbanization, education, and health facilities are factors connected with a far-reaching and relatively permanent change in the economic level of a society.

The relationship of short-term trends in the economy to fertility has also been investigated. Easterlin, for example, has interpreted the postwar baby boom as a response on the part of native white couples to the exceptionally favorable job-market conditions during that time.[31] Others have examined fertility and marriage rates in relation to business cycles over longer periods. While the impact of business cycles on fertility varies at different times and for different nations, most of this literature argues that birth and marriage rates show a direct response to rising and falling conditions in the economy. Silver, for example, has argued that this response occurs among most population subgroups in the United States, including foreign-born, Catholic, nonwhite, and farm residents.[32] Silver has also demonstrated this response of birth and marriage rates to business-cycle fluctuations for the United Kingdom and Japan.[33]

Along this line, some economists have argued that babies may be thought of as consumer durables like cars, new houses, or television sets.[34] Couples may plan their "consumption" of children in much the same way as they plan other expenditures. In this framework, "Can we afford it right now?" would be a question asked about an additional child, as well as about other household items. Others have maintained that there is something qualitatively different about the decision to have a child and the decision to buy a new appliance.[35] Societal values placed on children may change, causing rises and drops in the birth rate,[36] but tradeoffs between other goods and children are not made because the two are not comparable.

Whatever the strength of the business-cycle impact, birth and marriage rates do show ups and downs which parallel business trends. During the current period of birth rate decline in the United States, this is one of the hypotheses advanced to explain the rather precipitous drop in births just when the age distribution of the population would predict the opposite. Even if the baby-boom babies are now coming into the childbearing ages, current economic conditions may encourage them to postpone marriages and children.

Each of the variables we have considered above — natural environment and long- and short-term states of the economy — is a factor that is generally society-wide in its impact. We turn now to a consideration of factors that have their primary effect through special group membership.

Group Membership and Normative Influences

The factors discussed here operate selectively, affecting individuals differently depending on the special groups of which they are members or the special combinations of group memberships which they possess. They are most easily grouped into institutional areas.

MARRIAGE AND THE FAMILY

In spite of new ideas about the institution of marriage and occasionally approved reproductive unions which are nonmarital, the primary unit in which births occur is the family. Indeed, the very definition of the family centers around the act of birth and the allocation of responsibility for children. In most societies, marriage is considered the usual, if not the legal, prerequisite for parenthood.

Family units take many different forms. The United States pattern of a mother, father, and children living together is called a *nuclear family* and is actually a rather recent historical development. More common in history, and in many parts of the world today, is the *joint family*, in which one or more generations live together. Other forms of the family unit include clans, stem families, and other variations in the household unit, which might include uncles, in-laws, or multiple husbands and wives.

Some attempt has been made to determine the effect of each of these arrangements on fertility. This attempt has been somewhat thwarted, however, by lack of data from historical times and by the difficulty of separating out the effect of family composition. Certain forms of the family are more common with certain economic arrangements in societies, making it nearly impossible to separate out the effect of, say, an agricultural economy from the effect of joint-family living.

Nevertheless, while this generalization is not true for all societies, it seems that joint families have higher fertility rates than nuclear families.[37] This is apparently so because the nuclear-family system requires that the husband be able to support his family with land or housing of his own prior to marriage. Such economic independence is not necessary with a joint family arrangement, since the young couple can live with the parents. This makes youthful marriages possible. Since marriages tend to occur later in societies with a nuclear-family system, it again becomes difficult to distinguish the effect of age at marriage from the effect of nuclear-family interaction. Besides promoting marriage at an earlier age, some authors have speculated, child care is easier within joint or other large families, and this encourages mothers to produce more children.

This discussion highlights two variables besides form of the family that are important: the *percentage of women marrying* and the *age of first marriage*. Data from the United States population may be used to examine these trends in relationship to fertility. Overall, Americans are a marrying people (see Table 4.1). In 1974, only 4.7 percent of women aged forty to forty-four were still single. This percentage has de-

Table 4.1   Percent of women single, 15 to 44 years old, by age: United States, 1920 to 1960, and 1974

Age of woman	Year					
	1974	1960	1950	1940	1930	1920
15 to 19 years	—[a]	83.9	82.9	88.1	86.8	87.0
20 to 24 years	39.6	28.4	32.3	47.2	46.0	45.6
25 to 29 years	13.1	10.5	13.3	22.8	21.7	23.0
30 to 34 years	6.8	6.9	9.3	14.7	13.2	14.9
35 to 39 years	5.0	6.1	8.4	11.2	10.4 ⎫	11.4
40 to 44 years	4.7	6.1	8.3	9.5	9.5 ⎭	

[a] Data not reported in this age category, 1974.

Sources: Figures for 1920 to 1960 adapted from U. S. Bureau of the Census, "Fertility Indicators: 1970," *Current Population Reports*, Series P-23, No. 36, April 1971, Table 11. Figures for 1974 from U. S. Bureau of the Census, "Marital Status and Living Arrangements: March, 1974," *Current Population Reports*, Series P-20, No. 271, October 1974, Table C.

clined steadily since 1920. However, the proportion of single women in the younger ages has been increasing in this time period.

Median age at first marriage has exhibited variability (see Table 4.2). Between 1940–1944 and 1955–1959, years inclusive of the baby boom, median age at first marriage declined for Americans; then it began increasing slightly after 1959 as the birth rate began decreasing.

Table 4.2   Median age at first marriage[a] by sex: United States, five-year averages 1940 to 1969 and single-year data 1965 to 1970

| | Median age at first marriage[b] | |
Year	Men	Women
Five-year averages		
1965–1969	23.0	20.7
1960–1964	22.8	20.4
1955–1959	22.6	20.2
1950–1954	22.9	20.3
1945–1949	23.2[c]	20.4[c]
1940–1944	24.3[d]	21.5[d]
Single-year data		
1970	23.2	20.8
1969	23.2	20.8
1968	23.1	20.8
1967	23.1	20.6
1966	22.8	20.5
1965	22.8	20.6

[a] At present, first marriages constitute about three-fourths of all marriages for both men and women.

[b] Medians are based on data from the 1940 census and the Current Population Survey. Medians based on marriage registration data would be slightly different.

[c] Median is for 1947–1949.

[d] Median is for 1940.

Source: Adapted from U. S. Bureau of the Census, "Fertility Indicators: 1970," *Current Population Reports*, Series P-23, No. 36, April 1971, Table 9.

Another way to look at the marriage patterns of Americans is by using the cohort perspective. Using this approach, the age at marriage or the proportions of individuals with similar birth dates ever marrying can be examined. This kind of analysis has recently been performed for the United States by the Census Bureau[38] and interpreted by Glick and Norton.[39] These authors conclude that "a fundamental modification of life styles and values relating to marriage has been taking place."[40] This conclusion is supported by the findings that lifelong singleness may become more prevalent and that the proportion of women who end their first marriage in divorce has been rising for each successive birth group. While 12 percent of first marriages of women born in 1900 to 1904 have ended, or are expected to end, in divorce, the figure for women born in 1940 to 1944 may reach 25 to 29 percent.

It is too early to speculate on whether these trends do indeed signal changing patterns in family formation and dissolution, or to forecast what effect these changes will have on the birth rate. If women begin to marry later and spend less total time in marital unions, the low birth rates of developed countries where these patterns occur may drop even further.

Within the marital unit there are various *sex roles* and *norms* which have a direct impact on fertility. Traditionally, women have been responsible for homemaking tasks and child raising. One of their primary duties has been the bearing of children. Davis and Blake have argued that the extent to which a woman sees herself as feminine and suited for this role will influence her fertility.[41] An empirical test of this thesis with American women by Clarkson et al. lends support to this hypothesis.[42] This study found that women with more masculine self-concepts tended to have smaller completed families. Particularly important here was the extent to which women perceived themselves as competent, with those seeing themselves as more competent having smaller families.

These psychological approaches to sex-role socialization and fertility are complemented by a vast literature on the relationship of women's labor-force activity and fertility.[43] Some investigators have compared various nations,[44] while others have investigated female employment and fertility in cities.[45] All these studies show that the percentage of women employed and the number of economic opportunities for women are inversely related to birth rates or number of children ever born.

Extensive examination of this relationship has also been conducted for individuals. Still, as labor-force participation is greater, fertility is lower.[46] The ubiquity of this relationship on these different levels, for different areas, and at different times is a consistent finding. What has been unclear is whether fertility influences labor-force participation or the reverse. It is possible to reason that having more children leads women to drop out of the work force and assume greater responsibilities at home. On the other hand, it may be that the experience of employment leads to fewer children being born because women are interested in careers, economic rewards, or other benefits of working.

Recent investigations suggest that, in fact, this influence works both ways.[47] However, it appears that the influence of fertility on employment is stronger than the reverse. This finding dampens the policy recommendation that providing careers for women might make a significant impact on fertility.[48] Rather, this finding implies that if women were to have fewer children, more of them could be expected to enter the labor force.

Culturally defined roles of men may also have an impact on fertility levels in a society. In various contexts it has been noted that *manhood* may be defined by the number of children a man produces or, more particularly, by the number of male children he fathers. Defining manhood in this way may encourage men to shun any method of birth control or to have more children should they produce several girls.

The form of the family system and the appropriate roles within the family perceived by husband and wife both influence a couple's *family size preference*. As contraceptive methods have become more effective and more widespread, researchers have turned a great deal of attention to how many children a couple wants, considers ideal, expects, or desires.

One of the most interesting of these variables is expected family size. In the United States, interest has recently been sparked by reports of expected fertility that are lower than those of previous years, espe-

Figure 4.6 Number of births expected during woman's lifetime for wives reporting on birth expectations, June 1973

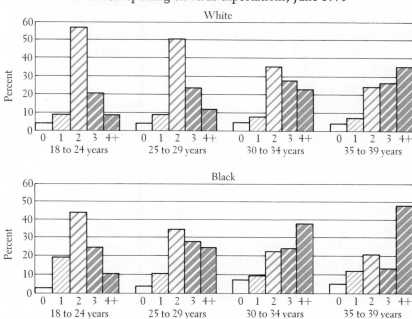

Source: U. S. Bureau of the Census, "Fertility Expectations of American Women: June 1973," *Current Population Reports*, Series P-20, No. 265, Figure 2.

cially for younger cohorts. Figure 4.6 shows some of these data. Although this is not true for older women, a majority of the younger women report that they expect no more than two children. While more Negro than white women anticipate having three or four children, a majority of Negroes in the eighteen- to twenty-nine-year-old group expect only two children. Still, these data also indicate no increase in the proportion of women expecting to be childless or to have only one child. Reductions in mean numbers of children expected are accounted for, then, by a greater proportion of women expecting to have two rather than three or more children.

If women perform according to these expectations, fertility in the United States may fall even lower than current levels. However, at least one author has suggested caution in that interpretation. Judith Blake has argued that since these data indicate no greater acceptance of one-child or childless families, changes from expectations are likely to be in the upward direction, leading to higher fertility than these expectations would suggest.[49]

SOCIOECONOMIC STATUS

Sociologists interested in the prediction of human behavior of many kinds have found that one of the most useful factors in such prediction is a person's socioeconomic status. Socioeconomic status (SES) refers to factors that contribute to the social and economic position of a person in a community, and may include education, occupation, income, style of life, place of residence, race, and many other variables. While SES has been measured in a variety of ways, it is repeatedly a good indicator of values, norms, attitudes, and behavior of individuals.

It is no surprise, then, that socioeconomic status (SES) is also related to fertility. Table 4.3 shows average number of children born in 1965 and 1972 to United States women aged thirty-five to forty-four

Table 4.3   Average number of children born to women aged 35 to 44 by color and socioeconomic status

	Average number of children born[a]			
			Negro &	
	white	white	other races	Negro
Socioeconomic status measure	1965	1972	1965	1972
Educational attainment[b]				
Elementary: less than 8 years	4.0	3.7	4.6	⎱ 4.8
8 years	3.5	3.4	4.8	⎰
High school: 1 to 3 years	3.2	3.4	4.0	4.5
4 years	2.9	3.0	3.2	3.6
College: 1 to 3 years	2.9	2.9	2.9	⎱ 2.6
4 years or more	2.8	2.6	2.2	⎰

Socioeconomic status measure	Average number of children born[a]			
	white 1965	white 1972	Negro & other races 1965	Negro 1972
Family income[b]				
Under $3,000	3.5	3.2[c]	4.2	
$3,000 to 4,999	3.5	3.5	4.5	4.4
$5,000 to $7,499	3.2	3.5	3.8	
$7,500 to $9,999	3.0	3.3	3.6	
$10,000 to $14,999	2.9	3.1	2.8	3.4
$15,000 and over	2.9	3.0		
Occupation of husband[c]				
Professional, technical, & kindred workers	2.9	2.9		
Managers, officials, & proprietors, excluding farm	2.9	2.9	3.1	2.9
Clerical and kindred workers	2.7	2.8		
Sales workers	2.9	2.8	2.9	
Craftsmen, foremen, & kindred workers	3.1	3.3	3.5	
Operatives and kindred workers	3.3	3.2	3.9	
Service workers, including private household	3.0	3.0	3.7	3.9
Laborers, excluding farm and mine	3.3	3.2	4.5	
Farmers and farm managers	3.6	3.6	[d]	

[a] The average number of children born refers to the group as a whole, and not to any one woman in this group. None of the women had 3.5 children.
[b] Figures in this group refer to women ever married.
[c] Figures in this group refer to wives.
[d] Figure does not meet standards of reliability due to small base.

Sources: 1965 data adapted from U. S. Bureau of the Census, "Fertility Indicators: 1970," *Current Population Reports*, Series P-23, No. 36, April 16, 1971, Tables 15, 16, 17. 1972 data are from U. S. Bureau of the Census, "Birth Expectations and Fertility: June 1972," *Current Population Reports*, Series P-20, No. 248, April 1973, Tables 17, 18, 20.

by race by three· traditional measures of SES — *educational attainment, family income,* and *occupation* of husband. First, reading across the table, it can be seen that Negroes and other races consistently have more children than whites in any of the classes of SES, except one.

Negroes and other races with four or more years of college have fewer children than whites with that amount of education.

Second, the figures showing fertility by education and income indicate an inverse relationship between SES and fertility. In general, those with low education or income had more children than those with higher education and income. The same general inverse relationship holds when occupation is used as a measure of SES, but it is more difficult to rank occupations in order of status than it is income and education. Generally speaking, however, it can be seen that professionals, managers, and clerical workers have fewer children than farmers, laborers, service workers, or operatives.

Why this consistent inverse relationship between fertility and socioeconomic status should appear, or if it will continue, is not entirely clear. One explanation has been that women in lower income groups, lacking education, simply do not know how to control their fertility should they desire to do so. While this hypothesis may have been valid in the past, data from the 1970 National Fertility Study indicate substantial increases in the percentages in all classes using contraception.[50] This increase has been particularly dramatic for black women. In addition, the 1970 data showed decreases in the educational differential in fertility, particularly for white women. These findings may mean that modern methods of birth control have filtered to all social classes in the United States, thus decreasing class differentials. Indeed, the 1970 data indicate that these reductions in class differentials have come about chiefly because of declines in unwanted births.

Another hypothesis to explain socioeconomic differences in fertility is that these women are not lacking in knowhow to control their births, but lack the motivation to do so. This hypothesis suggests that lower-class women greet new children with the same fatalistic attitude with which they view most of life. What chance would they have for better status, even if they controlled fertility? Sexual relationships, a pleasurable activity in what otherwise might be a difficult existence, are thus not likely to be interrupted or postponed in order to prevent future children. This hypothesis too would be consistent with lowered fertility in the future as it becomes increasingly possible to separate sex from childbearing.

In developed countries particularly, SES may be important in fertility because of the differing *style of life* associated with different levels of income, occupation, or education. Families with better means to engage in many activities and in a position to be mobile may find children more of a burden. Different tastes among the classes may lead to considerations of not only the quantity but the quality of children. A concern with being able to feed and care for children in one class may be manifested as a concern for properly clothing, expensively educating, and properly exposing them to new experiences in another class.

Exceptions to this strict inverse relationship between SES and fertility occur among some subgroups in the United States. The Indianapolis study found a direct relationship between fertility and SES among couples that completely plan their families.[51] Many studies have noted that among Catholic couples, the relationship between SES and fertility is a direct one.

There are exceptions to the inverse relationship between fertility and SES in other nations as well. In a study of villages in Poland, Stys has demonstrated that socioeconomic well-being and number of children are directly related.[52] In developing societies, this direct relationship might occur since those who are better off agriculturally would find children more of a benefit to them in cultivating the land.

RELIGION

Important as socioeconomic status is, the institutional area in society which defines morality, imparts values, and helps people cope with the unknown, namely religion, might be regarded as even more important. Many studies in the United States have documented religious differentials in fertility. Because of limited data on religious affiliation of the population, however, most of these studies have been small sample surveys conducted in limited areas. In 1957, for the first and only time to date, the United States Census Bureau asked for the religious affiliation of a nationwide sample of the United States population.[53] These data showed that Roman Catholics generally had higher fertility than either Protestants or Jews by the time they had completed their childbearing, and that Jews were conspicuously low in their fertility.

In the past these differences were due to many factors. It is widely known that the Roman Catholic church has looked with disfavor on the use of birth control techniques. Studies have also shown, however, that the Catholic church encourages families to have large numbers of children in more positive ways than prohibiting the use of birth control. Large families have been seen as blessings from God, as the right and proper function of marriage, and as a means of increasing the membership of the church.

This encouragement of large families has by no means been confined to the Catholic faith. Certain Protestant denominations, while not prohibiting the use of birth control techniques, are quite literal in their interpretation of the Biblical dictum, "be fruitful and multiply." Fundamentalist sects, small in number and predominantly rural in location, may also be of this persuasion. The Church of Jesus Christ of Latter-Day Saints, or Mormon Church, is another example of a religious institution that encourages large families through the glorification of children.

Religious influences can also confound the impact of other variables on fertility. We have noted above that, among Catholics, a reversal of the inverse relationship between fertility and SES occurs. Those Catholics with higher income and occupational status are more likely to heed their church's advice and have more children than Catholics in lower economic brackets. Higher-status Catholics not only can afford the additional children, but tend to have more frequent contact with their church and its schools.

While Catholics still have higher fertility than Protestants, most researchers are predicting reduction of this difference, largely due to radical changes in birth control practices among Catholics. By comparing the results of national survey data gathered in 1955, 1960, 1965, and 1970, Westoff and Bumpass have documented sharp rises in the percentage of Catholic women deviating from the teachings of their church relative to the use of birth control.[54] The proportion of Catholic women between the ages of eighteen and thirty-nine who in 1955 were using methods of birth control other than rhythm was 30 percent. This figure had risen to 68 percent by 1970, and had increased by seventeen percentage points between 1965 and 1970 alone. Westoff and Bumpass also looked at this trend for the various birth cohorts represented in their samples. In these studies, the percentage of women aged twenty to twenty-four not conforming to church teaching had risen from 30 percent in 1955 to 78 percent by 1970. As the women in each of the samples aged, they showed an even greater tendency not to conform to church teaching, presumably because controlling fertility became more important as desired family sizes were achieved or exceeded. This finding, along with the cohort data, led Westoff and Bumpass to speculate that the birth control practices of Catholics and non-Catholics may become "virtually indistinguishable" by the end of the century.[55]

In contrast with Catholics, the fertility of Jews has traditionally been lower than that of Protestants. To explain low Jewish fertility, many authors have pointed to the high value placed on education by Jews, which tends to raise their age at marriage and lower fertility. More speculative suggestions which might explain low Jewish fertility include the hypothesis that as a minority group in America, and one with a history of persecution, Jews might wish to limit their fertility in order to better their economic status, thus protecting themselves against oppression. This is an interesting suggestion, since a minority group which perceived its position as precarious might also try to outnumber the majority by producing many children. Another attempt to explain the lower fertility rates of Jews suggests that these lower rates do not represent a religious differential at all, but are a reflection of the higher socioeconomic status and urban residential patterns of Jews.

The Catholic-Protestant-Jewish differential in the United States is certainly not the only indication that religion has an effect on fertility. Several in-depth studies of religious subgroups and population processes have been conducted. We will cite only two of them here for illustrative purposes.

Moslem fertility has been noted to be generally high, very stable over time, and usually higher than the fertility of other groups in the same nations.[56] In an exhaustive study of Moslem natality, Dudley Kirk has noted some of the factors which explain these findings. Not all of these factors are strictly religious in nature. Moslem countries are very often developing nations, with joint family systems, high mortality rates, and agricultural economies in which sons are of great value. Religious influences include the Moslem belief that sexual relations are a God-given pleasure to be enjoyed, a belief in male dominance, encouragement of early remarriage for the widowed and divorced, and an early age at first marriage. These factors combined seem to produce the very high fertility rates observed among Moslem groups regardless of their particular national setting.

Another religious group that may have achieved something close to the biological limit of fertility is the *Hutterites*.[57] The average Hutterite woman has twelve children, which, when combined with low mortality and virtually no migration, creates a population increase of 4.1 percent per year. Such high fertility apparently comes about not because of any single factor, but because of the unique combination of many factors which are conducive to high fertility. Living in predominantly rural settings, the Hutterites avail themselves of good medical care. They believe that children have very positive value and that use of birth control is sinful. Their communal economy and high level of productivity allow each new addition to the population to be assured of support, and marriage is nearly universal. There is little separation of husband and wife, making for maximum exposure to conception. There are a few negative factors operating in Hutterite society to depress fertility. These include prohibition of premarital sex, a later age at marriage than in some cultures, and occasional surgical interference with reproduction to protect a woman's health. The length of this list of cultural practices influencing fertility makes it unclear whether the Hutterite fertility pattern should be interpreted more broadly as resulting from cultural, rather than only religious, practices. The cultural patterns shown here are certainly important, quite apart from their religious context.

GOVERNMENT

It has long been apparent to governments, as to religious groups, that the number of people in a nation heavily influences the options available. Depending on national goals, governments may find it advantageous to raise the birth rate or lower it, hoping for corresponding increases or reductions in the population. Few nations have tried to deliberately manipulate the death rate to produce the same results, and manipulating migration, while often practiced on a small scale, is not likely to make a substantial impact. The birth rate is most promising as a direct way to influence population growth and decline.

Attempts to raise the birth rate may be motivated by several concerns. First, there may be imperialistic ambitions. If the nation is interested in conquering the world, or even a substantial portion of it, it becomes necessary to maintain a large occupation force which can be spread out over acquired territory without crippling the forces left at home. Especially in early times when war was waged through hand-to-hand combat, it was important to be able to overwhelm the other side with superior numbers.

Besides imperialistic ambitions, nations sometimes need larger populations to facilitate economic development. Colonizing a new nation and trying to control and develop a large segment of land can be an impetus to greater births. Finally, national pride may equate the size of a nation with success and lead governments to encourage more births.

Given a pronatalist intent, there are several different strategies that might be employed. A government could pursue a negative or restrictive policy with regard to birth regulation. Such measures would include outlawing birth control, making abortion illegal, taxing bachelors or childless couples, and forbidding separation or divorce. Conversely, a government might try a more positive approach by instituting family allowances, paying families to have more children, glorifying children, exempting large families from taxes, and so on. Each of these policies and various combinations of them have been tried from time to time, with varying success.

One of the most famous attempts to raise the birth rate was the campaign undertaken by Hitler in Germany in the early 1930s.[58] The main elements of Hitler's program included baby bonuses, marriage loans, suppression of contraception and abortion, and an intensive propaganda campaign emphasizing the building of a master race. Women were encouraged to leave the labor force, and couples who married were given loans for furniture, housing, and other commodities. Part of these loans could be repaid by having many children. In addition, those with many children were given preferences in housing, travel accommodations, and the like.

Scholars are not in agreement on the success of these measures, although most cite German policies as more influential than many other programs.[59] The number of marriages and births in Germany did increase dramatically immediately after the policies went into effect. However, most of the increase in births came from first births. Although there was no appreciable long-term effect on the size of completed families, the collapse of the Nazi government abbreviated the time during which these policies were in effect.

France provides another example of a government that deliberately tried to raise the birth rate. The concern in France was prompted not by military ambitions, but by a real fear that the country would actually become depopulated.[60] The birth rate in France had fallen below replacement levels in the early part of this century, and government officials increased family allowances and payments to families based on the number of children. An attempt was made to keep the standard of living of couples with several children comparable to the standard of living enjoyed by those with no children. While the family allowance system may have achieved this goal, we have little evidence that it had a major impact on the birth rate in France.

More far-reaching population policies in France were enacted in 1939; the legislation was ahead of that of most other nations at the time.[61] The national family code included not only family allowances, loans for the establishment of households, and birth premiums, but also maternal and child protection provisions, demographic and medical education, and the establishment of maternity homes. Even the promotion of induced abortion was prohibited, whether or not an abortion actually followed. Only in 1967 were laws repealed which prohibited birth control information or the sale of contraceptives. In addition, abortion is now available in France.

Some authors have contended that the birth rate in France fell at a slower rate than it might have in the absence of these measures. Nevertheless, the birth rate has continued to fall throughout the century. The only interruption in this decline was a brief post-World War II resurgence of births, common in many Western countries.

Sweden has also had an extensive pronatalist program.[62] In an attempt to bring the birth rate up to replacement levels during the late 1930s and early 1940s, the Swedish government enlisted the aid of a special Commission on Population composed of experts in many fields. The commission took the view that every child in Sweden should be a wanted child and that the burden of replacement should be spread equally over all social classes in the country. Consequently, along with family subsidies, health centers for mothers and children, housing allowances, and free school books and lunches, the government also undertook an extensive birth control education program. While the Swedish birth rate has remained low, it is high enough to ensure replacement. Current assessments of the Swedish program report a shortage of family planning facilities and personnel, but because of the multifaceted nature of the Swedish program, one author has remarked, ". . . it appears fair to say that Sweden is as close as any country to the ideals of zero population growth with adequate provision for all."[63]

Some attempts to raise the birth rate have been quite recent. In 1967, the Province of Quebec in Canada instituted a new baby bonus. Concerned about a falling birth rate, the government offered to pay graduated allowances to families for each additional child.[64] However, this program seemed to have little immediate impact on the birth rate.

In 1967, the crude birth rate in Quebec was 17.3. By 1969 it had dropped to 16.0.[65]

A recent attempt to raise the birth rate in Rumania has had dramatic consequences.[66] Concerned about falling birth rates and possible labor force shortages, the government of Rumania issued a decree in 1966 banning almost all abortions and stopping importation of birth control pills and IUDs. Rumanian women had depended almost exclusively on abortion as a means of birth control, and many found themselves forced to carry to term pregnancies they had intended to have aborted. The result was that within eight months the birth rate doubled, and within eleven months it had tripled. (See Figure 4.7) The decrease in the birth rate since 1967 indicates that while the techniques used by Rumanian couples may have changed, use of birth control has not been abandoned. Even in 1973, however, the Rumanian birth rate was still above 1966 levels.

The strategy of each of the pronatalist programs described above has been different. Incentives, support services, penalties, and outright denial of services are used. Clearly the outstanding effect was achieved by the Rumanian effort, a success made possible by both the far-reaching power of government and the excessive dependence of couples on one method of birth prevention. Likewise, the scope of these programs has varied from general family support and betterment to short-term raising of births to support the labor force, war, or other efforts. Some of the programs have sought replacement fertility, others very high fertility. In every case the strategy chosen has reflected the form of government, the birth control and family histories, and the goals of the nations involved in these efforts.

More common in the last ten years have been *attempts to lower the birth rate*. The reader is no doubt familiar with some of the more popular reasons why nations undertake such a campaign. In many nations of the world today there is concern over *lack of resources*. Food, water, and fuel are in short supply in some countries and depleted in others. Governments have felt that reducing the birth rate might be the most direct way to slow down the consumption of such resources.

Figure 4.7 Monthly birth rates per thousand population,
Rumania: 1966–1970

Source: Henry P. David and Nicholas H. Wright, "Abortion Legislation: The Romanian Experience," *Studies in Family Planning*, Vol. 2, No. 10 (October 1971),
Figure 1.

Some areas of the world are concerned about *living space*. Overcrowding has become a problem. There are large metropolitan areas in
the United States suffering from high density. Some writers have gone
so far as to propose that these density levels contribute to crime,
juvenile delinquency, slums, and other problems. While it is not clear
how much density itself contributes to these problems, governments
have felt that some reductions would be desirable and have embarked
on campaigns to reduce the birth rate. In the developing nations of the

world these problems have been particularly acute. As noted above, economic growth may be being stifled by the press of population. A reduced birth rate should enable developing countries to use their resources for development as well as survival.

In still other countries, planners have been concerned over birth rate differentials among subgroups in the population. The United States is an example of a country where there is growing concern in this area. Reduction of the birth rate in this country has been seen by some as one way to reduce welfare rolls. Critics of this philosophy have charged that such thinking penalizes the lower classes or minority groups. Some have even charged that genocide, or the attempt to eliminate whole races of people, is the motivation behind such programs.

Each of these reasons for wanting to reduce the birth rate involves seeing growing population as an inefficient or deleterious situation because of lack of space or resources, or even because too many people are felt to be aesthetically undesirable. Various kinds of solutions to these problems have been suggested. The most popular movement, under way in many countries of the world now, is family planning. Basically, *family planning programs* involve several features. An educational program may be launched to provide information as to what kinds of family planning techniques are available and how they might be used. Propaganda campaigns may be instituted to encourage small families and create an atmosphere favorable to the adoption of family planning. Then some dissemination system is worked out so that the people may have access to the techniques they wish to use. The kind of dissemination system used depends on the particular country, the percentage of the people living in remote areas, the educational level of the people, and so on.

In any case, family planning programs, while generally highly organized and far-reaching, are entirely voluntary. Families wishing to reject the notion of family planning are free to do so. Some have argued that couples are not able to plan a nation's population growth, but rather only the size of their individual families.[67] Insofar as people wish to have more children than replacement levels would dictate, population will continue to grow in spite of the fact that couples are having only the number of children they want.

Other attempts to control births have revolved around the adjustment of a *law*. Some nations have legalized abortion, raised the age at which people may legally marry, or legalized sterilization. Even more extreme measures have been proposed by advocates of lower birth rates. Licensing of babies, compulsory sterilization, or the imposition of heavy taxes on babies have all been suggested as ways to directly and quickly lower the birth rate.

Those who oppose compulsory measures and lack faith in strictly voluntary measures have suggested still another alternative for reducing births. These advocates maintain that what is needed in many societies to reduce births is a total *change in attitudes* about families. They suggest that it is not sufficient to encourage couples to have fewer children. You must provide them with alternative methods of need satisfaction. Children are viewed by many as having intrinsic value to parents. They are enjoyed not as help on the farm, or as security in old age, but just because they are children. Women in many societies not only enjoy children, but define their own role in the family almost exclusively as mothers.

The best way to attack a high birth rate, some argue, is by *changing the role of women and deemphasizing the family* entirely. Careers for women have been suggested as one mechanism to accomplish this. Teaching parents to want leisure time for themselves is another. Societies might learn to regard being single as a desirable state, thus limiting the number of marriages and children. Childless couples might be regarded as wise instead of selfish. Each of these suggestions is a more indirect attack on the birth rate, but some maintain that this type of change is essential if any family planning program is to work.

An example of an effort to reduce the birth rate combining many of these measures is provided by India.[68] India's birth rate is about forty per thousand per year. Her death rate is only sixteen per thousand per year, producing a yearly population growth rate of 2.4 percent. This means that India's population doubles about every twenty-nine years.

That would make her population over one billion by the end of this century. With little land area and a shortage of resources to feed that staggering number, the result of continued growth of that kind could only be famine, overcrowding, economic disaster, and a rising death rate. This is already occurring.

In a desperate attempt to stop this tragedy, the Indian government has undertaken a massive family planning program. The undertaking is a difficult one since most of India's people are illiterate, most live in rural or remote areas and work the land, and they do not all speak the same language. In addition, the level of economic development is very low. No social security systems protect the population, so children are the principle insurance against starvation in old age.

Besides a massive propaganda campaign to promote the idea of a small family, India has introduced four major methods of birth control. These are sterilization on a voluntary basis, the IUD (intrauterine contraceptive device), the condom, and the pill. Clinics have been set up throughout the country for the free distribution of these devices, but other techniques are also being employed to reach those who will not or cannot come to the clinics. Schools, family welfare centers, and even postal carriers deliver the contraceptives.

Still, the administration of these programs has not been efficient. There has been resistance to India's program, and the birth rate is still high. Some of this resistance is religiously based, but some of it comes from the rural people who see children, and especially sons, as an economic asset to help work the land. Fear of death taking some of their children is still prevalent, and such fear encourages people to have extra children.

A stark contrast to the situation in India is provided by Japan. After the Second World War, Japan had a very high birth rate and a very small island. No longer having the possibility of expansion or the need for more and more people to conduct a war, Japan needed to reduce her birth rate a great deal. This was accomplished rather rapidly when abortion was legalized. Other factors operating in Japan during this period also contributed to a reduction of the birth rate. It is possible that psychological feelings of defeat may have discouraged the Japanese people from producing children. Rapid industrial development also occurred during this time. In addition, the Japanese adopted contraceptive practices, began marrying at older ages, and redistributed their population somewhat. It is difficult to assess the impact of each of these factors, but the combination of them seemed to be highly conducive to bringing down the birth rate rapidly.

An interesting aspect of birth control practice in Japan today is the heavy reliance on the condom to prevent conception. About 68 percent of couples in Japan use the condom as their major method of birth control, while only about 2 percent use birth control pills.[69] This preference for a male method of contraception is unusual at present, but it has benefits other than effective birth control in that the spread of venereal disease is greatly reduced. Recent analysis of condom use in Japan indicates that while disease prevention was the major reason for its popularity at the end of the nineteenth century, current promotion of the condom centers on its ability to enhance sexual pleasure.

The current showcase of family planning efforts in Asia is Taiwan.[70] As indicated in Figure 4.1, the birth rate in Taiwan was over forty per thousand in 1959 and has dropped to a present level of about twenty-seven per thousand. There is some argument among current scholars over how much of this decline has been due to the family planning program per se and how much has been due to other social and economic changes taking place in the country. It is true that the decline in the birth rate had begun before the family planning program became well organized or widespread. One of the major benefits of modernization in Taiwan has been increased education for women in recent years. Nevertheless, through the efforts of the family planning program, over 200,000 IUDs have been inserted. This is the major strategy of the program. Because Taiwan is one of the first developing countries to bring down its birth rate in recent years, it has been much studied. Demographers have been interested in watching the demographic transition take place in recent times.

The current level of the birth rate in the People's Republic of

China is estimated at about twenty-seven per thousand population, nearly the level of the birth rate in Taiwan. While demographers have been no less interested in watching fertility control programs in China, the data have not been easily obtained. While there are now several major works on demographic processes in China, the data used are largely constructed from popular publications, statements by officials of the Chinese government, personal visits, and United States government estimates.[71] Nevertheless, what we know about fertility policies in China is quite interesting.

Since the Chinese Communist assumption of power in 1949, China has had a stop-and-go policy on fertility. At first, it was thought inconsistent with Marxist ideology to proclaim population a problem. Rather, if shortages occurred, these were interpreted as reflecting an unequal distribution of goods and services, not an inadequate absolute supply. Under the Marxist government, redistribution of wealth, goods, food, and other commodities would eliminate the problems that were thought to be connected to population growth.

Not until 1954 was there some evidence of concern about population growth on the part of the Chinese government. By 1956 there had been an increase in the number of popular articles in China which discussed the pros and cons of birth control, and the Ministry of Public Health was assigned the responsibility for implementing a campaign for its use.

Surprisingly, in 1958 the government abruptly reversed its stand on the use of birth control and returned to its original statement that family limitation was an unacceptable notion. Scholars are in disagreement as to whether birth control programs disappeared entirely during this period or were simply downplayed.[72] In any case, this was the period of the Great Leap Forward, and the need for additional labor to undertake vast projects, plus general optimism, may have contributed to the ebbing of population growth fears.

By 1962, a full-scale effort to reduce births was once again begun. Financial difficulties and food shortages of huge proportions contributed to the reversal. Since 1962, the programs of the Chinese government have been rather consistently antinatalist. In addition to the emphasis on use of birth control techniques to limit the number of children, propaganda campaigns were begun to raise the age at marriage. Early marriage was touted as physically harmful or disastrous to careers, and premarital sex was strictly forbidden.

While the effects of these off-again–on-again measures are somewhat obscure, it would appear that the early efforts to limit births had little impact. Good evidence exists now, however, to indicate a rather substantial drop in Chinese births in recent years. Still, it is anticipated that the Chinese population will be about 965 million people by 1985.

What about fertility control in the United States? Fifteen years ago that question would have been answered only by reference to indirect influences on the birth rate. The United States had no organized family planning program, and in fact had no overall population policy of any kind. International migration was the only component of population change that was regulated directly. In 1959, President Eisenhower emphasized the hands-off policy of his administration by saying:

> I cannot imagine anything more emphatically a subject that is not a proper political or governmental activity or function or responsibility. This government has not, and will not as long as I am here, have a positive political doctrine in its program that has to do with this problem on birth control. That's not our business.[73]

In ten years, that position had changed. A Commission on Population Growth and the American Future was established, and Eisenhower had become honorary chairman of Planned Parenthood. In addition, a new agency has been created as part of the Department of Health, Education, and Welfare, specifically to deal with family planning. HEW expenditures for family planning increased from $8.7 million in 1965 to $56.3 million in 1969.[74]

In its final report issued in 1972, the Commission on Population Growth and the American Future stated:

> Our immediate goal is to modernize demographic behavior in
> this country: to encourage the American people to make popula-
> tion choices, both in the individual family and society at large
> on the basis of greater rationality rather than tradition or
> custom, ignorance or chance. . . . The time has come to chal-
> lenge the tradition that population growth is desirable: What
> was unintended may turn out to be unwanted, in the society as
> in the family.[75]

This statement is radical in one way and neutral in another. It is
radical in that it represents a departure from governmental silence on
fertility and population growth issues. It is neutral in that the recommendation of the commission stresses freedom of choice for individuals
and the desirability of changes that are good in and of themselves,
apart from their population relevance. The following are some of these:
1. Educational recommendations, including provision for education
    about population, family life, cost of children, and sex.
2. Child welfare recommendations, including provision of child care
    facilities, health and nutritional programs for children, the en-
    couragement of adoption, and the eradication of the different legal
    status of illegitimate children.
3. Women's status and rights recommendations, including encourage-
    ment of educational and occupational opportunity and passage of
    the Equal Rights Amendment.
4. Birth prevention recommendations, including removal of all prohi-
    bitions against dissemination of contraceptive information or sup-
    plies to minors or others, liberalization of abortion laws, removal of
    legal impediments to voluntary sterilization, funding for reproduc-
    tive research, and creation of programs to support family planning
    efforts.

Many other recommendations were made by the commission, but
these are the ones most directly connected to fertility. The response
of then-President Richard Nixon was to reiterate his opposition to
abortion and the availability of contraceptives to teenagers. Catholic

church leaders strongly denounced the report. Press reports were largely favorable.[76]

Since these suggestions, the only major action has been the 1973 Supreme Court opinion on abortion.[77] This opinion held that during the first trimester of pregnancy, the state did not have the right to interfere in a patient-and-doctor decision to terminate a pregnancy. During the second trimester of pregnancy, the state had the right to regulate who performs the abortion and under what conditions it is performed. In the third trimester of pregnancy, the Court held, every effort should be made to save the life of the fetus, since it is potentially viable in the seventh month. States may therefore prohibit abortion except to preserve the life of the mother during this final trimester. These divisions were made by considering the interests of the state in both the life of the mother and the life of the fetus.

The relatively unrestricted availability of abortion in at least the first three months of pregnancy is a new development in the United States, although abortion has played a major role in the efforts of many other countries to control fertility. It is difficult to tell at this time what the long-term impact on fertility will be. In New York, which liberalized its abortion law in 1970, Tietze has estimated that approximately one-half of the 23 percent decline in births from 1970 to 1972 was accounted for by abortions.[78] In addition, Tietze also argues that legalizing abortion has replaced "dangerous, discriminatory, undignified, and costly illegal abortions by legal abortions performed under medical auspices, accessible to and utilized by all the city's economic and ethnic groups."[79]

Still, the Supreme Court action has not been without controversy. In 1975, the Hogan-Helms Amendment, sometimes called the "Right to Life" amendment, was pending in the House of Representatives. This bill proposes that: "Neither the United States nor any state shall deprive any human being, from the moment of conception, of life without due process of law; nor deny to any human being, from the moment of conception, within its jurisdiction, the equal protection of the law."[80]

The introduction of this amendment has stirred much controversy.[81] Some have argued that women who are pregnant might be considered criminally negligent in the case of certain miscarriages. Babies conceived in the United States but born elsewhere might be considered citizens of the United States. Debates on the impact of the Supreme Court decision and this amendment have kept the abortion issue prominent in recent years. Nevertheless, the thrust of government policies on fertility in the United States has been marked first by laissez faire, and now by an increased effort to provide birth control services, education, and information to those who wish them. As controversy surrounded the earlier question of any government involvement, so it now surrounds the direction of government decisions and programs.

Like programs designed to raise the birth rate, programs that have tried to reduce the birth rate have differed in strategy. First, some nations have never stated an overt goal of fertility reduction. The United States, for example, even in the commission report, does not adopt a decline in births as its aim. India, on the other hand, has been explicit about the desired magnitude of fertility reduction. China presents still a third pattern, one of reversing goals within rather short time periods.

The specific fertility policies pursued have likewise varied. Indian policy has been eclectic and at one time or another has placed emphasis on nearly every technique of birth control, in addition to trying incentives and alternatives to childbearing. Legalization of abortion, provision for voluntary sterilization, and encouragement of contraceptive use were the main features of Japanese efforts to reduce fertility. The IUD has been most important in Taiwan, while provision of birth control techniques and encouragement of late marriage have been used by the Chinese. Rather broad recommendations were suggested by the United States Commission on Population Growth, centering on a policy of voluntary and wanted fertility.

Success rates have also varied. But the success or failure of each of these programs is clearly more dependent on general social and economic conditions in the society than on the particular strategies employed. Certainly strategies must fit the conditions of the time, but fertility reduction seems to proceed most quickly and surely when efforts to lower births are coupled with changes in the social structure, which in turn change the value of children.

The Individual

We have discussed societal-level influences on fertility and group and normative influences on fertility. In the end, however, the birth rate in a society depends on actions of individuals. It is the individual who mediates and synthesizes these influences and ultimately controls fertility. It is difficult for any individual in a society to escape the societal-level variables discussed above. The effects of the natural environment and the economic development of the society are presumably about the same on everyone. Each individual has different group memberships, however. The normative influences that result from these memberships are different for each person. In addition, each individual has a peculiar combination of group memberships, interacting with the societal-level variables.

These two kinds of influences acting on an individual's decisions about fertility do not exhaust the kinds of factors that could affect these decisions. We have barely touched on a whole host of psychological factors that could hold sway. A person's relationship with his or her parents or one's adjustment or stability could affect how many children that person wants to have. Psychologists have shown increased interest in researching these problems and have employed the concepts *attitude*, *value, motivation*, and *perception* to describe factors relevant to fertility behavior.[82] As one author notes: "The fertility of a population can be viewed as the result of many individual acts and decisions, made within a framework of biological and environmental constraints."[83] In addition to these psychological influences, there are also biological factors that affect fertility. A person's fecundity, or ability to have children, may be impaired. It is difficult to say how much influence biology has on the other factors we have mentioned above.

All of these are ways in which the individual is important in the process of fertility. It is important to remember that each child that comes into the world is the result of a decision — or the lack of a decision — about fertility. Such decisions are made by individuals but have an impact on all society.

The Prediction and Control of Fertility

It should by now be obvious to the reader that the prediction of fertility is no easy task. Whether on the societal level or the individual level, to try to weigh all the factors we have mentioned, and many we have not, and come up with a reasonable estimate of fertility is a staggering task. Even if one were to gather information on all the factors we have mentioned for a given society, how should they be weighted? And what about changes in these factors over time? What factors have we left out?

Even if we know the present level of economic development in a society, there may be many different religious groups represented, changing government policy, changing business cycles, and so on. Which of these is most important? Could we expect the relative influence of these factors to be the same for each country?

All of these are questions that are dealt with in research and in theory by demographers and others who have been asked to supply such predictions. The demand for reliable fertility forecasting is growing. Fortunately, the available research on which to base such predictions is also growing. The accuracy of past projections has not been particularly encouraging, however. While many countries were anticipating and taking measures to correct depopulation problems, the post-World War II baby boom occurred — surprising almost everyone. Birth rates rose drastically, and demographers began studying the phenomenon in retrospect.

Certainly our sophistication in such matters has improved in the last twenty years. The very demand for such projections has increased the interest and effort devoted to their production. Most commonly, fertility projections are made on the basis of several assumptions. We might assume that fertility will continue at its present rate. We might assume that it will lessen or increase by a specified amount. We might use current survey data on fertility expectations. The accuracy of our projections then hangs on the accuracy of those assumptions or the reasonableness of expectations data. Changes that are not anticipated could invalidate the effort.

The reader should be aware that even accurate prediction of future fertility, were we capable of that, would not ensure control. Deciding what will change fertility involves another set of assumptions and investigations into what kinds of policies will work. Much work is currently being done, on both an actual and a computer-simulated basis, to try out measures designed to control fertility. Governments and family planners have to surmise what would be the relative effects on the birth rate of raising the age at marriage or legalizing abortion. Their conclusions are based on all the factors that we have mentioned above and many more.

Notes

1. These estimates are contained in the *United Nations Demographic Yearbook: 1965*, New York, 1966, Table 12.
2. See, for example, T. E. Smith, "Cocos-Keeling Islands: A Demographic Laboratory," *Population Studies*, 14 (1960), 94–130.
3. A study which uses such records for its data is that by D. E. C. Eversley, "A Survey of Population in an Area of Worcestershire from 1660 to 1850 on the Basis of Parish Registers," *Population Studies*, 10 (1957), 253–279. There are many others.
4. *United Nations Demographic Yearbook: 1965*, New York, 1966, p. 1.
5. *United Nations Demographic Yearbook: 1965*, New York, 1966, p. 1.
6. See, for example, Dudley Kirk, "A New Demographic Transition?" in *Rapid Population Growth: Consequences and Policy Implications*, National Academy of Sciences, Johns Hopkins Press, Baltimore, 1971.

7. Leo Orleans, "China: Population in the People's Republic," *Population Bulletin*, Population Reference Bureau, Washington, 27, No. 6, 1971, p. 24.

8. H. Yuan Tien, *China's Population Struggle*, Ohio State University Press, Columbus, 1973.

9. For an early discussion of this phenomenon, see Ellsworth Huntington, *Season of Birth*, Wiley, New York, 1938. Huntington examines cross-cultural data to document seasonality of birth and discusses cultural and climatic factors as explanations of it. Attention is also given to subgroup differences in seasonality of birth and to the quality of those born in certain months.

10. For a complete discussion of the United States pattern, see Harry Rosenberg, *Seasonal Variation of Births: United States, 1933–1963*, Series 21, No. 9, National Center for Health Statistics, Washington, 1966.

11. See, for example, U. Cowgill, "Recent Variations in the Season of Birth in Puerto Rico," *Proceedings of the National Academy of Sciences, USA*, 52 (1964); or D. Kosambi and S. Raghavachair, "Seasonal Variation in the Indian Birth Rate," *Annual Eugenics*, 16 (1951–1952).

12. Ursula M. Cowgill, "The Season of Birth in Man," in *Man*, 1 (June 1966), 232–240.

13. See, for example, Rosenberg; J. Richard Udry and Naomi M. Morris, "Seasonality of Coitus and Seasonality of Birth," *Demography*, 4 (1957), 673–679; H. Hotelling and F. Hotelling, "Causes of Birth Fluctuation," *Journal of the American Statistical Association*, 26 (1931), 135–149; Huntington; K. Chang, S. Chan, W. Low, and C. Ng, "Climate and Conception Rates in Hong Kong," *Human Biology*, 35 (1963); or Melvin Zelnik, "Socioeconomic and Seasonal Variations in Births," *Milbank Memorial Fund Quarterly*, 47 (April 1969), 159–165.

14. For a discussion of this variable-cause hypothesis, see Cowgill.

15. United Nations, *Population Bulletin of the United Nations*, No. 7, 1963, New York, 1965, pp. 101–121.

16. One text does investigate this matter in detail. See Huntington.

17. J. M. Stycos, "Culture and Differential Fertility in Peru," *Population Studies*, 16 (1963), 257–270; or David M. Heer, "Fertility Differences in Andean Countries: A Reply to W. H. James," *Population Studies*, 21 (1967), 71–73.

18. David M. Heer, "Fertility Differences Between Indian and Spanish-Speaking Parts of Andean Countries," *Population Studies*, 18 (1964), 71–84.

19. W. H. James, "The Effect of Altitude on Fertility in Andean Countries," *Population Studies*, 20 (1966), 97–101.

20. Gordon F. DeJong, "Demography and Research with High Altitude Populations," *Social Biology*, 17, No. 2 (1970), 114–119.

21. Alan Berg, "Nutrition, Development, and Population Growth," *Population Bulletin*, 29, No. 1, Population Reference Bureau, Washington, p. 33.

22. Josue De Castro, *The Geography of Hunger*, Little, Brown, Boston, 1952.

23. Karl Sax, *Standing Room Only: The World's Exploding Population*, as quoted in Louise Young, *Population in Perspective*, Oxford University Press, New York, 1968, p. 74.

24. See, for example, Marston Bates, *The Prevalence of People*, Scribner, New York, 1955.

25. David M. Heer and Eba S. Turner, "Areal Differences in Latin American Fertility," *Population Studies*, 18 (1964), 279–292.

26. Heer and Turner, p. 290.

27. David M. Heer, "Economic Development and Fertility," *Demography*, 3 (1966), 423–444.

28. For a discussion of the interrelationship of these factors, see Carl E. Taylor and Marie-Francoise Hall, "Health, Population, and Economic Development," *Science*, 157 (August 1967), 651–657; and Carl E. Taylor, "Health and Population," *Foreign Affairs*, 43 (April 1965), 475–486.

29. Reynolds Farley, *Growth of the Black Population*, Markham, Chicago, 1970.

30. McFall, Joseph A., Jr., "Impact of VD on the Fertility of the Black Population, 1880–1930," *Social Biology*, 20, No. 1 (1973), 2–19.
31. R. A. Easterlin, "The American Baby Boom in Historical Perspective," *American Economic Review*, 51 (December 1961), 869–911.
32. Morris Silver, "Births, Marriages, and Business Cycles in the United States," *Journal of Political Economy*, 73, No. 3 (1965), 237–255.
33. Morris Silver, "Births, Marriages, and Income Fluctuations in the United Kingdom and Japan," *Economic Development and Cultural Change*, 14 (April 1966), 302–315.
34. G. S. Becker, "An Economic Analysis of Fertility," in National Bureau Committee for Economic Research, *Demographic and Economic Change in Developed Countries*, Princeton University Press, Princeton, N.J., 1960, pp. 209–231.
35. Judith Blake, "Are Babies Consumer Durables? A Critique of the Economic Theory of Reproductive Motivation," *Population Studies*, 22 (1968), 5–25.
36. Alan Sweezy, "The Economic Explanation of Fertility Changes in the United States," *Population Studies*, 25 (1971), 255–264.
37. For an example of a study that found this not to be true, see Moni Nag, "Family Type and Fertility," in *Proceedings of the World Population Conference*, 1965, Vol. II, ed. United Nations, pp. 160–163.
38. U. S. Bureau of the Census, "Marriage, Divorce, and Remarriage by Year of Birth: June, 1971," *Current Population Reports*, Series P-20, No. 239, September 1972.
39. Paul C. Glick and Arthur J. Norton, "Perspectives on the Recent Upturn in Divorce and Remarriage," *Demography*, 10, No. 3 (1973), pp. 301–314.
40. Glick and Norton, p. 301.
41. Kingsley Davis, "Population Policy: Will Current Programmes Succeed?", *Science*, 158 (November 1967), 730–739; Judith Blake, "Demographic Science and the Redirection of Population Policy," *Public Health and Population Change*, ed. Mindel C. Sheps and Jeanne C. Ridley, University of Pittsburgh Press, Pittsburgh, 1965.

42. Frank E. Clarkson, Susan R. Vogel, Inge K. Broverman, Donald M. Broverman, and Paul S. Rosenkrantz, "Family Size and Sex-Role Stereotypes," *Science,* 167 (January 1970), 390–392.

43. For a detailed summary of this literature, see Geraldine B. Terry, "The Interrelationship Between Female Employment and Fertility: A Secondary Analysis of the Growth of American Families Study, 1960," unpublished doctoral dissertation, Florida State University, 1973.

44. For example, J. D. Kasarda, "Economic Structures and Fertility: A Comparative Analysis," *Demography,* 8 (1971), 307–317; or for Latin America, David Heer and E. S. Turner, "Areal Differences in Latin American Fertility," *Population Studies,* 18 (1965), 279–292.

45. S. H. Preston, "Marital Fertility and Female Employment Opportunity," paper presented at annual meeting, Population Association of America, 1971.

46. See J. A. Sweet, "Family Composition and the Labor Force Activity of American Wives," *Demography,* 7 (1970), 195–209.

47. Terry, p. 233.

48. See Blake, *Demographic Science.*

49. Judith Blake, "Can We Believe Recent Data on Birth Expectations in the United States?" *Demography,* 11 (1974), 25–44.

50. Norman B. Ryder, "Recent Trends and Group Differences in Fertility," chap. 6 in Charles F. Westoff et al., *Toward the End of Growth,* Prentice-Hall, Englewood Cliffs, N.J., 1973, 62–66.

51. Pascal K. Whelpton and Clyde V. Kiser, eds., *Social and Psychological Factors Affecting Fertility,* vol. II, Milbank Memorial Fund, New York, 1950, p. 395.

52. W. Stys, "The Influence of Economic Conditions on the Fertility of Peasant Women," *Population Studies,* 11 (1957), 136–148.

53. U. S. Bureau of the Census, *Current Population Reports,* Series P-20, No. 79, February 2, 1958.

54. Charles F. Westoff and Larry Bumpass, "The Revolution in Birth Control Practices of U. S. Roman Catholics," *Science,* 179 (1973), 41–44.

55. Westoff and Bumpass, p. 44.
56. Dudley Kirk, "Factors Affecting Moslem Natality," in *Family Planning and Population Programs*, Bernard Berelson et al., University of Chicago Press, Chicago, 1966.
57. Joseph W. Eaton and Albert J. Mayer, "The Social Biology of Very High Fertility Among the Hutterites: The Demography of a Unique Population," *Human Biology*, 25 (September 1953), 256–262.
58. Discussions of the German program may be found in Frederick Osborn, *Preface to Eugenics*, Harper, New York, 1940, and in A. M. Carr-Sanders, *World Population*, Clarendon Press, Oxford, 1936.
59. See, for example, D. V. Glass, *Population Policies and Movements in Europe*, Clarendon Press, Oxford, 1940.
60. For a discussion of this possibility, see Joseph J. Spengler, *France Faces Depopulation*, Duke University Press, Durham, N.C., 1938.
61. Jean Bourgeois-Pichat, "France," *Country Profiles*, The Population Council, New York, 1972.
62. For discussions of the Swedish program, see Halvor Gille, "Recent Developments in Swedish Population Policy," *Population Studies*, 2 (June 1948), pp. 3–70; Gunnar Myrdal, *Population: A Problem for Democracy*, Harvard University Press, Cambridge, 1940; and Gertrude Svala, "Sweden," *Country Profiles*, The Population Council, New York, 1972.
63. Svala, p. 18.
64. Chicago Tribune, March 17, 1967, as quoted in *Population in Perspective*, Louise B. Young, Oxford University Press, New York, 1968, pp. 142–143.
65. *1972 Canada Yearbook*, Statistics Canada, Ottawa, March 1972, p. 241.
66. Henry P. David and Nicholas H. Wright, "Abortion Legislation: The Romanian Experience," *Studies in Family Planning*, 2, No. 10 (1971), 205–210.
67. Davis, p. 732.
68. For a discussion of India's program, see S. Chandrasekhar, "How

India Is Tackling Her Population Problem," *Demography*, 5, No. 2 (1968), 643–650.

69. Y. Scott Matsumoto, Akira Koizumi, and Tadahiro Nohara, "Condom Use in Japan," *Studies in Family Planning*, 3, No. 10 (1972), p. 254.

70. For a discussion of Taiwan's program, see Ronald Freedman and John Takeshita, *Family Planning in Taiwan: An Experiment in Social Change*, Princeton University Press, Princeton, N.J., 1969.

71. Orleans; Tien. This discussion relies heavily on the work of Orleans and John S. Aird, who reviews Tien's work in *Demography*, 11, No. 4 (1974), 695–701.

72. Orleans and Aird emphasize this reversal, whereas Tien does not.

73. Dwight D. Eisenhower, "The Presidential News Conference of December 2, 1959," U. S. Government Printing Office, Washington, pp. 787–788.

74. *Congressional Quarterly Weekly Report*, "Fact Sheet on Birth Control," 26 (October 11, 1968), pp. 2757, 2761.

75. *The Report of the Commission on Population Growth and the American Future*, Signet, New York, 1972, p. 7.

76. Charles F. Westoff, "Recent Developments in Population Growth Policy in the United States," chap. 14 in Charles F. Westoff et al., *Toward the End of Growth*, Prentice-Hall, Englewood Cliffs, N.J., 1973.

77. *Roe* v. *Wade* and *Doe* v. *Bolton*.

78. Christopher Tietze, "Two Years' Experience with a Liberal Abortion Law: Its Impact on Fertility Trends in New York City," *Family Planning Perspectives*, 5 (Winter 1973), 36–41.

79. Tietze, p. 41.

80. From a proposed amendment to the U. S. Constitution, H. J. Res. 261 and S. J. Res. 130.

81. See, for example, Harriet F. Pilpel, "The Fetus as Person: Possible Legal Consequences of the Hogan-Helms Amendment," *Family Planning Perspectives*, 6 (Winter 1974), 6–7.

82. For summaries of this literature, see James T. Fawcett, *Psychology and Population*, The Population Council, New York, 1971; and James T. Fawcett (ed.), *Psychological Perspectives on Population*, 2, Basic Books, New York, 1973.
83. M. B. Smith, *Social Psychology and Human Values*, Aldine, Chicago, 1969, p. 292.

Suggested Additional Readings

Useful summaries of trends and determinants of fertility are contained in:

Hawthorn, Geoffrey. *The Sociology of Fertility*. Collier-Macmillan Ltd., London, 1970.
United Nations. *Determinants and Consequences of Population Trends*. New York, 1973.

The Report of the United States Commission on Population Growth and the American Future is available from Signet, The New American Library, Inc., or from the Superintendent of Documents, U. S. Government Printing Office. In addition, there are six volumes of research reports that were part of the Commission's work, also available from the U. S. Government Printing Office.

Vol. I. *Demographic and Social Aspects of Population Growth.*
Vol. II. *Economic Aspects of Population Change.*
Vol. III. *Population, Resources and the Environment.*
Vol. IV. *Governance and Population.*
Vol. V. *Population Distribution and Policy.*
Vol. VI. *Aspects of Population Growth Policy.*

An autobiographical account of the beginnings of the birth control movement in the United States by Margaret Sanger is available in:

Sanger, Margaret. *An Autobiography.* Dover, New York, 1971. (First published by Norton, 1938.)

Useful summaries on population policy, family planning, and abortion are found in:

Berelson, Bernard (ed.). *Population Policy in Developed Countries.* McGraw-Hill, New York, 1974.

Lapham, Robert J., and W. Parker Mauldin, "National Family Planning Programs: Review and Evaluation," *Studies in Family Planning*, 3 (March 1972).

Nortman, Dorothy. "Population and Family Planning Programs: A Factbook." *Reports on Population/Family Planning*, No. 2 (4th ed.), September 1972.

Tietze, Christopher, and Deborah A. Dawson. "Induced Abortion: A Factbook," *Reports on Population/Family Planning*, No. 14, December 1973.

Recent collections of articles of fertility and related issues, including results of the 1970 National Fertility Study, are found in:

"The Human Population." *Scientific American*, 231, No. 3 (September 1974).

Westoff, Charles F., et al. *Toward the End of Growth.* Prentice-Hall, Englewood Cliffs, N.J., 1973.

By permission of John Hart and Field Enterprises, Inc.

5

Residential Mobility:
Trends and Determinants

Although fertility and mortality, together constituting natural increase or decrease, are often examined as a basis for gauging population change, no model of demographic change is complete without consideration of residential mobility, the third basic component. The movement of people from one area to another not only affects the size of populations but has an impact on the distribution and characteristics of people as well.

Because of the special terminology used by students of population movement, it is necessary to clarify the principal concepts and terms employed. Since most concerns about population size relate to the relatively permanent population of an area, it is the people who move to change their residence who are the subjects of population mobility studies. Those who make temporary moves (such as persons on vacation trips or on short business visits away from their home areas) are ordinarily not studied by demographers because their temporary moves have no lasting effect on the size of area populations.

People who change their residence are regarded as being *movers;*

151

the process is referred to as *residential mobility* or *geographic mobility*. People who change their permanent residence from one community to another, or from some other large geographical unit to another, are typically termed *migrants*; the process is referred to as *migration*. The intent is to define migrants as those who have severed connections with one area of residence and established connections in another. Given the limited number of geographical distinctions that can be made in official data, one type of geographical unit (the county, in the case of the United States) is chosen as the base for defining movements that involve severance of community ties. People who change their residence but do not cross a critical boundary which would identify them as migrants, are called *local movers*. Thus, someone who moves next door is a local mover, as is a person who moves several miles but does not cross a migration-defining geographical boundary (such as a county line in the United States). On the other hand, someone who moves only one block but thereby crosses a county line is regarded as a migrant, as is the person who shifts residence from one corner of a country to another. Actual distance moved is thus correlated with, but not an integral element of, the definitions.

Although migrants can be classified in any number of ways (e.g., by distance moved, direction of movement, number of geographical units crossed), one distinction looms large in the demographic literature, namely, the difference between intersocietal and intrasocietal movement. Movement between countries affects the population size and characteristics of the country; movement within a country leaves the country's population size unaffected but has an impact on the population size of areas within the country. The first type of movement is termed *international migration,* and the participants are called *immigrants* when they enter a country and *emigrants* when they leave a country. The second type of movement is termed *internal migration,* and the people involved are called *in-migrants* when they enter an area and *out-migrants* when they leave one. At times, these terms seem to be arbitrary, but they have become conventional in demographic analysis and serve to highlight some important aspects of population change.

International Migration

Historical Patterns of International Migration

Migrations between nations have been taking place since very early times, but it is only in the modern era that we have been able to assess the magnitude of these movements. The Woytinskys identified five major currents of international migration in modern times: (1) the emigration from Europe to North America beginning early in the seventeenth century; (2) emigration to South America and the Caribbean since the beginning of the sixteenth century; (3) emigration to South Africa, Australia, and Australasia in a somewhat later period; (4) importation of slaves from Africa to the New World since the sixteenth century; and (5) population shifts in the Far East, mainly from China and India to neighboring countries.[1]

These classic movements have largely completed their course in recent decades and have been replaced by migrations which are smaller in volume and different in direction but still significant in their impact. Typical of such movement was the readjustment of European peoples following the dislocations occasioned by World War II. Two general movements involving the resettlement of displaced persons were the return of German nationals living outside postwar German territory who had to return to Germany in accordance with the Potsdam agreement, and the migration back to their native countries of citizens of Poland, Czechoslovakia, and other European nations who had been uprooted from their homes during the war. The end of the war also opened up some of the channels of transoceanic migration. The United Kingdom and Italy were prime contributors to this overseas movement, directed largely toward North America and Oceania. In more recent decades, however, European nations have been receivers as well as senders of migrants.

The United States, Canada, Australia, New Zealand, South Africa, and Israel were the main receiving countries for emigrants from Northern and Central Europe and, later, from Southern Europe. Latin

America was also a destination for southern Europeans. At the same time, there were shifts between European countries, those most affected being the United Kingdom, Sweden, Belgium, France, and Switzerland.

Other significant international migrations have taken place in recent years in the Americas, Asia and the Middle East, and Africa. Dominant movements on the American continent have been the migrations from Mexico, Cuba, and Canada to the United States and a countermovement from the United States to Canada. Also observed in recent decades have been some sizable exchanges among South and Central American countries.

The most significant of the recent international migrations in Asia and the Middle East have been the shifts of people between India and West and East Pakistan, involving largely the movement of Hindus to India and Moslems to Pakistan; the population exchanges between Israel, Jordan, Lebanon, Syria, and the Gaza Strip resulting from the partition of Palestine and subsequent conflicts and boundary adjustments; the migrations of East Asian people to Japan; and the flow of Chinese people to Hong Kong and Taiwan. Finally, there have been the exchanges affecting Africa, namely, emigration of Europeans from African countries gaining independence and the mobility between African nations.[2]

International Migration and Population Change

All countries have experienced some immigration and emigration, yet international migration has had a significant impact on population change in only a minority of countries. For one thing, in many nations the inflow and outflow of people have substantially offset each other. Second, the rate of natural increase has frequently been so great that the net effect of immigration is dwarfed. Third, international migrations seem to be distributed unevenly over time; as a result, some countries are affected greatly by migration for only short periods of their history. Even so, there are some notable examples of countries whose populations were sharply increased or decreased by migration.

Ireland was remarkable in this respect, for not only did it contribute sizably to the emigration from Europe to the New World in the nineteenth century, but its population was halved in the process. In the 1850s, almost one and one-quarter million persons left Ireland, most of them headed for the United States, but some emigrating to Canada, Australia, and New Zealand. The movement was somewhat less voluminous in succeeding decades, but from 1846 to 1901 the Irish population was reduced from over eight million to just under four and one-half million.[3] This decline took place despite a continuing excess of births over deaths. As Isaac has put it: "Irish emigration thereby achieved the unenviable distinction of being the only migratory movement in modern history to have embraced a considerable proportion of a country's population and to have led directly to a definitive population decline."[4] Irish emigration tapered off during the twentieth century, and by 1970 natural increase had exceeded net emigration and produced a population increase in Ireland, a phenomenon for a long time unknown in that country.

The United States, the principal receiver of Irish emigrants during the late nineteenth century, is a nation that flourished on immigrant settlements. In addition to the early Spanish and French settlements that accompanied the sparse Indian population, the growing European and African migrations and the natural increase of these immigrants and their descendants swelled the population of the country to nearly four million by 1790, the time of the first census. Between 1819, when statistics on the topic first became available, and 1955, more than forty million aliens entered the country (Table 5.1). Except for periods of war and depression, the flow was substantial. The peak was reached at the turn of the century; in six of the eleven years from 1905 through 1915 there were more than a million immigrants.[5] Restrictive immigration legislation substantially curtailed movement into the country after 1920, yet significant numbers continued to enter. In recent years, the volume of illegal immigration is estimated to have equaled the volume of legal immigration.[6] Heavy emigration characterized some periods. Immigrants who had difficulty in adjusting to the new environment or whose economic success would place them in an exceedingly favorable position in their native countries were good candidates for returning to

Table 5.1   Immigration to the United States: 1820–1974

Year	Immigrants (000)	Year	Immigrants (000)	Year	Immigrants (000)
1820	8.4	1846	154.4	1872	404.8
1821	9.1	1847	235.0	1873	459.8
1822	6.9	1848	226.5	1874	313.3
1823	6.4	1849	297.0	1875	227.5
1824	7.9	1850	370.0	1876	170.0
1825	10.2	1851	379.5	1877	141.9
1826	10.8	1852	371.6	1878	138.5
1827	18.9	1853	368.6	1879	177.8
1828	27.4	1854	427.8	1880	457.3
1829	22.5	1855	200.9	1881	669.4
1830	23.3	1856	200.4	1882	789.0
1831	22.6	1857	251.3	1883	603.3
1832	60.5	1858	123.1	1884	518.6
1833	58.6	1859	121.3	1885	395.3
1834	65.4	1860	153.6	1886	334.2
1835	45.4	1861	91.9	1887	490.1
1836	76.2	1862	92.0	1888	546.9
1837	79.3	1863	176.3	1889	444.4
1838	38.9	1864	193.4	1890	455.3
1839	68.1	1865	248.1	1891	560.3
1840	84.1	1866	318.6	1892	579.7
1841	80.3	1867	315.7	1893	439.7
1842	104.6	1868	138.8	1894	285.6
1843	52.5	1869	352.8	1895	258.5
1844	78.6	1870	387.2	1896	343.3
1845	114.4	1871	321.4	1897	230.8

Note: From 1820 to 1867, figures represent alien passengers arrived; from 1868 through 1891 and 1895 through 1897, immigrant aliens arrived; from 1892 through 1894 and 1898 to the present time, immigrant aliens admitted. Since July 1, 1868, the data are for fiscal years ending June 30. Prior to fiscal year 1869, the periods covered are as follows: from 1820 to 1831 and 1843 to 1849, the years ended on September 30 (1843 covers nine months); from

Year	Immigrants (000)	Year	Immigrants (000)	Year	Immigrants (000)
1898	229.3	1924	706.9	1950	249.2
1899	311.7	1925	294.3	1951	205.7
1900	448.6	1926	304.5	1952	265.5
1901	487.9	1927	335.2	1953	170.4
1902	648.7	1928	307.3	1954	208.2
1903	857.0	1929	279.7	1955	237.8
1904	812.9	1930	241.7	1956	321.6
1905	1,026.5	1931	97.1	1957	326.9
1906	1,100.7	1932	35.6	1958	253.3
1907	1,285.3	1933	23.1	1959	260.7
1908	782.9	1934	29.5	1960	265.4
1909	751.8	1935	35.0	1961	271.3
1910	1,041.6	1936	36.3	1962	283.8
1911	878.6	1937	50.2	1963	306.3
1912	838.2	1938	67.9	1964	292.2
1913	1,197.9	1939	83.0	1965	296.7
1914	1,218.5	1940	70.8	1966	323.0
1915	326.7	1941	51.8	1967	362.0
1916	298.8	1942	28.8	1968	454.4
1917	295.4	1943	23.7	1969	358.6
1918	110.6	1944	28.6	1970	373.3
1919	141.1	1945	38.1	1971	370.5
1920	430.0	1946	108.7	1972	384.7
1921	805.2	1947	147.3	1973	400.1
1922	309.6	1948	170.6	1974	394.9
1923	522.9	1949	188.3		

1832 to 1842 and 1850 to 1867, the years ended on December 31 (1832 and 1850 cover fifteen months). For 1868, the period ended on June 30 and covers six months.

Source: U. S. Department of Justice, *1974 Annual Report, Immigration and Naturalization Service,* U. S. Government Printing Office, Washington, 1975, p. 25.

their original locations. At most points in United States history net immigration accounted for a small proportion of total population increase; at some points, however, the contribution was notable (Table 5.2). As much as two-fifths of population change during the 1880s could be attributed to the net effect of immigration. In the 1930s, there was actually net emigration. By the 1970–1972 period, when the rate of natural increase had dwindled, the continuing net movement to

Table 5.2   Components of population change in the United States:
1810 to 1972

Period	Total population change	Due to natural increase	Due to net immigration
1810–1820	100	97	3
1820–1830	100	96	4
1830–1840	100	88	12
1840–1850	100	77	23
1850–1860	100	68	32
1860–1870	100	75	25
1870–1880	100	75	25
1880–1890	100	60	40
1890–1900	100	72	28
1900–1910	100	61	39
1910–1920	100	82	18
1920–1930	100	88	12
1930–1940	100	101	−1
1940–1950	100	90	10
1950–1960	100	90	10
1960–1969	100	84	16
1970–1972	100	81	19

Source: Irene B. Taeuber and Conrad Taeuber, *People of the United States in the 20th Century*, U. S. Government Printing Office, Washington, 1971, p. 582; and U. S. Bureau of the Census, "Estimates of the Population of the United States and Components of Change: 1972," *Current Population Reports*, Series P-25, No. 499, p. 9.

the United States accounted for about one-fifth of the population growth.

Israel is a nation which has experienced what is perhaps one of the most rapid population buildups through immigration of any nation in history. Before statehood, the nation (then Palestine) was relatively unpopulated and had modest numbers of Jewish residents. The first wave of Jewish immigrants came following a series of massacres in Czarist Russia in 1880 and 1881. Though numbering no more than 20,000 to 30,000, these immigrants set a precedent for Jewish movement to the Holy Land. The second wave of immigration, from 1904 to 1914, added another 35,000 to 40,000 and brought with it the foundations of a new state. Events associated with World War I led to the emigration of many Jews, but a third wave of immigrants from 1919 to 1923 added 35,000 to the population, and a fourth wave in the 1924–1931 period introduced 82,000 to the new land. In the fifth wave, during Hitler's rise to power, more than 217,000 Jewish immigrants entered Palestine, and smaller numbers came up until 1948, when Israel emerged as a new state.[7] Thus, between 1919 and 1948 the Jewish population of Israel rose from 56,000 to 650,000, and 72 percent of this increase was attributable to net immigration.[8] In the four-year period following independence 687,000 immigrants entered Israel, more than the entire preindependence Jewish population of the country.[9] The new immigration included many non-Western as well as Western Jews. By the time of the 1961 Census, the Jewish population approached two million, and more than two-thirds of the total growth was accounted for by net immigration.

Internal Migration

The movement of people within nations will not have a direct effect on the size and composition of the national population, but it can serve to redistribute people within the country. As a consequence, the population size of geographic units inside the nation will be changed. Movement may be observed from one region to another, between states, from community to community, between rural and urban areas, and from urban centers to their periphery, as well as within a neighborhood.

The volume of internal migration in countries far exceeds that of international migration. It has been estimated that in Europe, in about 1930, at least seventy-five million inhabitants were living outside their native communities, while only about ten million were outside their countries of birth. Furthermore, numerous movements had taken place within communities.

Migratory flows change in size and characteristics as countries undergo the demographic transition. In general, one can say that the volume of migration increases as nations become more modernized, but the fact remains that the nature of migration in particular places and times is a consequence of the existing social structure and the character of social, economic, political, and cultural change.[10] There has been a tendency for internal migration in developing countries to be of two types: first, movement to settle new lands or exploit new resources, and second, movement in response to industrialization. In industrialized nations, internal migration is more likely to take the form of either movement of people from rural to urban areas or a shift of people from metropolitan centers to their suburbs.[11]

Migration within a country consists of individuals changing their residences, and yet so many of these individuals are involved in the same kind of move, in terms of the area of origin and area of destination, that one can discern both major *migration streams* and minor ones. The net effect of all these movements — some short, some long; some in one direction, some in another; some large in volume, some small — is the redistribution of the people living in the country.[12]

Streams of migrants are also composed of individuals with different migration histories. Movement from region A to region B, or from city X to city Y, during a particular period of time may include persons (1) who are moving for the first time or who have moved previously, (2) who are returning to a place they once moved from or who are coming to a place for the first time, (3) who are moving as individuals or who are changing residence with their families, and (4) who are part of a larger group or mass movement or who are moving independently of any group migration. Which of these categories movers can be placed in has an important bearing on the volume of net migration (moves in one direction — or of a particular stream — can partially or wholly offset moves in the opposite direction — or a counterstream) and on the overall characteristics of migration streams.

The Age Pattern of Mobility

As was the case with mortality and fertility, mobility is characterized by a typical age pattern. In contrast to mortality and fertility, the age configuration of mobility is not significantly determined by biological factors but depends more heavily on social and cultural factors. It is thus the case that the age curve of residential change may be more variable than that of deaths and births, but there are still general tendencies toward a predictable pattern.[13]

In this typical age pattern, mobility rates are relatively high in early infancy, decline somewhat but remain above average until the midteens, rise to a peak in the early twenties, remain high but decline progressively with the approach of middle age, and attain a moderately low but stable level from middle age onward.[14] This reflects variations in life cycle activities which are related to family and socioeconomic status. Thus, a high mobility rate for infants suggests the need for families to provide more adequate housing; the peak rate among those in their late teens and twenties is linked to finishing school, getting married, and taking a job; and the stabilizing of the rate in later years is indicative of more settled familial and socioeconomic stages.

Another way of looking at the age pattern of migration is to see how much of one's lifetime mobility is concentrated at various ages. Data for the United States for the 1966–1971 period reveal the probability of making a move during any one-year period. The graphs in Figure 5.1 are shown for all moves and, separately, for moves between states, between counties, and within counties. It is clear, first of all, that each of the graphs has the same form and that, therefore, age

Figure 5.1   Single-year-of-age probabilities of making various types of moves
during one-year periods, 1966–1971

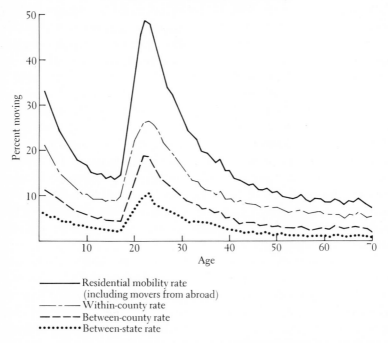

Source: Larry H. Long, "New Estimates of Migration Expectancy in the United
States," *Journal of the American Statistical Association*, Vol. 68, No. 341 (March
1973), 38.

patterns of mobility tend to be the same regardless of the kind of move.
The sharp peaks at infancy and, especially, in the early twenties are
striking.[15]

Examining the cumulative effects of mobility, it can be calculated
that by age eighteen a person can expect to have experienced about
one-fourth of lifetime residential mobility, and from age eighteen to
age twenty-five the person can expect to experience another quarter. By
the twenty-sixth birthday, the person will have completed half of all

the moves he or she will make. Just past age forty, three-fourths of the moves will have been accomplished.

That this age curve of mobility varies, even for national populations, can be seen in comparisons of the sexes, races, and countries. Women, because they generally marry slightly earlier than men, have somewhat higher mobility rates at ages seventeen to twenty-one. Blacks have higher rates of residential mobility than whites up to age nineteen and at age twenty-eight and over. This reflects the fact that blacks are less likely than whites to be migrants (between-county movement occurs frequently among people in their twenties), and what migration there is takes place over a greater part of the young adult age span.[16] The American population continues its mobility throughout the life cycle more than people in other countries. At age thirty-five an American has as many moves remaining in his or her lifetime as a Briton at age twenty-five and a Japanese at age one.[17] Apart from the higher level of mobility, these comparisons reflect varying age curves of residential change.

The unequal rates of movement by age are important in understanding the reasons why people move or do not move as well as the consequences of mobility for the community and society. When information on the age pattern of migration is combined with our knowledge of the age structure of mortality and fertility, we can perceive the relationship of the life cycle to population change.

Factors Affecting Mobility

Theoretical Considerations

Attempts at developing explanatory frameworks for residential mobility go back at least to before the turn of the century. E. G. Ravenstein, after analyzing census data for several Western societies, listed certain generalizations that could be derived from those data which he labeled "laws of migration." These included findings concerning the distance and direction of migration, the nature of migration streams and counterstreams, selectivity in the characteristics of migrants, and migration as a process which occurred in stages.[18] In succeeding years, others refined, modified, and added to these empirical generalizations. These inventories of research findings did not, however, provide a theoretical basis for studying migration.

A different approach to formulating principles of migration streams resulted in more rigorous statements about the relationship between the volume of migration and the distance between areas. Thus, the number of migrants was determined to be some mathematical function of the size of the population in areas of origin and destination and the distance traversed to get from one place to the other.[19] Stouffer conceptualized the relationship in terms of opportunities at a given place and the "intervening opportunities."[20] This general approach had empirical validity, but it has contributed little to a theory of residential mobility.

In an effort to give more structure to these earlier propositions and to generate others, Lee set down a general schema that could encompass findings about spatial movement.[21] He first classified the factors that enter into the decision to migrate and the process of migration under four headings: (1) factors associated with the area of origin, (2) factors associated with the area of destination, (3) intervening obstacles, and (4) personal factors. Whether or not an individual moves is seen as the result of a decision made by the individual, or by someone else for him or her, which is based on perceptions of positive or negative evaluations of conditions in the two areas and of the intervening obstacles. Perceptions of these values will differ according to the characteristics of the decision maker and other personal circumstances. This neat formulation helps to organize much of the foregoing literature on migratory behavior, but given the complexity of the phenomenon, it is too global to enable specification of the decision-making process itself and of the various social interactions which go into it.

Still other approaches have sought to identify factors affecting mobility by developing classificatory schemes. Petersen categorized migrations into five types which were of historical significance: (1) *primitive* migration (resulting from an ecological push to change the relationship between people and nature), (2) *forced* migration (deriving from a government policy affecting the relationship between people and the state which leaves the migrant no alternative), (3) *impelled* migration (also deriving from a governmental policy affecting the relationship between people and the state but from one which grants the person some option as to whether or not to leave), (4) *free* migration (based on the individual's will or aspiration, which may involve relatively small groups), and (5) *mass* migration (in which the aspirations of large groups of people produce social momentum that generates their migration from an area).[22] These five classes of migration are further divided according to whether the movement was designed to retain a way of life (conservative) or to bring about a new mode of life (innovating). This scheme sensitizes us to some of the distinctive types of migration in history and suggests the importance of attitudes and aspirations of individuals, as well as institutional factors, in determining migratory behavior.

In the remaining part of this chapter, residential mobility is viewed in terms of the classification used previously to survey factors affecting mortality and fertility. The broad societal effects are first examined, then normative influences of groups are assessed, and finally we reflect on the role of individual behavior.

Societal-Level Variables

Numerous conditions in the society and beyond provide a setting for prospective migration. Particular attention is paid here to *natural environmental factors, economic change,* and *political change.*

NATURAL ENVIRONMENTAL FACTORS

General environmental features of an area in which individuals live and those they must traverse in order to go elsewhere may facilitate or impede geographic mobility. It is less likely, for example, that residents of a nation in the Himalayas, who have to deal with mountain crossings and severe weather, will be migratory than will residents of plains countries where the climate is mild and travel is relatively simple, all other things considered. Not only *altitude* and *climate*, but *terrain*, *availability of water*, *natural resources*, and *condition of the soil* are relevant to migration opportunities. Historically, these factors played a crucial part in the wanderings of some early tribes and in the sedentary life of other peoples. They enabled many in the past to reach desired destinations, and they constituted barriers to mobility for some who would have preferred to relocate.

ECONOMIC CHANGE

Students of international migration in the late nineteenth and early twentieth century have recognized the role of the economy in the movement of people between nations. The industrialization that took place in "old" countries tended to inhibit emigration, and the industrialization in "new" countries had the effect of attracting immigrants. The flow of migration which evolved, however, can be seen as the consequence of optimizing the distribution of labor and capital on both sides of the Atlantic. Since labor and capital were plentiful in Europe relative to land and natural resources, and they were scarce in America, freedom to move and the available means of transportation enabled many to migrate westward.[23] As tne balance of these factors shifted over time, migratory flows were modified in volume and direction.

While the economy as a whole may be viewed as an effect on migration, it can also be seen in terms of three separate economic effects — seasonal, business cycle, and long-term.[24] The seasonality of international migration is related to the peak months of employment in receiving countries. The effect of the business cycle was revealed in the time lag between prosperity in America and increased immigration and between depressions and decreased immigration. In addition to annual fluctuations, longer-term economic changes, such as those associated with home and factory construction cycles, were related to long-term swings in migration.

Internal migration can also be affected by broad economic change. The Great Depression after 1929 reduced the attractiveness of the large cities, since jobs were limited and resources scarce. Urban areas, which had registered spectacular population growth during prosperity, had little or no increase; on the other hand, rural areas in almost all states reversed their population trends and began to show marked growth. It was not until the Depression subsided and the economy was stimulated again that migration to urban areas was resumed in the United States.

POLITICAL CHANGE

Although economic factors have generally been of principal importance in accounting for international migration, political factors have been of substantial consequence at particular points in time in given countries. For instance, the revolution in Germany in 1848 led to the emigration of a number of refugees, the massacres in Russia in the nineteenth century were followed by large-scale emigration of Jews, and the partition of India that created the country of Pakistan resulted in shifts of people from one area to another.[25]

An example of a political effect on internal migration is a period of military activity. During the three years and three months between December 1941 and March 1945 (a peak war period) in the United States, more civilians moved from one county to another than during the five years 1935 to 1940.[26] They were responding to a need for a shift of skilled workers, and their families, to production centers. In addition, the military buildup resulted in large flows of young men from all parts of the country to locations where there were military installations.

Group Membership and Normative Influences

Within the context of these general societal and community factors, residential mobility can be determined by a variety of group or normative effects. Bogue has written on a "catalogue of the objective situations that stimulate a change of residence from one community to another," in which he classifies events that may precipitate mobility into three categories: migration-stimulating situations for persons, factors in choosing a destination, and socioeconomic conditions affecting migration.[27] The last of these categories parallels our set of societal-level variables; the first category is akin to the normative considerations identified here. By and large, these refer to social-structural conditions that an individual faces at different stages of life and that guide decision making. The following discussion encompasses such group effects as those related to *the family, socioeconomic status, ethnic affiliation, health factors,* and *government.* These may be regarded as illustrative of group influences rather than as a comprehensive set of factors relevant to the migration process.

THE FAMILY

Migration is often associated with change in family status, from the occasion of marriage to the "empty nest" stage of family life when children are no longer in the household and the couple, or one of the spouses, survives the remaining years alone.

Mobility is often related to marriage because two people getting married will have come from different residences and, after marriage, will settle in one of those residences or in an entirely new location. During tight economic periods, newly married couples may "double up" with one set of parents until they manage to afford a home of their own. In the first stage one of the partners has become a mover, and in the second stage both have become movers. Migration at marriage may be culturally prescribed, as in traditional India. It is a widespread Hindu custom that a male take a bride from another village. Once married, the couple follows the practice of patrilocal residence; they reside in the same area as his relatives.[28] As a result, mobility is highly limited to women and serves to redistribute the female population extensively.

Even later in the family cycle, mobility is related to the structure and characteristics of family life (Table 5.3). Thus, a high proportion of movers are those who move in family units, usually with wives and

Table 5.3 Reason for move, by type of mobility, for male movers 18 to 64 years old: United States, March 1963 (percent distribution)

Reason for move	Intracounty movers	Migrants
All reasons	100.0	100.0
Related to job	11.6	58.1
To take a job	2.7	23.6
To look for work	1.0	9.6
Job transfer	0.4	7.3
Commuting and Armed Forces	7.5	17.6
Easier commuting	6.7	6.7
Enter or leave Armed Forces	0.8	10.9
Not related to job	88.4	41.9
Housing	60.4	11.3
Better housing	55.3	10.7
Forced move	5.0	0.6
Family status	19.1	16.3
Change in marital status	11.0	4.0
Join or move with family	8.1	12.2
Other	9.0	14.3
Health	1.1	2.8
All other reasons	7.9	11.5

Source: U. S. Bureau of the Census, "Reasons for Moving: March 1962 to March 1963," *Current Population Reports*, Series P-20, No. 154, p. 4.

children following husbands to more favorable job opportunities.[29] When persons move because of different housing needs, it is the family as a unit which responds to those needs.[30] Moreover, the decision to move takes account of the nature of interaction with the extended family after the move is completed.[31] The ties to one's relatives are a strong force in determining residential location.

Among men eighteen to sixty-four years old in the United States, reasons for moving were linked to family situations, but the type of move was crucial. Migration seems to occur primarily in response to circumstances relating to employment, whereas local mobility arises out of circumstances relating to what might be termed living arrangements.

As the family advances in its life cycle and its size diminishes as children leave home or spouses die, housing needs become more modest, and relocation is frequently an outcome. On the other hand, maintenance of the larger existing home may be the best way to provide a place for extended family members to visit and may enable those remaining in the household to continue their associations with kin and friends in a neighborhood.

Through all stages of the family cycle, the family is apt to be a strong influence on any family member's decision to move. Young people are socialized to norms of mobility behavior by the consequences for the family as well as for themselves.

SOCIOECONOMIC STATUS

It is obvious that status considerations play a vital role in determining the moving potential of individuals. Those seeking a better job or more prestige will frequently have to relocate in order to maximize their opportunity and adjust their locale to their aspirations. Also, it is more feasible for higher-status persons to move, particularly longer distances, as a means of maintaining or enhancing their status.

As a result of these factors, mobility tends to be selective of certain socioeconomic categories of the population. Thus, as shown in Table 5.4, the probability of moving is greatest at the lowest and highest levels of the education continuum. Those with higher education are more likely to move longer distances, while those with little education typically move locally. It has been calculated that the average American male with five or more years of college can expect to live in at least two different states during the remainder of his lifetime, whereas those not finishing high school will most probably spend the rest of their lives in the state where they are currently residing.[32]

From an occupational point of view, the highest mobility rates (especially of long-distance moves) are found among salaried professional workers and salaried managers and administrators; the lowest rates are found among self-employed professionals and proprietors of businesses.[33] Salaried employees frequently find themselves being relocated by their employers, a phenomenon not unusual in an economy in which businesses and industries standardize their employment activities but spread their commercial outlets and factories throughout the country. On the other hand, self-employed professionals will invest a great deal in capital equipment, clientele, customers, and actual or potential work and fringe benefits, which often tie them to a community and restrict their mobility.[34]

The chance to improve one's housing status has also been identified as a critical factor. Persons who have ascended in the socioeconomic scale, or who have aspirations to, frequently change their residences so that their families can interact with those of higher status and improve their level of living. Of course, housing changes are often responses to other physical and social needs as well, but they are generally linked to the web of socioeconomic characteristics that helps determine mobility patterns.

ETHNIC AFFILIATION

Racial, nationality, and religious factors are also related to mobility potential and to specific destinations. Bogue reports that nonwhite populations are more mobile than white populations in the United States, although the nonwhite mobility is heavily concentrated in local movement, a reflection of their lower average socioeconomic status. Movement across county borders is substantially less for nonwhites.[35] Of course, during some periods of time large numbers of American blacks have been migrants. Particularly during the middle decades of the twentieth century, large streams of blacks moved from southern rural areas and towns to northern cities. Once they arrived there, however, their movement was likely to be limited to the neighborhood in which they resided or to nearby areas of the city.

In a study done in the late 1960s, McAllister, Kaiser, and Butler examined twelve variables that might explain black-white mobility differences in metropolitan areas. These included age, education, family

Table 5.4   One-year rates of moving (percentages) and expected years
with moves by type of move, age, and years of school completed,
for men 25 years old and over

Age and years of school completed	Number of persons (000)	Percent moving			
		Total[a]	Within counties	Between counties[b]	Between states
Ages 25–29	36,793	37.9	22.5	13.5	7.0
Elem.: 0–7	1,736	39.8	25.6	11.9	5.2
Elem.: 8	1,876	42.3	28.2	12.6	5.7
H.S.: 1–3	5,719	37.2	24.3	11.6	5.2
H.S.: 4	14,844	33.7	21.5	10.7	5.2
College: 1–3	5,758	36.9	22.1	13.0	6.9
College: 4	3,888	44.8	20.2	20.5	11.3
College: 5+	2,972	49.6	22.4	23.9	15.6
Ages 30–34	32,467	26.0	15.6	9.1	4.5
Elem.: 0–7	2,369	29.1	20.1	7.4	3.1
Elem.: 8	2,038	26.7	16.8	9.1	3.3
H.S.: 1–3	5,318	27.0	19.0	7.5	3.7
H.S.: 4	12,363	22.5	13.4	7.9	3.6
College: 1–3	4,163	26.3	15.2	10.1	5.4
College: 4	3,527	27.2	13.0	12.7	6.8
College: 5+	2,689	34.5	17.9	13.6	7.5
Ages 35–44	68,348	17.0	10.3	5.9	3.0
Elem.: 0–7	7,237	21.1	15.2	5.1	2.0
Elem.: 8	6,615	17.3	21.1	4.6	2.0
H.S.: 1–3	12,242	16.0	10.9	4.8	2.1
H.S.: 4	23,095	15.6	9.3	5.3	2.7
College: 1–3	7,517	17.5	9.2	7.5	3.9
College: 4	6,453	16.6	7.9	7.7	4.6
College: 5+	5,189	19.4	9.0	9.0	5.4

Total[a]	Expected years with moves[c]		
	Within counties	Between counties[b]	Between states
7.27	4.53	2.46	1.17
8.38	5.87	2.17	0.90
7.58	5.09	2.29	0.88
6.94	4.74	2.08	0.92
6.51	4.07	2.17	1.01
7.41	4.35	2.80	1.39
7.74	3.82	3.43	1.92
8.47	4.11	3.80	2.30
5.44	3.44	1.80	0.83
6.47	4.64	1.60	0.65
5.53	3.72	1.68	0.61
5.14	3.56	1.51	0.67
4.88	3.03	1.65	0.75
5.63	3.29	2.17	1.06
5.57	2.85	2.44	1.37
6.05	3.03	2.64	1.54
4.19	2.70	1.36	0.62
5.07	3.68	1.24	0.50
4.25	2.92	1.24	0.45
3.84	2.65	1.15	0.49
3.80	2.39	1.27	0.58
4.37	2.56	1.68	0.80
4.26	2.22	1.82	1.05
4.38	2.16	1.98	1.17

Table 5.4 *(continued)*

Age and years of school completed	Number of persons (000)	Total[a]	Percent moving		
			Within coun-ties	Between coun-ties[b]	Between states
Ages 45–54	66,306	11.5	7.6	3.6	1.7
Elem.: 0–7	9,294	14.9	10.9	3.5	1.7
Elem.: 8	9,106	11.7	8.1	3.4	1.1
H.S.: 1–3	12,342	10.8	7.8	2.9	1.3
H.S.: 4	20,929	9.9	6.5	3.2	1.6
College: 1–3	6,663	12.0	7.3	4.5	2.2
College: 4	4,491	11.8	6.0	5.0	3.1
College: 5+	3,481	12.2	6.7	4.9	2.7
Ages 55–64	51,143	9.1	6.0	2.9	1.1
Elem.: 0–7	11,395	11.0	7.9	2.8	0.9
Elem.: 8	10,684	8.8	6.0	2.6	1.0
H.S.: 1–3	9,016	7.9	5.1	2.7	1.1
H.S.: 4	11,152	8.4	5.3	2.9	1.0
College: 1–3	3,986	9.5	6.3	2.9	1.2
College: 4	2,586	9.0	5.0	3.9	1.7
College: 5+	2,324	8.2	3.7	4.0	1.8
Ages 65+	49,380	8.3	5.6	2.6	0.9
Elem.: 0–7	17,770	8.5	6.2	2.2	0.7
Elem.: 8	13,325	8.6	5.6	2.9	0.8
H.S.: 1–3	6,003	7.3	5.0	2.3	0.9
H.S.: 4	6,362	7.6	5.0	2.5	1.0
College: 1–3	2,510	8.9	5.4	3.5	1.3
College: 4	1,956	9.2	5.5	3.3	1.9
College: 5+	1,454	7.8	4.1	3.7	2.8

[a] Includes movers from abroad.
[b] Includes movers between states.
[c] Expected years with moves in the age interval and all later ages.

Source: Larry H. Long, "Migration Differentials by Education and Occupation: Trends and Variations," *Demography*, 10 (May 1973), 245.

| | Expected years with moves[c] | | |
| | Within coun- ties | Between coun- ties[b] | Between states |
Total[a]			
2.62	1.75	0.82	0.34
3.12	2.28	0.78	0.31
2.64	1.80	0.82	0.27
2.36	1.64	0.71	0.29
2.35	1.52	0.78	0.32
2.76	1.72	0.99	0.44
2.73	1.50	1.11	0.62
2.58	1.33	1.14	0.67
1.67	1.12	0.53	0.19
1.87	1.35	0.48	0.16
1.67	1.12	0.54	0.17
1.46	0.98	0.48	0.18
1.54	0.99	0.53	0.19
1.77	1.13	0.62	0.24
1.76	1.01	0.69	0.35
1.54	0.75	0.75	0.45
1.33	0.90	0.41	0.15
1.36	0.99	0.35	0.12
1.38	0.90	0.47	0.14
1.16	0.80	0.36	0.14
1.22	0.79	0.41	0.15
1.42	0.87	0.55	0.21
1.47	0.88	0.52	0.31
1.25	0.65	0.59	0.45

size, socioeconomic status, duration of residence, tenure (owner or renter), family type, and social mobility commitment. Of these variables, only tenure status significantly affected black-white mobility differences.[36] Renters are more mobile than homeowners, and blacks are more likely to be renters than are whites. Viewed from another perspective, blacks are less likely to be able to arrange for the purchase of housing and, because of their impermanent situation, are more likely to be evicted by landlords or have their residences destroyed or removed for purposes of land development.

Ethnic groups of all types are affected to at least some degree by their cultural heritage and their ties to the traditions of the group; hence, where they will move will be partly determined by the movement of the group as a whole and their interest in being within traveling distance of the group. Such ethnic links are nicely demonstrated by the Macdonalds, who analyzed chain migration (that movement in which prospective migrants learn of opportunities, are provided with transportation, and have initial accommodation and employment arranged by means of primary social relationships with previous migrants) as it related to Italian neighborhood formation in the United States.[37] There were three types of this migration. First, some established immigrants who had achieved considerable status in the neighborhood helped male immigrants to get jobs in order to profit from them. They exploited the new immigrants directly or were paid a commission by American employers for providing labor. Second, new arrivals frequently went directly to the relatives and friends who had financed their passage and relied on them to find their first lodgings and employment. Such serial migration helped ensure integration into the community. Third, there was delayed family migration. Typically, males preceded their wives and children, or prospective brides, so that they might first provide an economic base for the family.[38] Chain migration thus made possible both the movement of people and their particular location in a homogeneous ethnic neighborhood.

HEALTH FACTORS

Physical well-being can play an important role in determining mobility status. Persons who are in poor health may move to seek a more favorable natural environment. Migrants to Florida, Arizona, and California often cite health reasons for moving. Even many local movers may leave their familial homes to seek medical aid and nursing care in a home for the aged or long-term institution. On the other hand, physical limitations may prevent some persons from being as mobile as they would like.

The relationship between mental health and migration has been a much-studied topic. It has been found that rates of first admission to mental hospitals are higher among migrants than among nonmigrants, even after such variables as age, sex, and color are controlled.[39] The obvious interpretation of this finding is that the stress of the migration process and the difficulties of adjusting to a new environment result in a high incidence of mental illness. However, one cannot discount the possibility that those with mental ailments are more likely to move or that the same factors that impel migration also contribute to mental illness.

GOVERNMENT

Among the groups which influence mobility behavior are the several kinds of governmental agencies. They enact laws and formulate policies governing migratory flows. Until recently, the interest of governments in migration related principally to immigration and emigration. Increasingly, however, norms concerning movement within countries are being formalized.

In considering appropriate policies on immigration, governments may specify the number of people that can be admitted, their areas of origin, and their characteristics. United States immigration policy has shifted over the years in these regards. In the earliest years, essentially free migration prevailed, although restrictions were imposed on paupers, criminals, prostitutes, and other stigmatized persons. The familiar quota system was introduced in 1921 with the stipulation that immigration from European countries be limited to 3 percent of the number of foreign-born of each nationality resident in the United States in 1910. A revision of the law in 1924 reduced the quota to 2 percent and based the distribution of nationalities on the 1890 Census. The aim of many congressmen was to further limit the numbers coming from the countries of Southern and Eastern Europe, whom they considered undesirable and who had migrated in large numbers after 1890. The change in the law succeeded in reducing the percent of immigrants from Southern and Eastern Europe from 45 to 12 percent. The Immigration and Nationality Act of 1952 maintained the national origins quota system but changed some of the features of the law. For example, a preference system was introduced that gave first priority, within the quotas, to highly skilled immigrants and their families. Families of United States residents were next in order of priority. The Immigration Act of 1965, which was first implemented in 1968, abolished the national origins quota system, continued a numerical ceiling on immigration (including that from the Western Hemisphere, which had been exempt earlier), changed the preference system to give greater priority to family relationships as a basis for selecting immigrants, and required employment clearances to ensure that a demand existed for the person's skills. As a consequence of the latter act, a significant change in the origin of immigrants took place, so that Southern European, Asian, and Caribbean immigrants make up a larger proportion of immigrants than previously.[40]

Although internal migration in the United States has generally been a matter of individuals and families freely moving to where they prefer to live, governments have become more concerned with mobility patterns and have begun to exert controls on some types of movement. Thus, in an effort to restructure cities, urban renewal programs have relocated large numbers of people from one part of the city to another. Public housing has provided mobility opportunities for some classes of the population, to the exclusion of others. Changing levels of public sector employment alter incentives for moving to new areas. Added to these factors affecting local mobility are government policies regulating interstate movements. Some states and counties are now passing legislation to monitor the flow of persons across their borders. Concerns with the environment, energy use, and diminution of space and privacy have led many citizens to support such restrictions. A national survey conducted by the Commission on Population Growth and the American Future in 1971 showed that half of those questioned favored government action designed to slow the growth of large metropolitan areas.[41] Some states have set up growth policies boards to shape legislation that will bring about optimal population distribution. It is apparent that attention to matters of distribution and migration of people will increase as preoccupation with population size is moderated.

Individual Effects

As broad societal changes take place, and various group structures and processes provide both guidance and pressures for action, the individual is engaged in a decision-making process that leads to mobility or nonmobility. Many of the decisions that are made are not entirely voluntary ones, in the sense that being imprisoned, evicted from the home, or ordered into military service prevents people from acting in an independent fashion. Similarly, a rational decision on the part of an individual as to whether or not to move may be tempered by the desires of family members and friends who impose constraints on the final outcome or by the individual's physical condition at the time. However, the decision as to whether or not to move is one typically made by an individual in the context of these other forces.

Kenkel has conceptualized the moving-decision process for families in terms of several steps. (1) Some circumstance or event raises the possibility of moving. (2) The family engages in a discussion in which the advantages and disadvantages of moving are elaborated. (3) A determination about moving is made, first by each family member and then by the family as a group. (4) If the decision is to move, the family selects the date, time, and location of movement.[42] Clearly, mobility decisions are not always made in such a logical fashion. Heads of families may decide about moving themselves and notify the family only after commitments have been made. Conflicts among family members may keep a group decision from being reached. Or the calculation of pros and cons of a move may be imperfect, that is, done without knowledge of some of the relevant information. Moreover, those who simply desire to move may create their own opportunities. Nevertheless, this process describes the general pattern of moving decisions.

How people decide whether or not to move when given an opportunity to do so may be determined, in part, by their psychological and
social predispositions. Kenkel has identified several types of persons
along these lines: the determined nonmovers, who have decided they
will stay where they are for a more or less indefinite period of time; the
tentative nonmovers, who have decided they will not move for the
present but who have certain reservations depending on new circumstances; the tentative movers, who have decided to move as soon as
specified conditions are met; the determined movers, who will move
very soon regardless of circumstances; and the unsettled, who cannot
reach a decision or have mixed feelings about moving.[43] They all begin
the decision-making process with a mental set concerning mobility.

These predispositions are determined, to a great extent, by the
socialization processes that have operated on individuals earlier in life.
Previous migration experiences, educational and career aspirations, the
attitudes toward moving of family members and friends, attachment to
particular communities and neighborhoods, and other normative factors
create images of desirable and undesirable moves and condition the
individual to an expected migratory history.

The inefficient operation of the mobility orientation process is reflected in data that relate desires, expectations, and actual movement.
Lansing and Mueller found that 20 percent of a national sample of
families desired to move, only 11 percent expected to move in the coming year, and only 5 percent actually made a move in that year.[44] They
also discovered that one-third of movers began thinking seriously about
moving only a month before they actually departed, and two-thirds
deliberated for half a year or less. Furthermore, only about one-third
of the movers considered any alternatives to the place they eventually
moved. Thus, decisions about residential mobility may be based on a
careful examination of alternatives, or on a relatively spontaneous reaction to the presentation of a novel opportunity to move, or on a
general feeling of dissatisfaction with one's present residence. The
configuration of decision making that emerges may be a function of
personality type or may depend on the intensity of feelings about one's
present situation at a point in time.

Future Mobility Prospects

Those responsible for making population projections for states and local areas are faced with the difficulty of estimating future residential mobility patterns. Traditionally, mobility is assumed to follow some past trend. For some periods of time and for some areas, this assumption of continuing past patterns of migration is valid; however, it is often not valid and is the cause of many inaccurate population projections for small areas.

The volume of immigration has been generally predictable in most countries because of government controls. Emigration has been less predictable, but levels have been fairly stable. Within nations, the movements of people are much too varied to be estimated accurately from past trends. As more surveys are taken which delve into the people's desires and expectations concerning mobility, and as data are collected regularly regarding changing employment opportunities, housing developments, and government actions in regard to residential location and mobility, we will have a basis for better predictive models of migratory behavior.

In the absence of such systematic information, we can only speculate about future mobility patterns for specific areas. It is safe to say, nevertheless, that migration will become an even more important component of population change in the future than in the past, owing to an increasing balance of births and deaths and further development and facility of modes of travel and relocation.

Notes

1. W. S. Woytinsky and E. S. Woytinsky, *World Population and Production*, Twentieth Century Fund, New York, 1953, pp. 67–83.
2. See "International Migration," chap. 7 in United Nations, *The Determinants and Consequences of Population Trends*, vol. I, New York, 1973, pp. 225–261.
3. Arnold Schrier, *Ireland and the American Emigration 1850–1900*, University of Minnesota Press, Minneapolis, 1958, p. 3.

4. Julius Issac, *Economics of Migration*, Oxford University Press, New York, 1947, p. 143.

5. Conrad Taeuber and Irene B. Taeuber, *The Changing Population of the United States*, Wiley, New York, 1958, pp. 48–52.

6. Judith Fortney, "Immigration into the United States with Special Reference to Professional and Technical Workers," in *Demographic and Social Aspects of Population Growth*, ed. Charles F. Westoff and Robert Parke, Jr., Vol. I of research reports of U. S. Commission on Population Growth and the American Future, U. S. Government Printing Office, Washington, 1972, pp. 211–212.

7. Judah Matras, *Social Change in Israel*, Aldine, Chicago, 1965, pp. 22–29.

8. Moshe Sicron, *Immigration to Israel, 1948–1953*, State of Israel, Statistical Supplement, Vol. II, Tables A2–A3, Jerusalem, 1957.

9. Matras, pp. 32–38.

10. Calvin Goldscheider, *Population, Modernization, and Social Structure*, Little, Brown, Boston, 1971, pp. 215–217.

11. Donald J. Bogue, *Principles of Demography*, Wiley, New York, 1969, p. 773.

12. Population redistribution is also a consequence of the balance of fertility and mortality. See Chapter 6 for a fuller discussion of this point.

13. In fact, the age curve for all three processes may vary depending on the geographic area and characteristics of those involved. One needs, however, to distinguish between the age distribution of a particular set of movers and the propensity to move at a given age. It is the latter that we are concerned with here.

14. Henry S. Shryock, Jr., *Population Mobility Within the United States*, Community and Family Study Center, University of Chicago, 1964, pp. 351–352.

15. Larry H. Long, "New Estimates of Migration Expectancy in the United States," *Journal of the American Statistical Association*, 68 (March 1973), 37.

16. Long, "New Estimates," pp. 40–43.

17. Larry H. Long, "On Measuring Geographic Mobility," *Journal of the American Statistical Association,* 65 (September 1970), 1195–1203.
18. E. G. Ravenstein, "The Laws of Migration," *Journal of the Royal Statistical Society,* 48 (June 1885), 167–235, and 52 (June 1889), 241–305.
19. Leading exponents of this approach were John Q. Stewart, "A Measure of the Influence of Population at a Distance," *Sociometry,* 5 (February 1942), 63–71; and G. K. Zipf, "The P_1P_2/D Hypothesis: On the Intercity Movement of Persons," *American Sociological Review,* 11 (December 1946), 677–685.
20. Samuel A. Stouffer, "Intervening Opportunities: A Theory Relating Mobility and Distance," *American Sociological Review,* 5 (December 1940), 845–867. This was later revised as "Intervening Opportunities and Competing Migrants," *Journal of Regional Science,* 2 (Spring 1960), 1–26.
21. Everett S. Lee, "A Theory of Migration," *Demography,* 3, No. 1 (1966), 47–57.
22. William Petersen, "A General Typology of Migration," *American Sociological Review,* 23 (June 1958), 256–266.
23. Brinley Thomas, "International Migration," chap. 22 in *The Study of Population,* ed. Philip M. Hauser and Otis Dudley Duncan, University of Chicago Press, Chicago, 1959, p. 531.
24. Thomas, pp. 526–527.
25. United Nations, *The Determinants and Consequences of Population Trends,* New York, 1953, p. 123.
26. Henry S. Shryock, Jr., and Hope Tisdale Eldridge, "Internal Migration in Peace and War," *American Sociological Review,* 12 (February 1947), 27.
27. Donald J. Bogue, "Internal Migration," chap. 21 in Hauser and Duncan, pp. 499–501.
28. Kingsley Davis, *The Population of India and Pakistan,* Princeton University Press, Princeton, 1951, pp. 111–112.
29. Shryock, p. 405.

30. Gerald R. Leslie and Arthur H. Richardson, "Life-Cycle, Career Pattern, and the Decision to Move," *American Sociological Review*, 26 (December 1961), 894–902.
31. Felix M. Berardo, "Kinship Interaction and Communications Among Space-Age Migrants," *Journal of Marriage and the Family*, 29 (August 1967), 541–554.
32. Larry H. Long, "Migration Differentials by Education and Occupation: Trends and Variations," *Demography*, 10 (May 1973), 247.
33. Long, "Migration Differentials," p. 248.
34. Jack Ladinsky, "Occupational Determinants of Geographic Mobility Among Professional Workers," *American Sociological Review*, 32 (April 1967), 253–264.
35. Donald J. Bogue, *Principles of Demography*, Wiley, New York, 1969, p. 763.
36. Ronald J. McAllister, Edward J. Kaiser, and Edgar W. Butler, "Residential Mobility of Blacks and Whites: A National Longitudinal Survey," *American Journal of Sociology*, 77 (November 1971), 452–453.
37. John S. Macdonald and Beatrice D. Macdonald, "Chain Migration: Ethnic Neighborhood Formation and Social Networks," *Milbank Memorial Fund Quarterly*, 42 (January 1964), 82–97.
38. Macdonald and Macdonald, pp. 84–90.
39. Everett S. Lee, "Migration and Mental Disease: New York State, 1949–1951," in *Selected Studies of Migration Since World War II*, Milbank Memorial Fund, New York, 1958, pp. 141–150.
40. Charles B. Keely, "Effects of the Immigration Act of 1965 on Selected Population Characteristics of Immigrants to the United States," *Demography*, 8 (May 1971), 157–169.
41. Sara Mills Mazie and Steve Rawlings, "Public Attitude Towards Population Distribution Issues," in *Population Distribution and Policy*, Vol. V of research reports of the U. S. Commission on Population Growth and the American Future, U. S. Government Printing Office, Washington, 1972, p. 612.
42. William F. Kenkel, "The Family Moving Decision Process," in

Family Mobility in Our Dynamic Society, Iowa State University Center for Agricultural and Economic Development, Iowa State University Press, Ames, 1965, p. 180.

43. Kenkel, pp. 191–192.
44. John Lansing and Eva Mueller, *The Geographic Mobility of Labor,* Survey Research Center, University of Michigan, Ann Arbor, 1967. See also the discussion of these and related data in Peter A. Morrison, "Population Movements and the Shape of Urban Growth: Implications for Public Policy," in Commission on Population Growth and the American Future, *op. cit.,* pp. 304–306.

Suggested Additional Readings

Shryock, Henry S., Jr. *Population Mobility Within the United States.* Community and Family Study Center, University of Chicago, 1964. A comprehensive review of trends and differentials in residential mobility in the United States through the middle of the twentieth century.

Taeuber, Karl E., Leonard Chiazze, Jr., and William Haenzel. *Migration in the United States: An Analysis of Residence Histories.* Public Health Monograph No. 77, U. S. Government Printing Office, Washington, 1968. An analysis of migration patterns based on data collected from the May 1958 Current Population Survey, which focuses on duration of residence as a factor in the mobility process.

Iowa State University Center for Agricultural and Economic Development. *Family Mobility in Our Dynamic Society.* Iowa State University Press, Ames, 1965. Deals primarily with the adjustment of families to migration, with particular emphasis on rural society.

U. S. Commission on Population Growth and the American Future. *Population Distribution and Policy.* Vol. V of Commission research reports, U. S. Government Printing Office, Washington, 1972. Includes several reports on the interrelationships of migration and social issues, and stresses the policy implications.

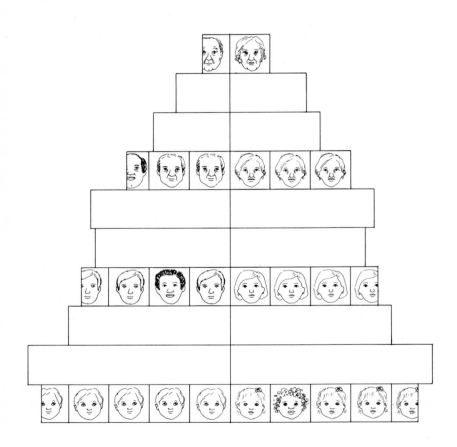

6

Population Composition and Distribution

In the preceding five chapters we have reviewed the major trends and components of population change. We turn now to a discussion of the structural components of population that can serve as both causes and consequences of population change. These are the composition and distribution of the population.

Population Composition

The *composition* of a population refers to the basic demographic characteristics by which the population may be divided or described. While there are many such characteristics we might consider, our discussion will be limited to those found to be most fundamental to population change — age, sex, and race or ethnic status.

We have already noted in discussing fertility, mortality, and residential mobility that age, sex, and racial or ethnic status are important explanatory variables related to these major components of population change. Each of the components varies among older and younger populations, among men and women, and among whites and nonwhites. In this chapter we will discuss in more depth how the age composition of a population, for example, can affect its birth and death rates. Fertility, mortality, and residential mobility can, in turn, change the composition of populations within small areas or within a whole country. Selective residential mobility by age, sex, and race can change the population composition of a nation. These and other ways in which population composition can be a consequence of population change or an influence on it will be examined.

While we discuss population composition as both a cause and a consequence of population change, the way in which population composition and change are related is really more of a circular process. High birth rates, for example, may create a younger population, which in time may again contribute to high birth rates or low mortality rates. The intertwining of these factors makes population composition an important structural component to consider in studying the process of population change in any society.

Age-Sex Composition

The age and sex compositions of a population are two factors that seem to be important as both causes and consequences of population change. We will discuss them together since various combinations of age and sex have special effects we might not notice were we to study them separately.

AGE-SEX DISTRIBUTION AS A CONSEQUENCE OF POPULATION CHANGE

One of the most useful devices for showing the past and present age-sex composition of the population is the age-sex pyramid. This device allows us to look at the percentage of the population which is in each age-sex category. Figure 6.1 shows these pyramids for the United States for 1900, 1940, 1960, and 1971. In the 1900 pyramid, for example, the bottom bar shows that males less than five years of age constituted 6.1 percent of the total population during that year, while females constituted 6.0 percent. If we compare the bars vertically, we are looking at the relative proportions of each age group in the population, while horizontal comparison allows us to see whether there were proportionally more males or females at each age.

Figure 6.1 Age-sex pyramids for the United States: 1900, 1940, 1960, and 1971

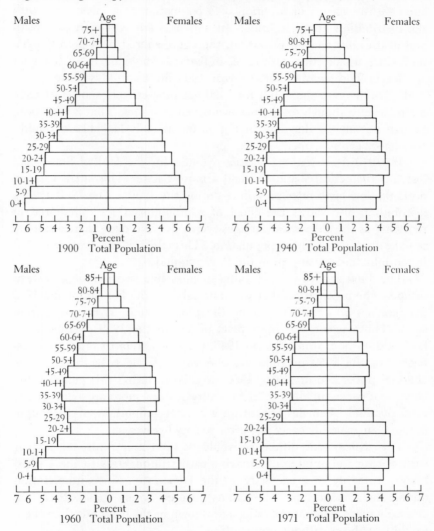

Source: Data are from U. S. Bureau of the Census, *U. S. Census of Population: 1960,* Final Report PC(1)-1B; *General Population Characteristics: U. S. Summary,* Washington, 1961, Table 47, p. 153. Figures for 1971 are from "Estimates of the Population of the United States by Age and Sex: July 1, 1971," *Current Population Reports,* Series P-25, No. 466, September 22, 1971.

Theoretically, age-sex pyramids are handy devices that allow us to compare the age-sex distribution of a population at a given time with the distribution at other times. In a population with constant birth and death rates and no migration, the figure should be a perfect pyramid, since usually there are fewer individuals surviving to each higher age level. The pyramid for the year 1900 illustrates this pattern very well. The bars on the graph for 1900 get progressively shorter at each higher level, although sometimes by uneven amounts. That is why, even though not all the drawings in Figure 6.1 actually look like pyramids, they have been so named.

By 1940, however, the age-sex pyramid for the United States had lost this theoretical shape and had a narrow base. This small base reflects the low birth rates prevailing during the 1930s. The 1940 age-sex distribution also shows the effect of a pronounced sex differential in mortality at the older ages. At age seventy-five and over, there are more females than males in the population. This effect of the sex differential in mortality did not appear in the 1900 pyramid.

The 1960 age-sex pyramid almost looks like two pyramids instead of one. The indentation that was noticeable at the bottom of the 1940 pyramid has advanced further up the 1960 pyramid as the population aged. Those twenty to thirty years of age in the 1960 pyramid were the children born from 1930 to 1940, years of low birth rates. Also reflected in the 1960 pyramid are the years of the baby boom. The children under age fifteen in 1960 were born during this period. The effect of the sex differential in mortality is even more apparent in the 1960 pyramid. Females constitute a greater proportion of the population than males at every age after twenty-five years.

This male-female difference would be even more pronounced if it were not for the number of surviving earlier immigrants to the United States, primarily over age sixty at the later date. Since immigration during the first part of this century favored young males, there are currently more males at the older ages shown in the pyramids than there would have been without immigration.

Finally, the 1971 pyramid shows each of the things reflected in the 1960 pyramid, advanced eleven years, but a change in the shape of the

Figure 6.2 Age-sex pyramid for Sweden, 1960

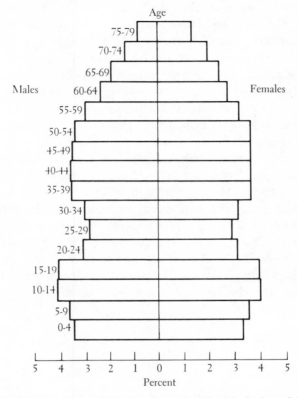

Source: Henry S. Shryock, Jacob S. Siegel, et al., *The Methods and Materials of Demography*, Vol. I, U. S. Government Printing Office, Washington, 1971, p. 240.

diagram has again taken place. Like the 1940 pyramid, the 1971 pyramid has an indented base because birth rates during the ten years before were lower than those during the twenty years which preceded that period. If birth rates continue to decline, the 1980 age-sex pyramid will begin to look inverted. This emerging age-sex structure is illustrated in the 1960 pyramid for Sweden, which has passed through that phase of demographic development.

Comparing the pyramids through this seventy-one-year period, another interesting phenomenon can be noted. The changing age composition results in a population which, as a whole, gets older during some periods and younger during others. A population is getting older when its average age rises and the proportion of people at older ages increases. A population is getting younger when its average age declines and the proportion of people at younger ages increases.

Examination of the sequence of age pyramids for the United States reveals continuing increases in the proportion of the population sixty-five years old and over. Also, as noted in Table 6.1, from 1900 to 1950 the median age of the population rose. By both of these criteria, the United States population was getting older during the first half of the twentieth century. Between 1950 and 1971, however, an apparent inconsistency in these criteria of aging can be noted. The percentage of the population at older ages continued to increase, while the median age declined. This anomaly was due to the fact that the renewed decline in the birth rate in the 1960s had reduced the relative numbers at the younger ages. Thus, the population has been getting both younger and older during the past couple of decades.

Table 6.1   Median age of the population, by sex:
United States, 1900–1970

| Year | | Median age in years | |
	Total	Males	Females
1970	28.1	26.8	29.3
1960	29.5	28.7	30.3
1950	30.2	29.9	30.5
1940	29.0	29.0	29.0
1930	26.4	26.7	26.2
1920	25.3	25.8	24.7
1910	24.1	24.6	23.5
1900	22.9	23.3	22.4

Source: U. S. Bureau of the Census, *Census of Population: 1970, General Population Characteristics*, Final Report PC(1)-B1, United States Summary, Table 53.

Similar trends in aging can be noted in many countries of the world. In the USSR, for example, the median age of the population increased from 24.4 in 1950 to 29.9 in 1970.[1] In the countries of Eastern Europe, where birth rates have declined drastically, a rise in the median age of the population has been noted and will most probably continue.[2] In less-developed countries, continued high birth rates coupled with declining death rates have produced very young populations (Table 6.2).

Table 6.2 Summary measures of age composition for selected developed and developing countries: around 1960

Country and year	Median age	Percent of total population		Ratio of aged persons to children (per 100)
		Under 15 years	65 years and over	
Developed countries				
France (1961)	33.3	25.4	12.1	47.8
Italy (1961)	31.6	24.6	9.5	38.8
Japan (1960)	25.6	30.0	5.7	19.1
Sweden (1960)	36.2	22.0	12.0	54.4
USSR (1959)	26.6	30.4	6.2	20.5
United States (1960)	29.5	31.1	9.2	29.7
Yugoslavia (1961)	26.4	31.5	6.1	19.3
Developing countries				
Chile (1960)	23.3	39.6	4.3	10.8
Ghana (1960)	18.4	44.6	3.2	7.1
Honduras (1961)	16.1	47.8	2.4	5.1
India (1961)	20.5	41.0	3.1	7.5
Iran (1966)	17.3	46.1	3.9	8.4
Syria (1960)	17.2	46.3	4.7	10.1
Taiwan (1956)	17.9	44.2	2.5	5.6
United Arab Republic (1960)	19.4	42.7	3.5	8.1
Venezuela (1961)	17.8	44.8	2.8	6.2

Source: Henry S. Shryock, Jacob S. Siegel, et al., *The Methods and Materials of Demography*, U. S. Government Printing Office, Washington, 1971, p. 234.

The greater proportion of older people and the higher average age in developed than in developing countries are principally due to the long-term decline in fertility. Lower birth rates mean relatively smaller numbers of people at the younger ages, with the reciprocal effect of relatively larger numbers at the older ages. One would also expect mortality reductions to contribute to the aging of a population. In fact, lengthening of life does add more people to the older segment of the population who would not otherwise have survived to be there, but mortality reductions are usually even greater during infancy and childhood than at older ages. Consequently, it is typical of societies proceeding through the demographic transition that mortality control will lead to even younger populations. In any event, changes in fertility over time are more important than changes in mortality over time in shaping the age structure. Selective age patterns of migration can also affect age composition, but historically they have had a rather small impact except in a few countries for short periods of time when immigration or emigration was substantially heavy.

Another way of looking at the age composition of a population is in terms of the *dependency ratio*. Dependency ratios are calculated by taking the ratio of the number of persons under fifteen and over sixty-four years of age to the number of persons aged fifteen to sixty-four, multiplied by 100. *Aged dependency* refers to the ratio of just those sixty-five and over to those fifteen to sixty-four, while *youth dependency* refers to the ratio of just those under fifteen to those fifteen to sixty-four. The term "dependency" is perhaps unfortunate. It presumably rests on the assumption that those under fifteen or over sixty-four years of age are dependent on those between those ages for economic or other sustenance. While some might argue that this is a reasonable rule of thumb, there are numerous cases of people between fifteen and sixty-four years old who are unable to support themselves. Likewise, many individuals over sixty-five are quite self-supporting, as are some under fifteen.

These shortcomings aside, the dependency ratio is another shorthand method of indicating something important about the age composition of the population. Table 6.3 shows these ratios for the United States from 1900 until the present. The youth dependency ratio in the United States moved steadily downward from 1900 until the decade 1940–1950, when it increased. High birth rates during this period created a rise in the youth dependency ratio that continued until 1960–1970, when it began to decrease again.

The aged dependency ratio, conversely, has been steadily rising throughout this century. This reflects the aging population discussed above. The rise in the proportion of aged persons in the population was quite small, however, between 1960 and 1971. This small increment is partly a reflection of the leveling off of mortality rates during the decade.

Sex ratios are another summarizing device for looking at the sex composition of a population. A *sex ratio* is the number of males per

Table 6.3 Dependency ratios in the United States, 1900–1970

Year	Total	Dependency ratios Youth	Aged
1970	62.2	46.2	16.0
1960	67.6	52.1	15.5
1950	53.9	41.4	12.5
1940	46.8	36.8	10.0
1930	53.4	45.1	8.3
1920	57.5	50.2	7.3
1910	57.3	50.5	6.8
1900	62.6	56.0	6.6

Note: The youth dependency ratio is defined as the ratio of population under fifteen to that fifteen to sixty-four years old. The aged dependency ratio is defined as the ratio of population sixty-five and over to that fifteen to sixty-four years old. The total dependency ratio is the sum of the youth and aged dependency ratios.

Source: U. S. Bureau of the Census, *Census of Population: 1970, General Population Characteristics*, Final Report PC(1)-B1, United States Summary, Table 53.

100 females in the population. A sex ratio greater than 100 thus indicates more males than females, while a sex ratio of less than 100 indicates fewer males than females.

In the United States, the sex ratio at birth is on the order of 105 males per 100 females. There are differences among subgroups of the population; for example, the sex ratio is about 106 for whites and 103 for blacks. Research on fetal deaths indicates that many more male than female fetuses die; therefore, the sex ratio prior to birth is much larger than that found at birth.

Table 6.4 shows the sex ratio of the United States population in 1970 by age and the overall ratio at ten-year intervals between 1900 and 1970. At the youngest ages, the number of males exceeds the number of females by four per hundred. By ages fifteen to nineteen, however, the sex ratio has dropped to ninety-eight and continues downward to about sixty-five at ages seventy-five and over. The effect of the sex differential in mortality on the sex composition of the population can be clearly seen in these figures. Table 6.4 also indicates that the sex ratio in the total population has been dropping since about 1910. As we noted in our discussion of differential mortality, the overall sex differential in death rates did not appear until about that time, but it has been increasing ever since.

A population component other than mortality has also played a role in determining the sex ratio. Prior to 1920, and before the cessation of massive immigration to the United States, the sex composition of the population was being affected by the selectivity in this migration. These migrants tended to be young, and about 60 percent of them were male.[3] The sex ratio of immigrants to the United States has become more balanced in recent years. Since 1920, with a great reduction in the numbers of migrants received each year, this component has played less of a role in changing the age-sex composition of the population.

AGE-SEX DISTRIBUTION AS A CAUSE OF POPULATION CHANGE

We have been discussing some of the ways in which change in the population components of fertility, mortality, and residential mobility

Table 6.4   Sex ratios for the United States population:
1900 to 1960, and by age for 1970

Date and age	Sex ratio
1970 total	95
0–4 years	104
5–14 years	104
15–24 years	98
25–34 years	96
35–44 years	95
45–54 years	93
55–64 years	90
65–74 years	78
75+ years	64
1960	97
1950	99
1940	101
1930	103
1920	104
1910	106
1900	105

Source: U. S. Bureau of the Census, *Census of Population: 1970, General Population Characteristics*, Final Report PC(1)-B1, United States Summary, Table 53.

can change the age and sex composition of the population. We turn now to some of the ways in which the age-sex composition of the population can have a direct impact on these components of population change.

In 1969 and 1970, the rising birth rate was a good example of how changing age-sex composition can affect fertility. As the baby-boom babies in the United States reached prime childbearing years, the birth rate rose slightly, resulting in a temporary departure from the recent trend.[4] Increased numbers of women of childbearing age in the population can cause such a rise in the birth rate. But that factor alone may be more than compensated for by other factors, as was true of the birth rate trends after 1970.

Failure to take into account the changing age structure of a population can cause very misleading interpretations of changing birth rates. In Hong Kong, for example, the crude birth rate fell from 35.5 in 1961 to 28.8 in 1965.[5] This decline was due almost entirely to changes in the age structure of the population, which left a smaller proportion of persons at reproductive ages, and not to real changes in fertility rates at each age level. Had this factor not been taken into account, demographers might have sought explanations for the decreased fertility in changing ideals, business-cycle changes, or some of the myriad other factors discussed earlier that might cause fluctuations in fertility rates.

The irregular age structure of the United States population will have an impact on future growth potential. Even if all women were to restrict themselves to two children each (approximately the level of replacement), it would take about seventy years for the nation's population size to level off. The reason for this phenomenon is that the number of females reaching reproductive age will vary over time. During some periods, the proportion of women of reproductive age will be "normal," and if each woman has two children, there will be a "normal" total number of births. In other periods, the proportion of women of reproductive age will be unusually large (e.g., when the baby-boom cohorts reach that age), and if each woman has two children, the total number of births will be relatively high. As a result, the population growth rate will fluctuate, being moderate at some times and high at others. After a number of decades (about seven), the constant number of births per woman will lead to greater stabilization of the age structure.

Another less direct, but still important, way in which age-sex composition can affect birth rates is by changing the number of men and women available to marry during a given period. Since women in the United States traditionally marry men somewhat older than themselves, a fluctuating birth rate can produce what demographers call a *marriage squeeze*. Since there were many more females born in 1946, for example, than there were males born in 1944, when those children reached marriageable age in the 1960s, there was a shortage of marriage partners for that cohort of women.[6] These women must then marry men their age or younger, or men considerably older, or remain unmarried. While these temporary imbalances in the sex ratios of potential marriage partners do not seem to produce long-term changes in marriage patterns, and hence in fertility rates, they are important on a short-term basis.

Like fluctuating birth rates, deaths of young males in wartime may also produce a marriage squeeze. An example of a country with an imbalance resulting from this effect is East Germany. In 1965, the sex ratio at ages twenty to forty-nine in this country was 85 as a result of very high losses of males during the two world wars.[7]

The age-sex composition of a population can also have a direct influence on its mortality rate. Since death rates usually increase at each older age after the first thirteen or so years of life, older populations will tend to have higher death rates than younger ones. This effect of age composition on the death rate can be seen clearly in Table 6.5. In the six states shown, the death rate varied consistently with the percentage of the population over sixty-five. Looking at just the crude death rates, without knowing about the age composition of these states, we might be led to hypothesize that Alaska has a healthier environment than does Florida, a hypothesis that does not have much intuitive appeal and is not consistent with comparisons of death rates at each age. We might also hypothesize, when looking at just the death rates, that Alaska has better medical-care facilities than Florida, and so on. While age is certainly not the only factor which explains the differences in death rates appearing in Table 6.5, it is one of the most important.

International differences in death rates can also be attributed partly to differing age compositions of populations. A few areas in 1970 had death rates as low as four per thousand population.[8] Hong Kong and Reunion (in Eastern Africa) are examples of such areas. These areas also had a very large percentage of their population under fifteen years of age.

Failure to take into account the age-sex composition of the population might also lead to errors in explaining cause-of-death patterns.

Table 6.5   Percent of population over 65 and crude death rates, for selected states, 1970

State	Percent over 65	Crude death rate
Alaska	2.3	4.8
Hawaii	5.7	5.5
Utah	7.3	6.9
Arizona	9.1	8.6
Arkansas	12.4	10.7
Florida	14.6	11.3

Source: Death rates are from *Monthly Vital Statistics Report,* "Annual Summary for the United States, 1970," (HSM)72-1121, 19, No. 13, September 1971, Table 2. Percent of population over 65 is from U. S. Bureau of the Census, *Census of Population: 1970, General Population Characteristics,* Final Report PC(1)-B1, United States Summary, Table 59.

Some causes of death are more characteristic of one age group than another. An older population might show higher rates of death due to heart disease, while younger populations might show higher rates of death due to accidents.

Since migration also shows selectivity by age and sex, the changing age-sex composition of a population might affect residential mobility rates. During the year 1969–1970, for example, 44.5 percent of those twenty-two to twenty-four years of age moved at least once.[9] This is contrasted with 8.6 percent of those sixty-five years of age and over moving during the year. Populations which are younger will therefore have greater potential for mobility.

FUTURE CHANGES IN AGE-SEX COMPOSITION

Determination of the future age-sex composition of the population is, of course, a complex matter. We may have a reliable basis for estimating the older segments of the population (which are already born), but we have a less reliable basis for estimating the younger segments (especially those not yet born).

In making projections of the population by age and sex, the United States Bureau of the Census often combines different estimates of future births, deaths, and migration to arrive at population counts for given years.

Two such estimates of the future age-sex composition of the population, made by the United States Census, assume varying rates of fertility.[10] If women have on the average 3.34 children each, by 1985 there will be an increasing proportion of children under five years old in the population (from 10.5 percent in 1965 to 12.1 percent in 1985) and a decreasing proportion of persons sixty-five or older (from 9.3 percent in 1965 to 9.1 percent in 1985). Conversely, if fertility rates decline to an average of 2.45 children per woman, a possibility that seems more likely given recent trends, then the proportion of young people under five in the population will be down to 9.5 percent and the proportion of persons sixty-five years of age and over will be up to 10.3 percent.[11]

The changes in sex ratios of the United States population are not expected to be great, at least until 1985. If birth rates become lower, the sex ratio is also likely to be lower, since decreasing birth rates mean an older population. We have already noted how much lower the sex ratio is among older persons in our population than among younger persons. The pattern of lower sex ratios at older ages may be modified further in the future, depending upon the extent to which mortality differences between the sexes change and the volume and selectivity by sex of immigrants is altered.

Racial-Ethnic Composition

The racial-ethnic composition of a population is another important variable, in some countries, as both a cause and a consequence of demographic change. Racial-ethnic composition encompasses several different variables. The *color* or *race* of persons in the United States, as measured by the Census Bureau (on which we are dependent for most of our data), is not based on biological classifications. Rather, the racial categories used in the census are a combination of color and nationality.

In 1970, for example, the Census Bureau reported that the United States population was made up of the following racial groups: White, Negro or Black, American Indian, Japanese, Chinese, Filipino, and several groups in the "all other" category such as Malayans, Polynesians, and Koreans. Obviously some of these are nationality groups. The census tabulations by race, therefore, reflect social convention as to what constitutes separate racial groups more than biological characteristics. Further, since the census figures for 1970 were gathered principally by self-enumeration, the data reflect the racial groupings that people recognize for themselves. (Published statistics from the census generally refer to "Negroes" rather than other identifying terms because historically census schedules used that term. In the 1970 Census, respondents could identify themselves as Negro or Black, whichever they preferred.)

In some tabulations by the Census Bureau, the categories "white" and "nonwhite" are used, or "Negro and other races" is substituted for "nonwhite." This distinction is not necessarily based on color of skin; it is created by grouping those who designate themselves as white with those of Spanish origin and Indo-European origin, and labeling all others nonwhite.

Ethnic origin of the population, on the other hand, has traditionally been determined by looking at data on place of birth, country of origin, language spoken, surname, and the like. More recently the Census Bureau has been reporting data on the ethnic origin of the population based on self-report.[12] The ethnic origin classifications are based, by and large, on nationality. On occasion, data are collected on religious affiliation, which is another indicator of ethnic origin.

Another census variable that is useful in analyzing racial-ethnic composition is *nativity*. Nativity indicates the place where the person was born and is generally differentiated by the categories "foreign-born" and "native." Included in the category "native" in the United States are all those persons born in the United States, Puerto Rico, and outlying areas of the United States, and persons not reporting their country of birth.

RACIAL-ETHNIC COMPOSITION AS A CONSEQUENCE
OF POPULATION CHANGE

The United States has often been called a nation of immigrants. Migration into the United States was the major force creating the nation and, hence, creating our present racial-ethnic composition.

We have already mentioned the important role that the quota system played in shaping the patterns of immigration to the United States. Table 6.6 underscores this point by showing the region of birth of the foreign-born population in this country for selected years from 1850 to 1970. At the beginning of this 120-year period, those who were born outside the United States were almost entirely from Europe, most particularly from Northern and Western Europe. By 1940, this picture had changed somewhat in that, while the majority of the foreign-born were still from Europe, a greater proportion of them came

Table 6.6 Percent distribution of the foreign-born population of the United States by region of birth: selected years, 1850–1970

	1850	1900	1920	1940[b]	1970
Total	100.0	100.0	100.0	100.0	100.0
Northwestern Europe	64.0	40.6	27.5	24.7	16.4
Central and Eastern Europe	26.1	40.0	44.1	43.4	30.2
Southern Europe	0.4	5.1	13.7	16.6	14.3
Other Europe	—[a]	—	—	0.2	0.4
Asia	—	1.2	1.7	1.3	8.9
Americas	7.5	12.7	12.4	13.2	28.1
Other	1.9	0.3	0.5	0.5	1.6

[a] Indicates that percentage rounds to zero.
[b] The figures for 1940 are for foreign-born whites only, but the exclusion of other races makes very little difference in the numbers.

Sources: U. S. Bureau of the Census, *Historical Statistics of the United States: Colonial Times to 1957*, U. S. Government Printing Office, Washington, 1960, p. 66; and U. S. Bureau of the Census, *Census of Population: 1970, Detailed Characteristics*, Final Report PC(1)-D1, United States Summary, Table 192.

from Southern, Central, and Eastern Europe. The foreign-born coming from other American nations, such as Central and South America, had increased also. Asian, African, and other nations were still contributing relatively small numbers to the population. By 1970, the proportion from Europe had dwindled and proportions from Asia and the Americas had increased appreciably.

As these data indicate, and as Table 6.7 further specifies, the United States has increasingly become a "melting pot" of ethnic groups. The principal countries of origin in early United States history (England, Germany, and Ireland) were represented by less than 30 percent of the population in 1969. Nearly half of those reporting did not identify with any of the eight specific groups indicated. There were as many Negroes as persons of English origin or German origin.

The racial composition of the United States population from 1790 through 1969 has undergone significant change (see Table 6.8). The

Table 6.7   Ethnic origin of the population of the United States, 1969

Ethnic origin	Number (000)	Percent
Total	198,214	—
Total reporting	180,579	100.0
English	19,060	10.6
German	19,961	11.1
Irish	13,282	7.4
Italian	7,239	4.0
Polish	4,021	2.2
Russian	2,152	1.2
Spanish	9,230	5.1
Negro	20,000	11.1
Other	85,633	47.4
Not reported	17,635	—

Source: U. S. Bureau of the Census, "Characteristics of the Population by Ethnic Origin: November 1969," *Current Population Reports*, Series P-20, No. 221, Table 1.

percentage of blacks in the population declined progressively from 19 percent to 10 percent between 1790 and 1920, was stable for several decades, and then went up slightly. The decrease in the percentage of blacks reflected the lower annual growth rates of blacks until 1930. Since that time, growth rates have been somewhat higher for blacks than for

Table 6.8   Population size and annual growth rates for whites and blacks, and the percentage of blacks in the total population, United States, 1790–1969

Year	Population (000)		Average annual growth rates for intercensal period (percent)		Percentage of total population black
	White	Black	White	Black	
1790	3,172	757	—	—	19
1800	4,306	1,002	3.06	2.80	19
1810	5,862	1,378	3.08	3.19	19
1820	7,867	1,772	2.94	2.51	18
1830	10,537	2,329	2.92	2.73	18
1840	14,196	2,874	2.98	2.10	17
1850	19,553	3,639	3.20	2.36	16
1860	26,923	4,442	3.20	2.00	14
1870	33,589	4,880	2.22	0.94	13
1880	43,403	6,581	2.56	2.99	13
1890	55,101	7,389	2.39	1.25	12
1900	66,809	8,834	1.92	1.79	12
1910	81,732	9,828	2.01	1.07	11
1920	94,821	10,463	1.48	0.63	10
1930	110,287	11,891	1.51	1.28	10
1940	118,215	12,866	0.70	0.79	10
1950	134,942	15,042	1.33	1.56	10
1960	159,467	18,916	1.67	2.29	11
1969	178,225	22,727	1.14	1.88	11

Source: Reynolds Farley, Growth of the Black Population, Markham, Chicago, 1970, p. 22.

whites. This is primarily due to differential fertility patterns for these two color groups. Since the period prior to World War II, the fertility of blacks has exceeded that of whites by a substantial amount. Very recently, as indicated elsewhere, the fertility differences among the racial groups have narrowed.[13]

While the death rate for blacks has traditionally been higher than the death rate for whites, this differential is narrowing and is not enough to compensate for the much higher birth rate of blacks.

In selected areas of the United States, the different migration patterns of blacks and whites are beginning to create racial compositions very different from those that had previously existed. The greatest change in racial composition has been taking place in the South. While blacks were 24 percent of Southern residents in 1940, they were only 19 percent of the Southern population in 1970. Three-fourths of all United States blacks lived in the Southern states in 1940, while only 53 percent were living there in 1970.[14] The Southern states of Mississippi, Alabama, South Carolina, North Carolina, and Georgia lost the greatest numbers of blacks between 1960 and 1970. New York, California, Illinois, Michigan, and New Jersey gained more blacks than any other states.[15]

Probably the most dramatic example of the effect that differential migration can have on the racial composition of an area is found in suburban-central city movement. Between 1960 and 1970, for example, black populations in central cities increased substantially, while the proportion of whites declined considerably as a result of out-migration. In 1970, four central cities in the United States had more than 50 percent black residents. These were Atlanta, Georgia, Newark, New Jersey, Gary, Indiana, and Washington, D.C., which was already more than 50 percent black in 1960.[16] Some blacks moved into the suburbs during the decade from 1960 to 1970, but this movement was very small compared with the flow of whites to the suburbs. This trend, if it continues, will produce greater residential segregation than has ever existed before, with whites living almost exclusively in the suburbs and blacks living almost exclusively in the central cities.

RACIAL-ETHNIC COMPOSITION AS A CAUSE OF POPULATION CHANGE

As the population components of fertility, mortality, and residential mobility operate to change the racial-ethnic composition of nations and areas, so the racial-ethnic composition in those areas and nations can influence fertility, mortality, and residential mobility.

Areas such as the Southern United States that have high percentages of blacks have had generally higher birth rates. As blacks continue to move into central cities, if their birth rates remain higher than those of whites, it is possible that central cities, which have long been known for low birth rates, will become areas of high birth rates. On the other hand, it must be recognized that changes in social conditions can affect the fertility desires and behavior of groups with previously high fertility and lead to a decline in fertility.

As Figure 6.3 shows, racial and ethnic groups have had differing birth rates, which not only have influenced the numbers of each ethnic group in the population over time, but may have had a great impact on areas with large concentrations of one group or another. The most fertile of the ethnic groups has been those of Mexican descent, followed by those of Puerto Rican, Irish, German, English, Italian, Polish, and Russian descent. It should be remembered that these data refer to self-reports of ethnic origin and may not necessarily refer to the place of birth of the respondent or his or her parents. Nevertheless, such differences in fertility among racial and ethnic groups are evident and have influenced the total population structure.

FUTURE CHANGES IN RACIAL-ETHNIC COMPOSITION

For at least the past two decades, the percentage of the population that is black has been steadily increasing. This increase has been primarily due to the relatively high birth rates of blacks, as was pointed out above. The main problem in projecting the future racial-ethnic composition of the population is in estimating whether this birth rate differential will persist or decline. Indeed, there is some evidence to support narrowing of the differential. For example, it has been shown that the most rapid declines in fertility between 1957 and 1970 in the

Figure 6.3   Fertility variations by ethnic origin: November 1969

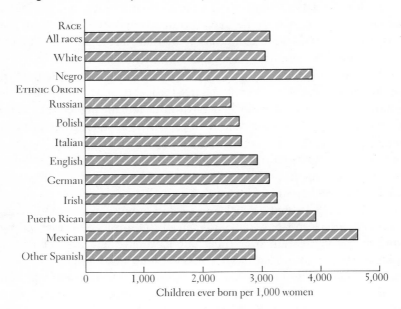

Children ever born per 1,000 women

Source: U. S. Bureau of the Census, "Fertility Variations by Ethnic Origin: November 1969," *Current Population Reports*, Series P-20, No. 226, November 1971.

United States took place among blacks, American Indians, and Mexican-Americans.[17]

Moreover, a recent report by the Census Bureau shows that, among young wives (eighteen to twenty-four years old), there was only a small difference between whites and blacks in lifetime births expected. Among whites, 2,154 lifetime births were expected by each thousand wives, whereas the corresponding figure for blacks was 2,215.[18]

Still, an outstanding characteristic of the present black population of the United States is its young age. High birth rates produce younger populations, which in turn put more women of childbearing age into the population at successive dates. Thus, even if the average number of births of blacks were to decline, in proportion to whites they would still have more women bearing children for some time to come, and the overall birth rate levels would differ. It is most likely, therefore, that the percentage of the population which is black will continue to increase for a number of years. The United States Census Bureau estimates that the black population could be as high as 14.2 percent of the total population by 1985.[19] Estimates made for the United States Population Commission range from 10 to 15 percent, with 13 percent seeming most likely.[20]

Changes in ethnic composition of the population are likewise difficult to predict. As a result of the enactment in 1968 of a new immigration policy in the United States, it is likely that over many years the ethnic origin of the population will not be so heavily Northern and Western Europe. As in the past, wars, natural disasters, and other events which stimulate refugee movements may be expected to contribute temporary influxes of persons from a variety of nations.

Racial and ethnic composition will also be affected by the rate of intermarriage among groups. Although marriage among people in different racial categories has been rare in the United States, the rate has been increasing. Among whites, marriage across nationality and religious lines is much more frequent and also increasing. Because of these trends, racial and ethnic categories of the population will become even less "pure" in the future than at present.

Population Distribution

The distribution of a population refers to how that population is spread over a given land area. Our discussion of population distribution includes the relative numbers of people in different geographical units, the extent to which people tend to be heavily concentrated in some areas, and the patterns by which population distribution changes over time.

It will be clear from the text materials that follow that population distribution at a point in time is the result of initial settlement patterns in an area, subject to subsequent modifications by births, deaths, and residential mobility. The basic processes of population change thus serve to determine population distribution. In turn, the basic population processes are affected by the distribution of population because, as indicated in earlier chapters, distinctive cultural and social structural factors associated with particular areas have an influence on fertility, mortality, and residential mobility.

World Population Distribution

The distinction that can be made between international and intranational population distribution, like that between international and intranational (or internal) migration, is based partly on the extent of available data and partly on the different distributional patterns which can be observed in the world and within nations. The lack of adequate population information for some parts of the world makes world population distribution difficult to describe except in the broadest terms. In particular countries, especially those with advanced demographic reporting systems, the information on population distribution is generally more complete and more complex, thereby permitting more detailed analyses. Also, the increasing specificity of areas (that is, the ability to identify smaller units and their linkage to other units) enables us to describe distributional patterns and processes and understand their causes and consequences more readily. It is only through the intensive study of individual nations that this can be accomplished.

In our examination of world population distribution, we will follow the framework elaborated earlier, paying attention to relative numbers of people in different areas, the extent of population concentration, and the components of population redistribution.

THE SPREAD OF POPULATION AMONG NATIONS

The topic of world population distribution is not new to you if you have read our overview of population trends in Chapter 1. A glance back at that section and at Appendix B will show the uneven distribution of people among nations and broader regions of the world. Table 1.1 acquainted us with the fact that populations of some areas of the earth have been growing in size at a more rapid rate than those of other areas, and that, as a consequence, there have been shifts in population distribution among nations and regions over time.

The percentage distribution of world population in Table 6.9 highlights those changes. Although Asia contained more than half of the world's population in 1950, the proportion of population in that continent had actually been declining over the previous two centuries. This decline was most noticeable in the most populated areas of the continent, the People's Republic of China and the combined areas of India and Pakistan. By 1973, however, rapid population increase in the smaller countries of Asia helped to raise Asia's share of total world population. A decrease in the relative share of world population can also be observed in Africa between 1750 and 1900. During the twentieth century, Africa increased its proportion, with the most rapid increases taking place in central and southern Africa. Europe's share of world population grew most perceptibly during the nineteenth century, but by 1950 it was about the same as it had been during the earlier periods, and by 1973 its proportion was considerably smaller. Sharp increases over time in the percentage of world population are noted for the USSR and the Americas, and a small rise in its proportion was recorded for Oceania. The USSR reduced its share during the twentieth century, and North America declined relatively after 1950. The greatest relative increases were in Middle and South America.

Thus, during two hundred years of the modern era, a modification of the world's population distribution took place that shifted relative numbers of people away from Asia and Africa toward the developing areas of the world, most notably the USSR and the Americas. After 1950, this process began to change as population growth started to stabilize in North America and the USSR and rapid population growth took place in parts of Asia, Africa, and Middle and South America.

CONCENTRATION OF POPULATION: INTERNATIONAL COMPARISONS

When we speak of the relative numbers of people in different countries, it is obvious that we are not assuming that the population is spread out over the same distances in each country. The size and shape

Table 6.9   Percentage distribution of the world's population
among major areas, 1750–1973

Area	1750	1800	1850	1900	1950	1973
World total	100.0	100.0	100.0	100.0	100.0	100.0
Asia (excluding USSR)	63.0	64.4	63.5	56.1	54.9	56.9
China (Mainland)	25.2	33.0	34.1	26.4	22.3	20.8
India and Pakistan	24.0	19.9	18.5	17.3	17.3	17.3
Japan	3.8	3.1	2.5	2.7	3.3	2.8
Indonesia	1.5	1.3	1.8	2.5	3.1	3.4
Remainder of Asia (excluding USSR)	8.5	7.1	6.9	7.2	9.0	12.6
Africa	13.4	10.9	8.8	8.1	8.8	9.8
North Africa	1.3	1.1	1.2	1.6	2.1	2.4
Remainder of Africa	12.1	9.8	7.6	6.4	6.7	7.4
Europe (excluding USSR)	15.8	15.5	16.5	17.9	15.6	12.3
USSR	5.3	5.7	6.0	8.1	7.2	6.5
America	2.3	3.2	5.1	9.5	13.0	14.0
North America	0.3	0.7	2.1	5.0	6.6	6.1
United States	0.2	0.5	1.8	4.6	6.0	5.5
Remainder of North America	0.1	0.2	0.3	0.4	0.6	0.6
Middle and South America	2.0	2.5	3.0	4.4	6.4	8.0
Oceania	0.3	0.2	0.2	0.4	0.5	0.5

Source: Table 1.2; and U. S. Bureau of the Census, World Population: 1973; Recent Demographic Estimates for the Countries and Regions of the World, U. S. Government Printing Office, Washington, May 1974.

of land area varies among nations, and the relationship of population to land area provides us with another dimension of world population distribution. Among a number of measures of population concentration, we shall examine two which are widely utilized in demographic analysis: population density and urbanization.

The first measure, *population density*, refers to population per square unit of land area. A glance at Table 6.10 shows that in 1964 countries with large population sizes did not necessarily have the largest population densities. Conversely, some countries with small populations were densely settled. For example, India's nearly half billion people had a density of only 155 per kilometer of total land area, and the nearly two hundred million in the United States represented a population density of merely 21 per kilometer of total land area. On the other hand, Hong Kong had a comparable population density of 3,578, and for Malta it stood at 1,024. When agricultural land, rather than total land, is used as the base for these calculations, densities become larger. In some countries, such as the United Arab Republic, Japan, and Iran, the relatively small ratio of agricultural to total land area raises the population per square kilometer considerably when agricultural, instead of total, land area is the base for the density statistic.

Comparisons of population densities cannot be properly interpreted without considering the social and cultural settings in which the ratios exist. That is, such densities must be viewed not only in terms of the degree of intensity of physical contact, but also with regard to social organization, values, and lifestyles; the individual's status and class position within the society; and personal and social expectations regarding a desirable way to live. For these reasons, moderate population densities (such as those in the United States) may not indicate any greater carrying capacity than high population densities (such as those in the Netherlands).[21]

The second measure of population concentration, *urbanization*, refers to the proportion of a population resident in urban areas or in areas with a given concentration or higher. In a more dynamic sense, urbanization can be viewed as a process involving the multiplication of points of concentration and the increases in the size of individual concentrations.[22]

The growing urbanization of the world's population can be seen from the figures in Table 6.11. As the population grew from 1.8 billion to 3 billion between 1920 and 1960, the fraction found in localities with 20,000 or more inhabitants increased from 14 percent to 25

Table 6.10 Population density per square kilometer of total area
and of agricultural area, for selected countries, 1964

Country	Estimated population (thousands)	Area (square kilometers)		Population per square kilometer	
		Total land	Agricultural land[a]	Total land	Agricultural land
Africa					
Algeria	10,975	2,381,741	454,710	5	24
Gabon	459	267,667	1,270	2	361
Libya	1,559	1,759,540	112,850	1	14
Morocco	12,959	445,050	155,100	29	84
Nigeria	56,400	923,768	217,950	61	259
South Africa	17,474	1,221,037	1,024,480	14	17
United Arab Republic	28,900	1,000,000	25,060	29	1,153
North America					
Barbados	242	430	300	563	807
Canada	19,271	9,976,177	628,480	2	31
Mexico	39,643	1,972,546	1,029,090	20	39
United States	192,120	9,363,353	4,413,660	21	44
South America					
Argentina	22,022	2,776,656	1,378,290	8	16
Brazil	78,809	8,511,965	1,267,280	9	62
Colombia	17,482	1,138,338	196,530	15	89
Peru	11,298	1,285,215	200,990	9	56
Asia					
Ceylon	10,965	65,610	18,860	167	581
China, Taiwan	12,070	35,961	8,930	336	1,352
Hong Kong	3,692	1,032	130	3,578	28,400
India	471,624	3,046,232	1,768,850	155	267
Indonesia	102,200	1,491,564	176,810	69	578
Iran	22,860	1,648,000	180,000	14	127
Japan	96,906	369,661	69,900	262	1,386
Korea, South	27,633	98,431	21,530	281	1,283
Pakistan	100,762	946,716	257,610	106	391
Philippines	31,270	300,000	112,100	104	279
Singapore	1,820	581	130	3,133	14,000
Thailand	29,700	514,000	106,040	58	280

Country	Estimated population (thousands)	Area (square kilometers)		Population per square kilometer	
		Total land	Agricultural land[a]	Total land	Agricultural land
Turkey	30,677	780,576	543,780	39	56
Vietnam, North	18,400	158,750	20,180	116	912
Europe					
Czechoslavakia	14,058	127,869	68,190	110	206
France	48,411	547,026	341,090	88	142
Germany, East	16,028	107,896	64,350	149	249
East Berlin	1,068	403	120	2,651	8,900
Germany, West	56,097	247,973	141,210	226	397
West Berlin	2,193	481	135	4,559	16,244
Hungary	10,120	93,030	69,790	109	145
Italy	51,090	301,255	204,620	170	250
Malta	324	316	160	1,024	2,025
Netherlands	12,127	33,612	22,680	361	535
Poland	31,161	312,520	201,300	100	155
Romania	18,927	237,500	147,420	80	128
Spain	31,339	504,748	351,880	62	89
United Kingdom	54,213	244,030	196,640	222	276
Yugoslavia	19,279	255,804	147,730	75	131
Oceania					
Australia	11,136	7,686,810	4,793,460	1	2
USSR	227,687	22,402,200	5,999,750	10	38

[a] Agricultural land includes "Arable land and land under permanent crops" and "Permanent meadows and pastures." Unused but potentially productive land is excluded. Details of definition differ among countries.

Source: Henry S. Shryock, Jacob S. Siegel, et al., *The Methods and Materials of Demography*, U. S. Government Printing Office, Washington, 1971, p. 134.

percent. Both urban and rural areas shared in the population growth
of the period, but the gains were more rapid for urban areas. Yet, only
a minority of the world's people can be said to be urbanized even
today. It has been calculated that, in 1970, about 61 percent of the
people on earth lived in rural areas, 39 percent were urban (given each
country's definition of "urban"), and 24 percent lived in cities of 100,000
or more.[23] On an absolute numerical basis, the extent of urbanization
appears more vividly. Between 1920 and 1960, the world's urban population tripled each decade, on the average, while the rural population
grew at a more nominal rate.

The extent of urbanization differed by regions of the world. In
1960, roughly half of the population in North America and Oceania

Table 6.11   Percentage distribution of world population
by size of locality, 1920–1960

Size of locality (number of inhabitants)	1920	1930	1940	1950	1960
Total population	100.0	100.0	100.0	100.0	100.0
Number (in millions)	(1,860.2)	(2,069.3)	(2,296.9)	(2,516.8)	(2,994.4)
Under 20,000	86.4	84.1	81.4	78.9	74.8
20,000 and over	13.6	15.9	18.6	21.1	25.2
100,000 and over	8.6	10.5	12.5	14.3	17.5
500,000 and over	5.1	6.5	7.7	8.9	11.7
2,500,000 and over	1.6	2.3	2.9	3.3	4.7
12,500,000 and over	—	—	—	—	0.9
20,000–99,999	5.0	5.4	6.1	6.8	7.6
100,000–499,999	3.5	4.0	4.9	5.4	5.8
500,000–2,499,999	3.5	4.1	4.8	5.6	7.1
2,500,000–12,499,999	1.6	2.4	2.9	3.3	3.7
12,500,000 and over	—	—	—	—	0.9

Source: United Nations, *Urbanization: Development Policies and Planning*, New
York, 1968, p. 10.

lived in localities with 20,000 or more inhabitants, whereas the proportions were two-fifths in Europe, one-third in the Soviet Union and Latin America, one-fifth in East Asia, and one-seventh in South Asia and Africa.[24] Distinguishing countries by their stage of development helps to sharpen the comparison. Comparing 43 developed and 171 developing countries in 1970, about 69 percent of the population in the former and 26 percent in the latter were in urban areas. Also, 44 percent of the people in the developed nations, and only 16 percent in the developing ones, resided in cities of 100,000 or more.[25]

COMPONENTS OF WORLD POPULATION REDISTRIBUTION

Each of the basic processes of population change (mortality, fertility, and residential mobility) can account for variations in population distribution among nations over time. Although migration between countries is the most obvious redistribution process, population distribution can also be modified by differences in rates of births and deaths. In areas like North America and Oceania, high net immigration levels, combined with substantial natural increase, raised their share of the world's population significantly up until 1950. (See Table 6.9) In areas like China, India, and Pakistan, moderately high death rates and emigration were more than compensated for by high birth rates and immigration, but the net effects were not as great as in other areas, thus reducing their share of the world's population. Indonesia's relatively high birth levels and sharply declining death levels accounted for its increased percentage of the world's population. It is, therefore, apparent that any combination of the basic population components might produce a population change rate that differs from the world average and thereby leads to population redistribution.

One can also identify the relative contributions of migration and natural increase or decrease to changing urbanization patterns. As indicated by Goldstein:

> In 1960, the world's rural population had considerably higher birth and death rates than did the urban population, but be-

cause of a greater relative differential in death rates, the natural increase of the urban and rural population was comparatively close, 16 and 21 per thousand respectively. A major factor, therefore, accounting for the higher urban growth rate (33 per thousand) compared to the rural (12 per thousand) lay in the differential patterns of population transfer. In 1960, the net shift resulting from population transfers amounted to 17 per thousand for the urban population in contrast to an actual loss of 8 per thousand for the rural parts of the world. In effect, therefore, population transfers for the urban population doubled the growth resulting from natural increase, whereas the losses sustained from population transfers in rural areas had the effect of reducing the natural increase by as much as 40 percent.[26]

In the less developed regions of the world, population transfers (through both migration and reclassification of areas from rural to urban) constituted the major force generating the high rate of urban growth, although natural increase was substantial. In more developed regions, however, natural increase played a slightly more important role in producing continued urbanization.[27]

FUTURE CHANGES IN WORLD POPULATION DISTRIBUTION

There is every reason to expect that the trend of urbanization experienced in the recent past will continue during the next few decades. Some slackening of natural increase combined with further transfers of population from rural areas may accelerate the trend. Projections put 51 percent of the world population in urban areas by the year 2000. In the more-developed regions, it is expected to be about 81 percent, and in the less-developed regions, in the neighborhood of 43 percent by the turn of the century.[28]

With regard to population distribution among nations, the slow-down in international migration in recent years will shift attention to natural increase or decrease as the principal determinant of population shifts. The proportions of the world population in Asia, Africa, and

Latin America should increase, while those in the USSR, Europe, and North America should decrease. The United States' share of world population should continue to decline as a result of continued restrictions on immigration and declines in natural increase. The magnitude of distribution changes will depend, of course, on the extent of reductions in the birth rate in different areas.

Population Distribution Within Nations

The description of distribution patterns within societies requires considerably more detailed information than is necessary for the description of overall national distribution character. How extensive that information should be is a function of the kinds and numbers of geographical units that are meaningful for analysis.

Typically, official population statistics are provided for divisions of a country along political lines as well as along nonpolitical lines. The classification system for the United States is representative of those for nations with broad land area. Included among politically defined areas are states, counties, cities, towns, smaller urban places, and minor civil divisions. The importance of these units for the analysis of population distribution rests on the significance of legal residences and governmental functions. The population base of an economy, the population eligible to vote in an election of governmental representatives, people holding automobile licenses, the number of property owners, and the number of children attending schools are examples of demographic statistics which are keyed to political boundaries.

Political units may be combined in various ways for statistical purposes, even though the combined area has no political identity. *Metropolitan areas*, or other functional groupings of counties with urban character, give us a basis for describing urbanization trends that go beyond city boundaries. *Regions* of the country are groupings of states corresponding to broad sections of the nation that have historical as well as contemporary importance (e.g., the South, the West).

Often, these political units and their groupings are not adequate for indicating general distribution patterns or changes in population. *Farm-nonfarm* residential distinctions are an important part of distributional analysis. The simple urban-rural dichotomy in demographic data does not respect political boundaries. Some large urban conglomerations are more accurately defined by a land area that cuts across geographical lines. An *urbanized area* in United States Bureau of the Census parlance is that area encompassing a large city and its urban hinterland; it does not necessarily conform to county boundaries.

Finally, we are often interested in population distribution within the smallest political units, particularly where populations are very concentrated and we wish to describe or explain their distributional forms. How is population distributed over *city blocks* or *census tracts* (which are groups of blocks that correspond to neighborhoods or other subsegments of a city)? How geographically patterned are land uses and the characteristics of residents of an urban area?

THE SPREAD OF POPULATION AMONG GEOGRAPHICAL UNITS

Illustrations of population distributed across these several types of units, and changes over time, can be given for the United States. The uneven distribution and dynamics of change may not be characteristic of all societies at all periods of time, but these illustrations serve to point out that the distribution of population by area has significant implications for the study of demographic and social changes in a nation.

The graph in Figure 6.4 shows vividly the shifting proportions of population in the four major regions of the United States over time. At the time of the first census in 1790, with only the Eastern coast of the present land area then settled, almost half of the population was in the Northeast and half in the South. Development of the North Central region and its incorporation into the nation led to an increasing share of the country's people being in that area. With the settlement of the West, beginning in the mid-1800s, that region's share of the national population began to increase. By 1970, the four regions were approaching parity in their proportions of the United States population, although significant differences remained.

Figure 6.4   Percent distribution of population by region, 1790–1970

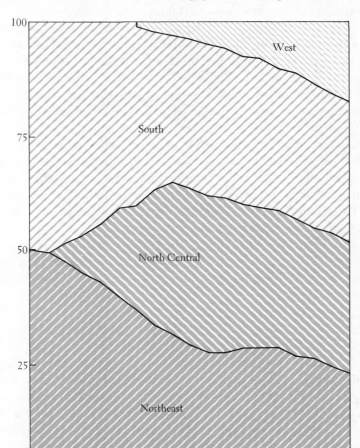

Source: U. S. Bureau of the Census, *U. S. Census of Population, 1970*, Final Report, PC(1)-A1, U. S. Government Printing Office, Washington, 1971, p. 19.

An examination of county populations in the United States will likewise show disparities in population size and changes in them over time. One would expect differences because of unequal amounts of land area among counties and variations in economic bases, but these factors can account only in part for the distribution changes from one point in time to another. Figure 6.5 reveals that substantial gains and losses took place in the United States counties between 1960 and 1970, which resulted in realignments of population distribution by county over the decade. These changes reflect the movement away from rural counties and toward urban (mainly metropolitan) counties.

The urban or rural character of counties is a major factor in determining variations in total population sizes. In Figure 6.6, it can be seen that although almost three-fourths of the United States population was classified as living in urban areas in 1970, a large number of counties contained no urban population whatever, and a vast majority had a percent urban less than the United States average. There was a tendency for most of the American people to congregate in a limited number of metropolitan areas that cover a very small portion of the nation's land area.

CONCENTRATION OF POPULATION: INTRANATIONAL COMPARISONS

As already indicated, the concentration of population can be measured in at least two ways: by comparing population density (population per square unit of area), and by comparing levels and rates of urbanization. Population densities vary considerably from one part of the United States to another. Compared with an average density of about fifty-five per square mile in the United States, densities are as low as one per square mile or less in many rural areas and as high as seventy-five thousand per square mile in New York County (Manhattan Island), and still higher in some neighborhoods.

Measures of urban change indicate what population densities do not, namely, the growing attraction of people to a small number of areas. Between 1900 and 1960 in the United States, while total population increased two and a half times, urban population increased al-

Figure 6.5 Percent of change in total population by counties, 1960–1970

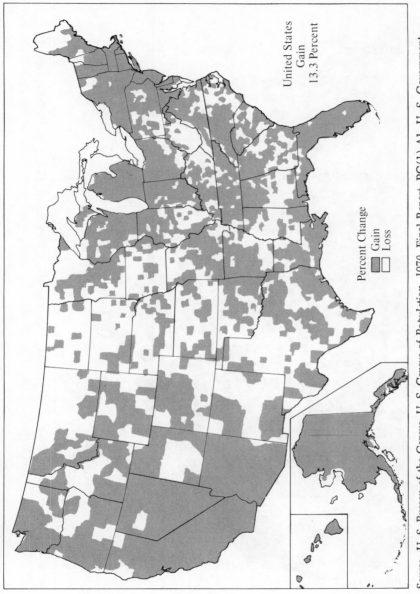

United States
Gain
13.3 Percent

Percent Change
Gain
Loss

Source: U. S. Bureau of the Census, *U. S. Census of Population, 1970*, Final Report, PC(1)-A1, U. S. Government Printing Office, Washington, 1971, p. 27.

Figure 6.6   Percent of population urban by counties, 1970

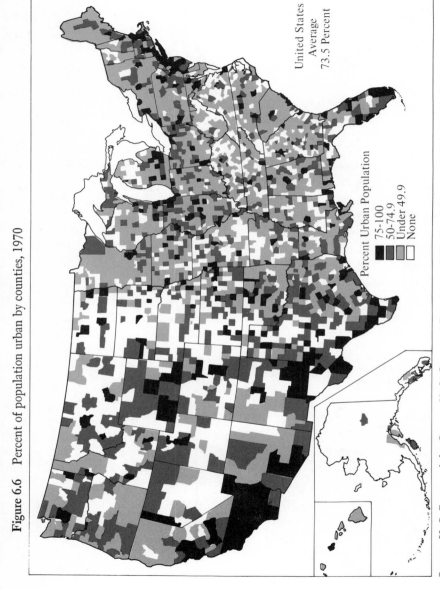

Percent Urban Population

75–100
50–74.9
Under 49.9
None

United States
Average
73.5 Percent

Source: U. S. Bureau of the Census, *U. S. Census of Population, 1970,* Final Report, PC(1)-A1, U. S. Government
Printing Office, Washington, 1971, p. 33.

most fourfold, metropolitan area population (which includes that in central cities of 50,000 or more and the surrounding areas) increased more than fourfold, and large metropolitan area population (including one million or more people) increased fivefold.[29]

We have stated that urbanization is a worldwide phenomenon. Even in predominantly rural parts of Asia, urbanization is proceeding apace. In Thailand, for example, although the overall level of urbanization is low (perhaps between 10 and 15 percent in 1970), the rate of urban growth is high. As in the United States and most other nations, however, there is a tendency for extreme concentration of people in a few places. Of about 116 municipal areas in Thailand in 1960, ten of these areas had accounted for two-thirds of the urban growth between 1947 and 1960. Moreover, Greater Bangkok alone absorbed a majority of the national urban increase, reinforcing its status as the principal city.[30] Thus, Thailand, like the United States, continued to urbanize, with a tendency for concentration in the large urban areas.

The growth of metropolitan areas in the United States must be understood in terms of the locus of growth within those areas. Among the largest metropolitan areas in the 1950–1960 and 1960–1970 periods, the population of the central cities remained constant or declined, while the populations outside the cities continued to grow. In the 1950s, the metropolitan rings around cities grew about four and a half times as fast as the cities they surrounded and captured approximately three-fourths of the total increase for metropolitan areas. In the 1960s, the rings grew at an even faster pace and captured slightly more of the overall growth.[31] When one considers further that many cities had annexed territory from the hinterland during those decades, it is clear that population growth away from the centers of the metropolitan areas was even greater than it appeared. The growth of metropolitan areas is thus accompanied by a decentralization process within these areas, in which the suburbs and other outlying areas have been built up most rapidly.

A parallel development in metropolitan growth in the United States has been the merging of once discrete metropolitan areas as they expanded geographically. The term *megalopolis* has been introduced to refer to the densely populated urban chains from Boston to Washington and from Chicago to Pittsburgh.

Growing population concentration, especially in the form of urbanization, can take place even while a population is becoming more dispersed. That is, concentrations may be developing in a number of places even though the greatest concentrations are in a few areas. Nine-tenths of the black population of the United States in 1910 was within the Southern region. By 1960 the proportion had been reduced to just over half. However, while Southern blacks were predominantly in rural residences, the increasing numbers of blacks outside the South were overwhelmingly urban.[32] Increasingly, as indicated earlier, blacks have become a numerical majority or near-majority in many of the nation's large cities. They have not, however, emerged in great numbers in the suburbs, a phenomenon reflecting important social processes of the past few decades.

COMPONENTS OF POPULATION REDISTRIBUTION WITHIN NATIONS

If one examines the relative distribution of population in a society at different points in time, it becomes apparent that a dynamic process is at work redistributing the population. It may not be obvious, however, that redistribution is the result of the additive effects of the three basic components of population change, and that the relative importance of each component varies by area and time period. Two illustrations of these effects in developing areas are given below.

Vaidyanathan attempted to account for the sources of differential urban growth in India between 1951 and 1961.[33] The population of defined urban areas of India had grown from 61 to 70 million during that time, but the urban growth rate varied from 16 percent for Madras to 49 percent for Greater Assam. Nationally, two-thirds of the urban growth was due to natural increase and about one-third to migration. At the state level, however, the relative contributions varied. The states that had relatively low rates of urban population increase had relatively low rates of net migration and moderate levels of natural increase (excess of births over deaths). The states with sizable urban growth rates gained substantially from migration, but they had high rates of natural increase as well. In fact, in only three out of the sixteen states was migration the principal factor. Thus, in a country like India with a high rate of natural increase, whatever shifts in residence take place are likely to be more than matched by natural growth. In rural areas, which may be experiencing net out-migration, continued population growth will be solely the result of natural increase.

A similar study of urban growth in Latin America reinforces the findings for India and adds some clarifications to an understanding of the basic processes.[34] First, urban population increase in Latin America (principally between 1940 and 1960) was caused by both rural-urban migration and a positive rate of urban natural increase. Second, migration was a relatively more important factor in large metropolitan centers than in smaller urban areas. Third, some urban growth came about through reclassification as urban of areas that were previously rural; hence, neither migration nor natural increase really determined that element of change. And fourth, some natural increase contributing to urban growth was the result of births and deaths of recent migrants. Therefore, in a sense part of the urban natural increase might not have occurred had it not been for migration.

These studies reveal that migration is not always the principal source of population redistribution, but that it contributes to changes in the distribution of people both directly and through the reproductive processes of the migrants.

POPULATION DISTRIBUTION WITHIN URBAN AREAS

The changing balance of population in metropolitan areas between central cities and the surrounding territory is, of course, not the only significant aspect of intraurban population distribution changes. Populations within cities assume varying geographical patterns, and these shift over time.

There have been numerous attempts to describe the population structure of cities in general terms. Burgess surveyed some large North

American cities and, on the basis of these, posited a *concentric zonal hypothesis*, namely, that there will be differentiation of functions as one moves away from the center of cities. Concentric layers emanating from the central point will form the central business district, industrial areas, lower-class working homes, areas of better residences, and commuter suburbs. Burgess provided a reasonably accurate portrait of many American cities that were growing during the first part of the twentieth century. Later studies in Latin America showed that cities there traditionally had a different gradient pattern, with higher-status residences in the center of the city and lower-class residences toward the periphery. With population growth and changes in social and economic organization, these cities changed their population spatial form and began to assume the North American pattern.[35]

Alternative descriptions of population distribution have been offered. Hoyt emphasized sector development resulting from arterial transportation patterns. Others have pointed to the effects of both natural features of the land (water, parkland, etc.) and cultural effects (such as ethnic neighborhoods that cut across social lines) on land use. In any event, all cities may exhibit some common demographic features as well as some unique ones that result from the particular set of historical events that affected the city and the precise period of time during which the city developed. In recent years, much attention has been devoted to the intervention of governments in restructuring cities and thus altering population distribution. Urban renewal, subsidized housing, environmental control, and tax incentives and disincentives are examples of government policies which have had some impact on the distribution of people within urban areas.

FUTURE CHANGES IN POPULATION DISTRIBUTION WITHIN NATIONS

The determinants of future changes in urban population distribution are so numerous and varied that it would be highly presumptuous to specify future directions in this area. There is good reason, however, to anticipate continuation of the growth of cities, since that has been a long-term trend. We might also expect population patterns within cities to be a function not only of government policies of the types already mentioned, but also of availability of critical natural resources, such as those necessary for the operation of transportation vehicles and the construction of homes and industries. Many believe that continuing population growth can be accommodated only through the expansion of smaller cities and the creation of new ones. The complexities of the factors involved warrant considerable caution in extrapolating what appear to be present-day trends.

Notes

1. U. S. Bureau of the Census, "Projections of the Population of the U.S.S.R., by Age and Sex: 1969–1990," *International Population Reports*, Series P-91, No. 18, December 1969.
2. U. S. Bureau of the Census, "Projections of the Population of the Communist Countries of Eastern Europe, by Age and Sex: 1969–1990," *International Population Reports*, Series P-91, No. 18, December 1969.
3. See U. S. Bureau of the Census, *Historical Statistics of the United States: Colonial Times to 1957*, U. S. Government Printing Office, Washington, 1960, p. 62.
4. National Center for Health Statistics, *Monthly Vital Statistics Report; Annual Summary for the United States, 1971*, Vol. 20, No. 13, August 30, 1972.
5. For a discussion of the Hong Kong situation, see Ronald Freedman, D. N. Namboothiri, and A. Adlakha, "Hong Kong's Fertility Decline: 1961–68," *Population Index*, 36 (January–March 1970), 3–18; and Sui-Ying Wat and R. W. Hodge, "Social and Economic Factors in Hong Kong's Fertility Decline," *Population Studies*, 26 (November 1972), 455–464.
6. For calculations on the marriage squeeze over time, see Donald S. Akers, "On Measuring the Marriage Squeeze," *Demography*, 4, No. 2 (1967), 907–924.

7. U. S. Bureau of the Census, "Projections of the Population of the Communist Countries of Eastern Europe, by Age and Sex: 1965–1985," *International Population Reports*, Series P-91, No. 14, 1965.

8. See World Population Data Sheet, Appendix B.

9. U. S. Bureau of the Census, "Mobility of the Population of the United States: March 1969 to March 1970," *Current Population Reports*, Series P-20, No. 210, January 15, 1971.

10. U. S. Bureau of the Census, "Summary of Demographic Projections," *Current Population Reports*, Series P-25, No. 388, March 14, 1968.

11. "Summary of Demographic Projections," Table C.

12. See U. S. Bureau of the Census, "Characteristics of the Population by Ethnic Origin, November, 1969," *Current Population Reports*, Series P-20, No. 221, April 30, 1971.

13. U. S. Bureau of the Census, "Fertility Indicators: 1970," *Current Population Reports*, Series P-23, No. 36, April 1971, Table 2.

14. U. S. Department of Commerce, *Commerce News*, March 3, 1971, pp. 2–3.

15. *Commerce News*, March 3, 1971, Tables 2 and 3. For a thorough discussion of the contributions to changes in the racial composition of the population, see Reynolds Farley, *Growth of the Black Population*, Markham, Chicago, 1970.

16. U. S. Department of Commerce, *Commerce News*, February 10, 1971, pp. 1–2.

17. James A. Sweet, "Differentials in the Rate of Fertility Decline, 1960–1970," *Family Planning Perspectives*, 6 (Spring 1974), 103–107.

18. U. S. Bureau of the Census, "Prospects for American Fertility: June 1974," *Current Population Reports*, Series P-20, No. 269, September 1974.

19. U. S. Bureau of the Census, "Summary of Demographic Projections," *Current Population Reports*, Series P-25, No. 388, March 1968, p. 9.

20. Reynolds Farley, "Fertility and Mortality Trends Among Blacks in the United States," in *Demographic and Social Aspects of Popula-*

tion Growth, Vol. I of research reports of the U. S. Commission on Population Growth and the American Future, U. S. Government Printing Office, Washington, 1972, pp. 111–132.

21. Alice Taylor Day and Lincoln H. Day, "Cross-National Comparison of Population Density," *Science*, 181 (September 14, 1973), 1016–1023.

22. Hope Tisdale, "The Process of Urbanization," *Social Forces*, 20 (March 1942), 311.

23. Kingsley Davis, "The Role of Urbanization in the Development Process," *International Technical Cooperation Centre Review* (Tel Aviv), 1 (July 1972), 1–13. (Issued as Reprint No. 408 of International Population and Urban Research, University of California at Berkeley.)

24. United Nations Department of Economic and Social Affairs, *Urbanization: Development Policies and Planning*, New York, 1968, p. 12.

25. Davis.

26. Sidney Goldstein, "An Overview of World Urbanization, 1950–2000," in International Union for the Scientific Study of Population, *International Population Conference, Liege 1973*, Vol. 1, IUSSP, Liege, 1973, p. 183.

27. Goldstein, pp. 184–185.

28. Goldstein, p. 179.

29. Philip H. Hauser, "Urbanization — Problems of High Density Living," in *World Population — The View Ahead*, ed. Richard N. Farmer et al., Indiana University, Graduate School of Business, 1968, p. 191.

30. Sidney Goldstein, "Urbanization in Thailand, 1947–1967," *Demography*, 8 (May 1971), 205–223.

31. Leo F. Schnore and Vivian Zelig Klaff, "Suburbanization in the Sixties: A Preliminary Analysis," *Land Economics*, 48 (February 1972), 25.

32. Reynolds Farley, "The Urbanization of Negroes in the United States," *Journal of Social History*, 2 (Spring 1968), 241–258.

33. K. E. Vaidyanathan, "Components of Urban Growth in India,

1951–1961," *Proceedings of the International Population Conference, London 1969*, International Union for the Scientific Study of Population, Liege, 1971, pp. 2941–2947.

34. Robert H. Weller, John J. Macisco, Jr., and George R. Martine, "The Relative Importance of the Components of Urban Growth in Latin America," *Demography*, 8 (May 1971), 225–232.

35. Leo F. Schnore, "On the Spatial Structure of Cities in the Two Americas," in *The Study of Urbanization*, ed. Philip M. Hauser and Leo F. Schnore, Wiley, New York, 1965, pp. 349–398.

Suggested Additional Readings

Bogue, Donald J. "Color-Nativity-Race Composition." Chapter 7 in *The Population of the United States*. The Free Press, Glencoe, Ill., 1959. Presents data on the color-race-nativity composition of the United States and the distribution of various groups over time.

Davis, Kingsley. *World Urbanization 1950–1970: Vol. I: Basic Data for Cities, Countries, and Regions*, and *Vol. II: Analysis of Trends, Relationships, and Development*. Population Monograph Series Nos. 4 and 9, Institute of International Studies, University of California, Berkeley, 1969, 1972. The most comprehensive survey of world urban demographic patterns which unravels some of its complexities.

Hauser, Philip M. and Leo F. Schnore, eds. *The Study of Urbanization*. Wiley, New York, 1965. Interdisciplinary perspectives on urban research throughout the world, which focus on urban processes and their consequences.

Kiser, Clyde V. "The Aging of Human Population: Mechanisms of Change." In *Social and Psychological Aspects of Aging*, ed. Clark Tibbitts and Wilma Donahue. Columbia University Press, New York, 1962, pp. 18–35. A description of the demographic process of "aging populations" and characteristics of aged people.

U. S. Bureau of the Census. "Projections of the Population of the United States by Age and Sex: 1972 to 2020." *Current Population*

Reports, Series P-25, No. 493, December 1972. A series of projections compiled by the United States Bureau of the Census which allow the reader to make estimates of what the future age-sex composition of the population of the United States is likely to be.

U. S. Commission on Population Growth and the American Future. *Population Distribution and Policy.* Vol. V of Commission research reports, U. S. Government Printing Office, Washington, 1972. Discussions of urban trends and their implications for policy formulation in the United States.

"*Edgar! For God's sake! You can't just take population control into your own hands!*"

Drawing by Ross; © 1972 The New Yorker Magazine

7

Population Impacts:
Education, the Economy,
and the Environment

In the preceding chapters we examined some of the factors that influence population size, growth rates, composition, and distribution. In addition, we looked at societal, group, and individual influences on fertility, mortality, and mobility. But that is only half the picture. Demographic processes in turn influence these various factors. This chapter and Chapter 8 will explore some of the ways in which population size, growth rates, composition, and distribution influence other processes in society.

Specifically, we shall examine how demographic processes affect education, the economy, the environment, the polity, religion, and the family. Of course, some population processes are more important than others in each area. For example, the size of the population may be an important factor in the form the educational or political system takes, but the growth rate of the population may be more important in determining the economic patterns in the society. Likewise, the level at which population influences each of these areas also varies. While the impact of population on the economy may be most evident at societal or national levels, the impact of population on the family may

235

be most important at the group or individual level. Thus, no single framework can be used to discuss all these institutions and how they are affected by population processes.

For this reason we have chosen to deal in this chapter with the impact of demographic processes on the development and deterioration of education, the economy, and the environment at the societal level. We will largely ignore subgroup or individual perspectives on population and these three areas, even though population does influence the education, the economy, and the environment of subgroups and individuals. Population growth, for example, can affect both the economic development of a nation and individual socioeconomic status. But the subgroup and individual manifestations of these institutions and how they are influenced by population processes will be dealt with in conjunction with the family, since these circumstances are likely to be manifested in that setting.

In Chapter 8, we will deal with the impact of population on the polity, religion, and the family at all three levels—society, group, and individual. In such a context we can discuss, for example, both demographic impacts on the importance of the family as an institution and the impact of fertility on the family budget and siblings.

Population and Education

In demographic literature, three measures of educational status are generally found: (1) *school enrollment*, or the number or percentage of the population enrolled in school by age, sex, or other characteristics; (2) *educational attainment* of the population, or years of school completed; (3) and *literacy*, or the number or percentage of the population who are able to read and write in any language. These measures are not independent of one another, but are different in some senses.

Overall literacy rate in a population is a crude measure, since ability to read and write is a rather minimum standard against which to measure educational achievement. School enrollment is a measure of how many persons in the population are currently receiving formal education, or if projected, how many persons may be expected to receive education. The educational attainment measure, on the other hand, reflects the level of education achieved by people already old enough to be out of school. Both school enrollment data and figures on educational attainment refer to participation in the formal educational system, and do not include other kinds of learning. We will use each of these measures to describe population and education relationships.

Population Size and Education

When societies were small and undifferentiated, and residential mobility was low, education usually consisted of apprenticeship. Fathers passed skills along to sons, mothers to daughters; or, in a more developed form, masters of given trades agreed to train a limited number of apprentices in their occupation. Education was thus highly individual and very different from the large classes common in universities at the present time.

As societies grew, it became more efficient to organize education at specific locations and to license or certify those who were educators. With growing populations, more skills and specialization became necessary. Societies needed to separate out those who were most able to learn given skills from among all those who wanted training.

As population grew still larger, one-room schoolhouses containing all six elementary grades gave way to single grades in multiclassroom schools. Training thus changed from individual tutelage, to small classes for the elite, to large schools where students may number in the thousands.

As schools accommodated more and more students, they also became more formalized. There was a need not only to teach and evaluate great numbers of students, but to develop procedures to select teachers as well. Volunteer teachers or those selected by community consensus were replaced by teachers trained in the school system specifically to assume these positions. Whether these changes are seen as beneficial to education or not, their connection, at least in part, to growing population is clear.

Some societies have not been able to simply provide more places in schools and more educators for the greater number of children coming into each generation. In these societies, the rates of school enrollment, educational attainment, and literacy have remained low. In such societies, education is still the privilege of a few. We shall discuss this problem more fully below.

Population Growth Rates and Education

The mere size of a population is perhaps not as important for the development and maintenance of its educational system as the rate at which that population grows and the stability of the growth pattern. Rapid or erratic growth creates problems for educational systems, as it does for other societal institutions.

Examples of *rapid* population growth influencing education are plentiful. In an analysis of the development and cost of education in the United States, Sweden, and Latin America, for example, one author makes a startling statement:

> The handicap that the Latin American demographic characteristics have represented for educational purposes will continue in the future. The goals for rapid educational development will be jeopardized by the high fertility of these populations. Even those Latin American countries that will rapidly reduce fertility up to the year 2000 . . . will have an education cost 47 percent higher than that in the Swedish case in 1965.[1]

The impact of population growth rates on education is thus quite important. Even the United States had an education cost per worker

10 to 18 percent higher than did Sweden, owing to slightly higher levels of fertility and mortality from the 1800s to 1960.[2]

These costs occur because in rapidly growing populations, more and more resources have to be consumed to maintain a constant standard of living for each generation. Thus increased expenditures on education to provide instruction to a greater *proportion* of children becomes more difficult when the *number* of children is also increasing. Thailand illustrates this problem well. About 4.3 million children were enrolled in school there in 1960.[3] This number had grown to 6.1 million in 1970, but because of rapid population growth, this large increase in the number of children enrolled in school represented only a very slight increase in the proportion of children enrolled.

Pressure on school systems to accommodate more and more young people can be felt in developed nations as well. While in developing countries this pressure is directed toward the acquisition of primary and secondary education, in developed nations pressure is felt most at higher levels of the educational system. Figure 7.1 illustrates this phenomenon in the United States by showing projected college enrollment figures from 1973 to the year 2000.

The four population projections in Figure 7.1 are made by assuming different levels of fertility between now and the year 2000. In addition, Figure 7.1 assumes that the proportion of young people going to college will continue to grow as it has in the past. The series E projection is the lowest, and assumes an average of 2.11 children per woman. The series B projection, on the other hand, assumes an average of 3.10 children per woman. Before 1985 these figures are shown as a single line, since the children to be enrolled in college in 1985 are already born, and this projection can be made rather safely. Notice, however, that by the year 2000, the number of persons enrolled in college if current trends in enrollment continue is vastly different under the different fertility assumptions. Even the difference between 2.11 children and 2.45 children (series E and D) will make a difference of about 1.7 million students enrolled in college. If fertility assumptions differ

Figure 7.1   Projections of college enrollment, 1973 to 2000. (Projections based on the assumption that women will bear the following number of children, on the average, during their lifetime: $B = 3.10$; $C = 2.78$; $D = 2.45$; $E = 2.11$.)

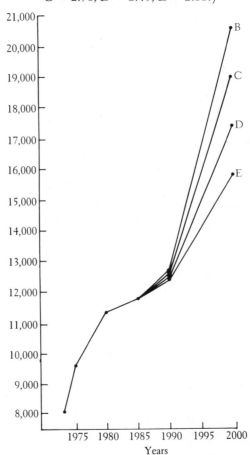

Years

Sources: 1973 data are from U. S. Bureau of the Census, "School Enrollment in the United States: October, 1973," *Current Population Reports,* Series P-20, No. 261, March 1974, Table 4. All other data are from U. S. Bureau of the Census, "Projections of School and College Enrollment: 1971 to 2000," *Current Population Reports,* Series P-25, No. 473, January 1972, Table A-2.

by as much as one child per woman (series E and B), the college enrollment difference by the year 2000 would be about five million students.

Erratic population growth produced by rising and falling fertility rates also requires adaptations of the educational system. Fluctuations in numbers of young people change the needs for teachers, classroom space, and monetary expenditures from year to year, making effective development of the educational system difficult. This is a problem particularly for developed countries that have experienced erratic fertility in the last fifty years. In the United States, for example, the post-World War II baby boom filled classrooms to capacity as these children reached school age. Portable classrooms, temporary teachers, and buildings designed for other purposes were all pressed into service to meet the demand. By the 1960s the educational system had nearly caught up with this demand, only to be faced with a period of declining fertility. Many of the extra classrooms and facilities built to cope with baby-boom children are relatively empty in the 1970s following ten years of fertility decline.

An even more striking example of erratic growth is provided by Rumania. When abortion clinics were closed by the government in 1967, Rumania's birth rate tripled in less than two years. (See Chapter 4.) As these children reached school age, the burden on the educational system was increased threefold, but only for a short period of time since the birth rate declined sharply again. Such variations in the numbers of children to be educated, a direct result of erratic fertility rates, produce problems for communities and nations trying to improve, or at least maintain, an acceptable level of education.

Population Composition and Distribution and Education

We have seen that both the numbers of people to be educated and the rates at which those numbers change are important considerations. What kinds of persons are to be educated, where they come from, and where they are located are also important.

Age composition of the population is one such consideration. High-fertility populations are also young populations, as we have learned above. In young populations, the dependency burden is high because there are relatively fewer middle-aged workers in the population to support the education of large numbers of young persons. This factor contributes to a higher cost per worker for education and a greater overall burden for the system.

Racial-ethnic composition of the population may also influence the educational system. In cities where a heavy influx of immigrants is common, needs for curriculum changes may emerge, such as teaching English as a second language. In central city schools, greater proportions of black students give rise to requests for more teachers who can satisfy the curriculum needs of the students.

The great movement of citizens from rural to urban areas has of course created burdens for the urban schools, but problems have arisen in rural systems as well. Where these systems are becoming depopulated, the demand for teachers is lessened. In addition, teachers in rural schools are more likely to need broad skills in a variety of areas than are teachers in urban schools, who may teach only one subject to a variety of classes each day.

In each of the ways we have discussed above, and in many more, population size, growth rates, composition, and distribution have an impact on the educational system. In spite of the importance of the population variables, it is ironic that the educational system itself is at present doing very little to educate students about these processes. In a survey conducted for the Commission on Population Growth and the American Future, it was found that knowledge about population processes and facts among Americans was very low.[4] In addition, few secondary schools have courses or even units included in the curriculum to teach students about population processes.[5] While it is not entirely clear that knowledge about population processes would make a difference in, say, the fertility or mobility behavior of individuals,[6] it would seem that since it is one of the major recipients of population consequences, the educational system would profit from exploring ways of spreading knowledge about those processes and their results.

Population and the Economy

For residents of many developed countries, and for Americans in particular, "bigger" has long been synonymous with "better." Towns have pointed with pride at the new residents and industry they have been able to attract. More people has meant larger markets for goods and services, ensuring economic growth. Truly, the major part of the nation's history reflects a belief in the growth ethic.

Only recently has the inevitability of the connection between population growth and economic growth been questioned. This questioning has taken place not only in the developing countries, where growth has become a rather obvious burden, but also in developed countries, where "more" has sometimes meant "dirtier" and "poorer," as well.

The Commission on Population Growth and the American Future concluded in its report:

> We have looked for, and have not found, any convincing economic argument for continued national population growth. The health of our economy does not depend on it. The vitality of business does not depend on it. The welfare of the average person certainly does not depend on it.
>
> In fact, the average person will be markedly better off in terms of traditional economic values if population growth follows the two-child projection rather than the three-child one.[7]

Still, there are those who have maintained that stable population growth would mean a disrupted, if not a stagnant, economy.[8] What are the mechanisms, then, by which population processes affect the economy? How can we sort out these arguments?

The issues involved in the more recent discussions of population changes and economic development seem to vary, depending on whether the nation in question is developed or developing. For developing countries, some have argued that priority should be given to developing the economy in order to lower birth and death rates, while others have maintained that lowering high birth rates first would greatly aid these nations in developing their economic structures. In developed countries, on the other hand, the debate seems to center around whether economic stagnation would result from slowly growing or even decreasing populations. The impact of increasing numbers in these countries is seen as primarily related to demand for goods and services, the composition of the labor force, and potentials for creative technological development.

Because concern over the economic impact of population processes has taken different forms in societies at different stages of development, we will discuss these concerns separately for developed and developing countries. In addition, we will consider some population processes that influence nations in somewhat the same way, regardless of their economic development level.

Population and Developing Economies

There is some agreement among economists and demographers that the economic growth rate of some of the less-developed countries during the past few years has been impressive. Gross national product (GNP) is the most common summary measure of economic well-being; it refers to the total volume of goods and services produced in a society during a given period of time. We have used unadjusted gross national product and gross national product per capita in Figure 7.2 to illustrate the role of population in the economic development of a nation. This figure shows the percentage change in each of these measures for the countries in the continents or areas indicated. Note that

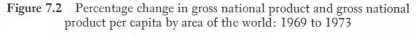

Figure 7.2   Percentage change in gross national product and gross national
product per capita by area of the world: 1969 to 1973

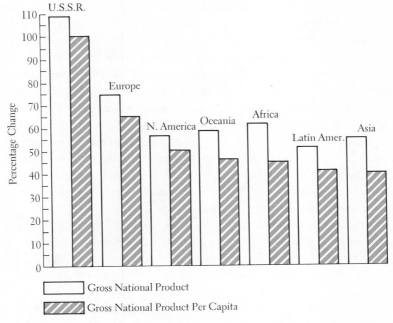

Source: Figures computed from Population Reference Bureau, Inc., *1973 World
Population Data Sheet*, Washington, D.C., 1973.

in the developing areas, Oceania, Africa, Latin America, and Asia, the
growth in gross national product between 1969 and 1973 has been
rather large. But the difference between the change in gross national
product and the change in gross national product per capita is the
portion of this growth taken away by increasing population. While in
the USSR, Europe, and North America the differences between these
two figures are not large, in Africa the difference is seventeen percentage
points. Figure 7.2 shows rather clearly that had population remained

constant and GNP been the same, the percentage gain in gross national product per capita in each area would have been larger. This is a phenomenon we noted above with regard to educational gains. As one author states the problem, "It is a matter of running up the down escalator; it is possible to reach the top, but the effort involved is much greater than it would be if the escalator were halted."[9]

The connection between population growth and economic development in these developing nations has been described as cyclical. As some writers reason, having too many children makes it difficult for a family to accumulate savings and thus limits investments. Lack of investments prevents capital from growing, does not help unemployment, and further perpetuates the cycle of poverty. With lowered fertility, the cycle should be broken, since the family would then have greater savings and would be able to make more investments in such items as education for their children.

This reasoning has led to what one author calls the "magic formula," namely that "a decline in fertility necessarily will have a favorable impact on the rate of social and economic development."[10] Whether this formula is in fact "magic" has been much debated in the literature.

With regard to Latin America, for example, some have questioned the link between reduced fertility and savings.[11] Those arguing this point say that the relative contribution of household savings to total savings of a country is very small. Further, family investments are only a small part of total national investment. In making investments, there is no guarantee that families will use what additional savings they have for long-term investments that would really help the economy, such as education.

To make the issue even more confusing, there are some countries whose economic development seems to have been helped by increases in population. In Guyana, for example, the rice industry was able to develop because of an expanded labor force and an expanded demand for goods, both largely furnished by population increase.[12] Australia has certainly grown and developed as a nation through increased population growth from migration.[13]

The other point of contention with regard to the effects of reduced population growth on economic development is how long-term such effects would be. Some say that increased savings by families after fertility is reduced would only be temporary.[14] Others have suggested that in the long run decreased fertility may lower the time countries require to develop economically, but in the short run it will worsen unemployment because of lower demands for goods and services.[15]

A rather thorough debate on these issues occurred in China during the 1950s. As noted in Chapter 4, China's birth control policies have been erratic, in part reflecting ideological debates on the propriety of introducing birth control programs in socialist states. It will be recalled that Marxian philosophy indicates that the Malthusian view of population processes is not correct; that is, population problems arise from unequal distribution of resources, not from the numbers of people alone.

China has had economic development goals that have been seen by some as incompatible with indefinitely increasing population. Thus, arguments ensued over the necessity and/or desirability of bringing down the birth rate to facilitate economic development or for some other purposes. In support of many births as a facilitator of economic development, one Chinese writer argued:

> In the past, many Malthusian scholars once displayed a "scientific" facade and concluded that the territory of China could supply consumption materials to maintain at most 200 million to 280 million persons. This fallacious thesis has been shattered by actual events. Because of the revolutionary victory and the expansion of production, we have within a short period of time abolished hunger for the first time in the history of our nation as well as solved, step by step, the unemployment problem and appreciably raised the level of living of the entire people, though our nation's population has passed 600 million.

Moreover, since national liberation, under comparatively backward technological circumstances, we have rapidly made large strides in the national economy. This would have been inconceivable had there not been such a massive source of manpower.[16]

But that view was not to be the prevailing sentiment in China. It remained for others to justify birth planning and limitation for ideologically acceptable reasons:

Someone has made a preliminary estimate that if we would have to support only 500 million people, our nation's productive capacity would suffice and enable them to enjoy fine clothing and abundant food. As it is impossible for China's population to be reduced to 500 million, we have no recourse but to control reproduction. If we would manage to keep the population below 700 million within fifteen years, and positively fulfill our nation's economic construction plans, then in 1972 the whole people would be able to have a good life of fine clothing and abundant food.[17]

This statement reflects concern with a standard of living for individuals, as well as with the general economic growth of the society. It argues, as does Figure 7.2, that while economic growth may be possible under conditions of rapidly growing population, improvement in the level of living of a people will be accelerated if population growth is curtailed. Still, the conditions are different for each country at different points in time.

A more middle-ground approach to the question of the relationship between fertility control and economic development of the developing nations is taken by Easterlin:

The existing state of knowledge does not warrant any clearcut generalizations as to the effect of population growth on economic development in today's less developed areas. Some theoretical analyses argue that high population growth creates pressures on limited natural resources, reduces private and public capital formation, and diverts additions to capital resources to maintaining rather than increasing the stock of capital per worker. Others point to positive effects such as economies of scale and specialization, the possible spur to favorable motivation caused by increased dependency, and the more favorable attitudes, capacities, and motivations of younger populations compared to older ones. The actual evidence . . . does not point to any uniform conclusion.[18]

Easterlin would say we just don't know. While the majority of writers would argue that reductions in fertility would bring economic benefits of some kind, even if only short-run, to the developing nations, others say that only if economic conditions are improved will fertility go down.

Population and Developed Economies

In the economically developed countries, recent concern has centered on falling birth rates and their impact on at least two major areas of the economy: size and rate of growth of the GNP, and composition and size of the labor force.

First, with regard to growth of the GNP, it is clear that the volume of goods and services produced is larger with rapid population growth than with zero population growth. This lower overall growth of the GNP will affect industries differently. Families with two children clearly require fewer diapers, jars of baby food, pediatricians, and cribs than do three- or four-child families. Industries catering to the needs of young children, at least in some cases, will suffer from reduced fertility.

The decreased business of these industries will be buffered in at least two ways. First, many companies make not only baby food, but other products such as ketchup, mustard, and hot dogs. These are "leisure foods," commodities for which demand is increasing and will increase further as families decrease fertility and have more money and time for leisure activities. Secondly, parents tend to spend more money on the first child, requiring other children to reuse or share toys, furniture, or other items.[19] Replacing the three-child family with the two-child family thus creates greater problems for those industries producing nonreusable or nontransferable goods for children.

Other sectors of the economy, on the other hand, would benefit. We have already mentioned leisure foods. Likewise, sporting goods manufacturers and retailers, travel industries, and other recreational businesses will have more customers. The net effect on the GNP will be negative, but because of these mixed factors, the magnitude of the effect is unclear.

More important than the total GNP, however, is the GNP per capita. If real income remains constant and the same proportions of income are absorbed by government, this is almost certain to rise with decreased population growth rates. This occurs because there are not more and more new persons in each generation to share incomes. This effect also takes place, however, because of the changed age composition of populations with low or zero growth. Since they contain a greater proportion of middle-aged people relative to dependent aged or young people, these populations have more workers available to produce goods and services to share with nonproducers. With larger incomes per family, even the business of child-related industries may increase.

The second area of concern is labor force size and composition. It is not clear whether future technologies will require more or fewer workers than are presently available. If full employment is important as a societal goal, however, higher birth rates may generate more problems than lower birth rates. The Commission on Population Growth and the American Future stated the following:

It seems clear that labor force trends under the three-child projection can be expected to generate greater pressure for increased production, employment, and consumption, and correspondingly greater problems associated with the social and environmental consequences of such increases.[20]

By contrast, some have argued that in a stable population with a constant number of persons available for the labor force, mobility will be much less than before.[21] Since the average age of workers in the labor force will rise, the overall productivity of the labor force may decline. Conversely, an older work force may be more experienced and skilled. These prospects, coupled with fear of a decreased GNP, have caused concern in many European nations as well as in the United States.

Sweden, however, provides an example of high GNP increases coupled with slow population growth.[22] Sweden has experienced slower population growth rates than the United States for some time, but average productivity has consistently risen by rates that are high by any world standard. Now that Sweden's fertility is at or slightly below replacement levels, it will be interesting to view the economic results.

It is difficult to predict the influence of population on the economy with accuracy in the developed countries, since no long-term historical precedent exists for the stable demographic processes envisaged. Nevertheless, the Commission on Population and the American Future anticipated massive changes in the economy, whether population stabilizes or not.[23] Their report expressed faith that the economy would find healthy ways to adjust to lower population growth and would even benefit from these changes in some areas.

Population and Creativity

One of the resources any nation has for its economic and general social development is those citizens who are especially gifted, bright, or creative. Such persons innovate, lead social change, and develop technological and social tools that help the society. This resource is important for both developing and developed economies. Some people have argued that decreased population growth lessens the number of such persons in a society. In addition, this argument contends that some population pressure, by producing a continual need to cope with problems, stimulates creativity. Young people often provide impetus for social change. If the population becomes older, these people fear, society will become stagnant and conservative, not open to new ideas and new ways.

Such speculations are, of course, hard to validate. It is possible to reason in the opposite direction — that decreasing the dependency burden and rate of social change will lead to creative and intelligent, rather than emergency, solutions for problems. Which, if any, of these results will occur remains to be seen.

One of the ways in which population processes have already affected the number of creative or particularly able people available to a nation is selective migration, often called "braindraining." The most able in each nation may move to places where they have better opportunities. Nations such as the United States attract the best students from developing countries, who want to stay beyond their school years since pay is higher and facilities for many occupational pursuits are superior to those in their home countries. Recently, the United States has passed new laws to restrict the number of foreign students who can stay in the country.

On the other hand, unskilled workers who are unemployed may leave areas seeking new opportunities. This kind of selective migration can be a stimulus to economies in the areas from which emigration takes place, since it lessens the unemployment burden.

Selective migration can thus be a stimulus or a hindrance to economic development, in both the place of origin and the destination. While international migration policies have long existed to regulate these flows between countries, only recently have many nations like the United States begun to consider internal migration policies or incentives that would change the direction, composition, or amount of migration within the nation.

Population and Environment

In assessing the impact of population on the natural environment, the economic factors just discussed make conclusions difficult. It is clear that it is people who pollute, use resources, invent chemicals with adverse side effects, and create waste. Without people there would be no environmental catastrophes such as filthy rivers, dirty air, or poisoned animals and plants. The difficult question thus is not whether people create pollution, or even whether more people create more pollution than fewer people, but how many environmental problems are created by numbers and distribution of people and how many by the ways in which those people live. It has been asked whether changes in population processes or changes in economic systems would produce more beneficial results for the environment. The majority of writers seem to feel that changes in economic systems will produce the greatest impact, while many argue that changes in both are ultimately necessary.

In the developing nations, the primary environmental problems seem to be resource shortages, particularly food shortages and living space shortages. In developed nations, environmental problems include energy and mineral shortages, pollution, and difficulties arising from population concentrations in certain areas. We will discuss these problems separately.

Environment in Developing Nations

In the late 1960s, a host of writers predicted that massive famine would occur in much of the developing world within ten years. The following illustrates such projections:

> The battle to feed humanity is over. Unlike battles of military forces, it is possible to know the results of the population-food conflict while the armies are still "in the field." Sometime between 1970 and 1985, the world will undergo vast famines —

hundreds of millions of people are going to starve to death. That is, they will starve to death unless plague, thermonuclear war, or some other agent kills them first. Many will starve to death in spite of any crash programmes we might embark upon now. And we are not embarking upon any crash programme.[24]

Such predictions were not very optimistic but were rather common. Then for a brief period it seemed these estimates were in error. Because of something called the Green Revolution, the threat of massive famine appeared to have abated. The Green Revolution refers to the development of new higher-yielding strains of wheat, rice, and other products. These new grains made possible greater yields from the same amount of land under cultivation. The change in the amount of food produced by some nations was so dramatic that some that had been net importers of food became self-sufficient or even exporters.

The Green Revolution was not a permanent answer to population pressure on food supplies. These new grains required massive amounts of fertilizer and water, and new techniques of agriculture had to be learned if the farmer was to use them effectively. In addition, in the most tradition-bound societies where fertility is the highest, commitment to the old agricultural ways is also strong. The impact of the Green Revolution was further limited by the inefficiency with which governments distributed the grains and provided the instruction necessary for their cultivation. Even when seed and fertilizer were supplied by other nations, the bureaucratic morass in some countries prevented their utilization.

Norman Borlaug, Nobel Prize winner for the development of the new grains, estimated that the Green Revolution, if used to its utmost, would stave off famine for thirty years.[25] Thirty years is certainly not very long, but this appears now to be an overestimate. The developing nations of the world are again facing massive starvation and are likely to continue to do so unless population growth is reduced drastically. This has led writers to speculate on whether the developed nations can continue to feed both themselves and these developing nations indefinitely. The answer to that question is clearly no. What is in doubt is how much more time technology or foreign aid can buy for these rapidly growing nations that face continual food shortages.

The other difficult problem in developing nations is crowding and the consequent environmental damage. In the cities of India, for example, millions live in the streets, with sanitation facilities sadly lacking and disease rampant. Poor diet and poverty are the rule. To properly clothe, educate, and employ these millions is a nearly impossible task. The environmental conditions themselves work against such changes.

That problems of environmental strain and food shortage exist in these nations no one denies. Differences in viewing these problems center on the degree of urgency perceived and the solutions envisioned. These differences are not unlike those we found when we examined economic issues. Some authors suggest that direct attacks on population growth rates are the key. Others argue that assaults on the environment will have greater impact. Still others believe that only with massive economic aid for development can either population or environmental issues be attacked. That the three areas are inextricably intertwined everyone agrees.

Environment in Developed Nations

As we noted above, growth in GNP has been the sought-after goal of most developed nations. But this growth has exacted certain prices — among them, environmental deterioration. To make this point and to illustrate the degree to which economic growth and environmental problems are connected in developed nations, Ehrlich writes:

> More important than what the GNP is, however, is what it is *not*. It is not a measure of the degree of freedom of the people of a nation. It is not a measure of the health of a population. It is not a measure of the state of depletion of natural re-

sources. It is not a measure of the stability of the environmental systems upon which life depends. It is not a measure
of security from the threat of war. It is not, in sum, a comprehensive measure of the quality of life.[26]

Because of these links between prosperity and environmental damage,
Ehrlich and others have suggested that nations forego some amount of
economic growth in the future to insure the maintenance of other
valued goods and conditions.

Population changes, too, can contribute to environmental damage,
although the Commission on Population Growth and the American
Future estimated that in almost all environmental areas, the impact of
economic growth was much greater than that of population growth.
Relative to consumption of valuable resources, one author has estimated for the United States that:

A one percent reduction in population would reduce consumption of resources in the year 2000 by 0.2 to 0.7 percent, whereas
the equivalent percentage reduction in per capita GNP would
reduce consumption in that year 0.6 to 3.5 percent.[27]

It is clear that population processes play an important role in several environmental areas, even if not as important a role as economic
development. In the United States, for example, several minerals will
shortly be or are at present in limited supply. Under a two-child
rather than a three-child family model, demand for these minerals will
be reduced by 1 to 8 percent by the year 2000. By the year 2020,
the demand would be reduced by 14 percent.[28]

In looking at pollution control, it is again clear that lower economic
growth rates would produce greater benefits than reduced population
growth. In addition, an active attack on pollution in the form of an
abatement or regulatory policy would produce greater impacts on clean
air, water, etc., than would population control.[29] Nevertheless, those
areas with the greatest pollution problems also have high population

concentrations. As population concentrates in urban areas more and more, strategies such as staggered work hours, forced use of mass transit, or special taxes on car use will be required in order to keep hydrocarbon emissions at acceptable levels. These changes alter our style of life and are clearly made necessary by population changes as well as by economic activity.

Other considerations in developed nations include the amount of land available for recreational use. It has been estimated that if all the land in the United States were divided up equally between the population of 1972, for example, each citizen would have 11 acres.[30] If families average three children between now and the year 2000, that number will shrink to 7 acres. By 2020, it will be down to only 5 acres. Under a two-child model, there will be 7.5 acres per person in 2020. As population grows, regardless of the rate, the amount of land available for leisure uses like parks, forests, preserves, and the like diminishes.

Developed nations also use massive quantities of water, not only for personal use but for industrial uses as well. Water shortages already exist in the southwestern United States, and the Commission on Population anticipated that such shortages would spread. With a two-child family model, savings in water by the year 2000 would be 23 percent over the three-child model, a substantial difference.[31]

In addition to these environmental considerations, there is a set of pollutants about which little is known except that they are extremely dangerous. This set of pollutants includes radioactive wastes, pesticides, and various chemicals emitted by industry, all of which continue to have an impact over a long period of time. The environmental damage wrought by these pollutants may be far worse than the standard emissions from combustion processes because of their long-lasting nature, because of their ability to affect large areas, and because their effects take a long time to appear. While it is difficult to project the exact impact in this case of reducing population growth, at least there would be more time in which to carefully test and evaluate advanced technology and its side effects.

Each of these environmental problems is influenced by population processes. Some of them are tightly bound to population growth; others are more loosely connected through economic processes. In every case, few environmental benefits seem to result from continued population growth. Even larger improvements in the environment would result from slower economic growth — a difficult solution for the developed nations.

Other Environmental Problems

Developed and developing nations share the burden of unequal distribution of people and resources among nations. Many of the nations with the largest populations have the fewest environmental resources. The inequality of population and resource distributions create problems of support for the "haves" and problems of scarcity for the "have-nots." Both problems contribute to tension in international relations.

In addition, both developed and developing nations have pressing environmental problems that could be alleviated by slower rates of population growth. In developing nations, the frantic search for newer technological developments to push back the ever-present specter of famine could be alleviated in part by slower population growth. The developing nations must implement new programs without time to watch for side effects or to test other results. The wholesale introduction of fertilizer, for example, may create water supply or ground damage.

In developed nations, too, time is often precious. Energy crises, made worse by large populations, demand instant solutions. Such instant solutions sometimes have devastating long-range effects. As we noted in discussing education and economic development, the effect of technological gains is lessened by increasing populations, so that overall progress is slow.

To say that the economy, education, and the environment can develop indefinitely if population keeps growing rapidly is absurd. To say that the world will die from starvation or pollution tomorrow, or to argue that developed economies can never cope with stable populations, is equally silly. The middle ground seems to be recognition that population processes play a part in educational, economic, and environmental well-being. This recognition can be the first step toward making effective planning decisions to reach societal goals in these areas.

Notes

1. Eduardo Arriaga, "Impact of Population Changes on Education Cost," *Demography*, 9 (May 1972), 283.
2. Arriaga, p. 279.
3. Manasvi Unhanand et al., "Thailand," *Country Profiles*, The Population Council (March 1972).
4. Carl C. Hetrick, A. E. Keir Nash, and Alan J. Wyner, "Population and Politics: Information, Concern, and Policy Support Among the American Public," in *Governance and Population: The Governmental Implications of Population Change*, Vol. IV of research reports of the U. S. Commission on Population and the American Future, U. S. Government Printing Office, Washington, 1972, pp. 301–332.
5. Stephen Viederman, "Population Education in Elementary and Secondary Schools in the U. S.," in *Aspects of Population Growth Policy*, Vol. VI of research reports of the U. S. Commission on Population and the American Future, U. S. Government Printing Office, Washington, pp. 433–458.
6. A study for the U. S. Commission on Population and the American Future, for example, found that knowledge about population was not related to concern about it. See Hetrick, Keir Nash, and Wyner.
7. Commission on Population and the American Future, *Population and the American Future*, Signet, New York, 1972, p. 53.
8. Arguments of this sort are made by Harold H. Barnett, "Population Problems: Myths and Realities," *Economic Development and*

Cultural Change, 19 (July 1971), 545–559. A suggestion that rapidly achieved stability would be disruptive is made by Ansley J. Coale, "Man and His Environment," *Science,* 170 (October 9, 1970), pp. 132–136.

9. Gavin W. Jones, "Effect of Population Change on the Attainment of Education Goals in the Developing Countries," in *Rapid Population Growth: Consequences and Policy Implications,* ed. Roger Revelle, Johns Hopkins, Baltimore, 1971, p. 317.

10. As noted in Mercedes Pedrero Nieto, "Reviews of Papers Presented to the Conference: Jack Harewood, 'Algunos pensamientos acerca de los probables efectos de las disminuciones recientes de la fecundidad y el crecimiento de la poplacion en el Caribe Britanico,' " *Concerned Demography,* 2 (January 1971), 7–8.

11. As noted in Eric R. Weiss-Altaner, "Reviews of Papers Presented to the Conference: Angel Fucaraccio, 'El control de la natalidad y el argumento del ahorro y la inversion,' and Paul Israel Singer, 'Combios de poblición y producción,' " *Concerned Demography,* 2 (January 1971), 8–11.

12. Jay R. Mandle, "Population and Economic Change: The Emergence of the Rice Industry in Guyana 1895–1915," *Journal of Economic History,* 30 (December 1970), 785–801.

13. Allen C. Kelley, "International Migration and Economic Growth, Australia, 1865–1935," *Journal of Economic History,* 25 (September 1965), 333–354.

14. John Isbister, "Birth Control, Income Redistribution, and the Rate of Saving: The Case of Mexico," *Demography,* 10 (February 1973), 85–97.

15. Richard Blandy, "Population and Employment Growth: An Introductory Empirical Exploration," *International Labor Review,* 106 (October 1972), 347–366.

16. Yang ssu-ying, "The Premise of Birth Control Advocacy Is Not Malthusianism," quoted in *China's Population Struggle,* H. Y. Tien, Ohio State University Press, Columbus, 1973, p. 222.

17. Chung Hui-nan, in *People's Daily*, March 7, 1957, as quoted in Tien, p. 193.
18. Richard A. Easterlin, "Effects of Population Growth on the Economic Development of Developing Countries," *The Annals of the American Academy of Political and Social Science*, 369 (January 1967), p. 98.
19. Ritchie H. Reed and Susan McIntosh, "Costs of Children," in *Economic Aspects of Population Change*, Vol. II of research reports of the U. S. Commission on Population Growth and the American Future, U. S. Government Printing Office, Washington, 1972, pp. 336–350.
20. *Population and the American Future*, pp. 49–50.
21. Lincoln H. Day, "The Social Consequences of a Zero Population Growth Rate in the United States," Commission on Population Growth and the American Future, Research Reports, Vol. 1, *Demographic and Social Aspects of Population Growth* (Washington: (U. S. Government Printing Office, 1972), pp. 661–674.
22. Gertrud Svala, "Sweden," *Country Profiles*, The Population Council (July 1972).
23. *Population and the American Future*, p. 45.
24. Paul R. Ehrlich, "Paying the Piper," *New Scientist*, 36 (December 14, 1967), 652–655.
25. Population Reference Bureau, "The Techno-Population Race: Who Needs It," PPB Selection No. 40 (July 1972).
26. Paul R. Ehrlich and Anne H. Ehrlich, *Population, Resources, Environment: Issues in Human Ecology*, Freeman, San Francisco, 1970, pp. 279–280.
27. Ronald G. Ridker, "Resource and Environmental Consequences of Population Growth in the U.S.: A Summary," in *Population, Resources and the Environment*, Vol. III of research reports of the U.S. Commission on Population Growth and the American Future, U.S. Government Printing Office, Washington, p. 23.
28. Ridker, p. 23.

29. Ridker, p. 26.
30. Ridker, p. 27.
31. Ridker, p. 28.

Suggested Additional Readings

For further reading on education and population see:

Jones, Gavin W. "Effect of Population Change on the Attainment of Educational Goals in the Developing Countries." In Roger Revelle, ed. *Rapid Population Growth: Consequences and Policy Implications.* Johns Hopkins, Baltimore, 1971, pp. 315–367.

Lane, Mary Turner, and Ralph E. Wileman. *A Structure for Population Education.* University of North Carolina Press, Chapel Hill, 1974.

Muhsam, H. V., ed. *Population and Education: Mutual Impacts.* Ordina Editions, Liege, 1975.

A set of readings on economic consequences of population patterns is found in:

U.S. Commission on Population Growth and the American Future, *Economic Aspects of Population Change,* Vol. II of research reports, U.S. Government Printing Office, Washington, 1972.

Three readings relevant to population impacts on the economy are found in:

Roger Revelle, ed. *Rapid Population Growth: Consequences and Policy Implications.* Johns Hopkins, Baltimore, 1971. These include T. Paul Schultz, "An Economic Perspective on Population Growth"; Harvey Leibenstein, "The Impact of Population Growth on Economic Welfare — Nontraditional Elements"; and Paul Demeny, "The Economics of Population Control."

Further reading on population and the environment can be found in:

Bahr, Howard M., Bruce A. Chadwick, and Darwin L. Thomas. *Population, Resources and the Future: Non-Malthusian Perspectives.* Brigham Young University Press, Provo, Utah, 1972.

Ehrlich, Paul R., and Anne H. Ehrlich. *Population, Resources, Environment: Issues in Human Ecology.* Freeman, San Francisco, 1970.

U. S. Commission on Population Growth and the American Future, *Population, Resources and the Environment,* Vol. III of research reports, U. S. Government Printing Office, Washington, 1972.

"Boy, did I have an afternoon! The census man was here."

Drawing by George Price; © 1940, 1968 The New Yorker Magazine

8

Population Impacts:
The Polity, Religion, and the Family

In Chapter 7 we examined some of the ways in which population processes influence societal changes in education, the economy, and the environment. Now we turn to three other important institutional areas: the polity, religion, and the family. These are the institutions that regulate the use of authority and power, morals and conceptions of ultimate meaning, and sexual behavior and reproduction, respectively. We will begin with the most global of these institutions, the polity, and later discuss religion and the family.

Population and the Polity

It is certainly true that population processes affect the form, effectiveness, and relative world positions of governments. Although this is not an exhaustive consideration of the ways in which this occurs, we will examine three primary influences of population on the polity: (1) population effects on national power, (2) population effects on governmental processes, and (3) population effects on internal political disputes within nations.

Population and Power

The sheer size of its population has long been thought an important determinant of a nation's strength. Ancient Romans, for example, were strongly pronatalist since conquering territory for the empire demanded vast armies. Even for present-day power, not so entirely determined by the number of fighting men, population is an important contributor. Kingsley Davis, for example, has noted that large population size contributes to a nation's power in four major ways.[1] First, it provides a larger labor force to make economic contributions to a nation. Second, in a large population there are greater advantages of scale from a system of mass production and distribution, making modern economies more profitable. Third, a larger military force can be maintained for defense and security purposes. Finally, if new territory is gained by military or other action, large occupational forces can be sent to the new land to maintain its allegiance to the state. These factors have been cited by other authors as well. In a recent analysis of developing countries, Hendershot finds a strong relationship between a nation's military power and the size of its population.[2]

A more refined examination of the relationship between national power and population size has been accomplished by Organski, Mesquita, and Lamborn for the Commission on Population Growth and the American Future.[3] These authors note that to truly measure the relationship of population to power in a nation, one must consider only those persons in the population who contribute to the furthering of national goals, the "effective" population. People effectively utilized by a country contribute to its influence over others, whereas those who only consume and drain a country do not. When looked at in this more refined way, population seems to be related to power in a conditional way.

How many persons a country needs to effectively achieve political or other goals varies, of course, with the social organization and technological development of the society. The personnel requirements of different technologies are not the same. A large population may be an asset in some settings and a liability in others, depending upon the circumstances.

Nevertheless, what nations believe about population and power has enormous practical consequence for population growth and decline. Nations that believe their power to be directly connected to their level of population growth or the size of their population would of course pursue different fertility, mortality, and migration control policies than those that feel that extra people are an additional burden on the nation.

Population and Governmental Processes

Just as a nation's population makes a difference in international politics, so the number of people being governed in a nation affects the possible forms of internal government. For example, participatory democracy, or all persons in the society voting on each issue, is not a feasible form of government when the population is large and/or widely dispersed. Recent technological innovations have raised questions about whether we might not all be able to vote on each issue pending in Congress by remote computer, but this suggestion remains a part of science fiction for the present.

In the United States, several authors have analyzed the growth of the nation and the result of that growth on the governmental processes in the country. Davidson, for example, has noted that in 1870 the number of representatives in the Congress was 106.[4] The present number in the House of Representatives is 435. That fact alone changes the nature and form of deliberations possible for the House.

The workload of each session is now greater, and the time it takes each legislator to do what was originally conceived of as a part-time job has grown longer. Politics has now become a career, with less turnover of persons in office. More and more committees become necessary, as do more and more rules for writing bills and conducting debate. Legislators are not often available to their constituents, since even in the smallest states the number of people represented by a senator or a representative is quite large. Data such as these are not, of course, measures of the quality of representation or government. These changes may have resulted in the same quality of government or even raised the quality of representation. They are nevertheless changes made necessary by population dynamics.

These considerations have led some authors to speculate on how large governmental units should be if they are to effectively communicate with people and deliver needed services. Elazar, for example, has estimated that for local governments to function effectively in communication and delivery, their optimal population size should be 40,000 to 200,000, a size many communities exceed.[5] States, says Elazar, should have approximately 2.5 to 10 million persons to facilitate these two goals. Larger size results in greater concentration of power in the hands of a few. Whether the numerical estimates of Elazar are correct or not, the important point here is the recognition that population size does influence the nature of governmental processes.

The cost of government services has also escalated tremendously. This is true not only because of the growth of the population, but because of other population processes as well. Grumm puts the argument succinctly:

> There is no question that population change has a profound impact on the costs of state governmental services. If only people did not migrate, have so many babies, or wait so long to die, government costs could be reduced . . . the mere movement of population from state to state and even from county to county produces conditions eventuating in increased government costs.[6]

Population redistribution also affects the general character of governmental processes. As the proportion of rural representation in Congress falls, for example, more support may be gained for programs put forth by the Department of Housing and Urban Development than for those put forth by the Department of Agriculture.

Population and Internal Disputes

We have seen ways, then, in which population processes affect international and domestic politics. Population also has an impact on political processes and disputes within national subgroups. For example, the very high rate of natural increase of non-Jews in Israel is causing concern among Jews there. Natural growth among non-Jews is two and a half times that of Jews.[7] Unless immigration of Jews to Israel continues at a rapid pace, non-Jews will soon have a greater power position in the nation and a potentially larger voice in political decisions.

The United States provides another example of how population processes and, more recently, population policies affect ethnic fears and disputes. Some prominent black leaders in the nation have claimed that the current family planning movement is genocidal in its intent toward blacks.[8] Dick Gregory, H. Rap Brown, the Black Panthers, and the Black Muslims have all voiced this fear. A quote from the Black Panther publication illustrates this view:

> Black people know that part of our revolutionary strength lies in the fact that we outnumber the pigs — and the pigs realize this too. That is why they are trying to eliminate as many people as possible before they reach their inevitable doom.[9]

Within the black community this view has been debated. The following illustrates some of the counterarguments to this genocidal interpretation:

> At this point a few members of my community will tell me that legalized abortion is simply another white man's trick to foster racial genocide. They will say that we need to reproduce as many black children as possible — which only adds numbers. There is no magic in a home where someone has reproduced five or more black babies and cannot manage economically,

educationally, spiritually nor socially to see that these five black
babies become five highly trained black minds.

. . . under slavery, blacks were encouraged to reproduce to
assure an adequate supply of muscle energy people. Wake up,
brothers and sisters, America no longer needs muscle energy
people.[10]

This latter argument seems to be more appealing to the majority of
the black community. Black women have been receptive to family
planning programs in their communities. In addition, as early as 1960,
national fertility surveys found that 90 percent of black women had
either used or intended to use contraception.[11]

The white community, on the other hand, has also voiced fears of
the relative balance of ethnic power being changed by population
processes. Feeling threatened by the larger natural increase of blacks
in the nation, whites have on occasion argued for increased white reproduction. In addition, the redistribution of the black and white populations, creating a black majority in some central cities in the nation,
has had political repercussions. These changes have fostered not only
fears as to who will be elected to various offices from such districts,
but also fears of "takeovers" as well.

At an earlier time in United States history, changing population
distribution also contributed to changes in power. Farley has pointed
out that "slavery was not compatible with an urban environment."[12]
This was so because in the cities, blacks could more easily escape, get
other jobs, and congregate with other blacks for protection.

What appears in each of these situations, then, is fear on the part
of ethnic groups within a nation that differentials or changes in population processes will contribute to differentials in power between their
own group and others. Open warfare, attempts at regulation, or resistance to population policies may be the results of such fear.

The USSR, on the other hand, illustrates how population processes
like migration and distribution patterns may contribute to greater communication between various ethnic groups in a nation. Silver has

examined how the process of "Russification," or the learning of Russian in addition to one's native tongue, has been impeded or speeded up by various patterns of migration and population distribution in the USSR.[13] His analysis showed that those who had migrated outside of their native area or who lived in urban areas learned Russian more often than those who did not migrate or live in urban areas. In addition, Silver found that those who lived in urban areas outside of their native areas experienced the greatest impact of Russification. These migratory and population distribution patterns may then have an effect on nationalistic ties. Sharing a common language may increase understanding between various groups in the USSR.

We would not suggest here that the panacea for nations' political ills is reduced population growth or redistribution of population. What seems to be clear, however, is that population processes have a definite and important impact on political processes — effectiveness, forms, and power — within and between nations.

Population and Religion

In the chapters above, it has often been noted that religion is an important influence on population processes. The ways in which population can in turn influence religion may be less obvious. Two current influences will be discussed here: (1) the impact of population distribution on religion, and (2) the influence of population on religious doctrine and commitment.

Population Distribution and Religion

Originally the United States population was almost entirely Protestant, with few Catholics, Jews, or others. However, because of changing immigration patterns and differences in natural increase of religious groups, the population is now more heavily Catholic than it was in the early years. Particularly in urban areas, where large numbers of Jewish and Catholic immigrants settled, the Protestant majority has been scaled down.[14]

In addition to these consequences of international migration, internal residential mobility also influences religion. We have noted the increasing urban-to-suburban movement of people in developed countries. This means that the central city areas become populated with more and more blacks, members of other minority groups, and low-income whites. In addition, high proportions of older people are left in the central cities. Such movement has an impact on the formerly large and wealthy churches located in central city areas. Left with congregations that have low incomes, these churches may no longer be able to support the large buildings and varied programs that were offered before the exodus of higher-income and younger families.

In addition, however, people of different social classes are not distributed evenly among religious denominations. People of higher economic status, for example, are more often Episcopalian, Unitarian, Congregationalist, or Presbyterian, while people of low economic status more often join small sect groups or fundamentalist branches of the Baptist or Lutheran churches. As the concentration of people of low economic status in central cities has increased, there has been a large growth of "storefront" churches and sects of various kinds in these areas. Such groups tend to be temporary, and turnover of leaders and members is high. The practices and beliefs of such groups may be tailored to the needs and circumstances of the central city resident. Their financial survival is, of course, tenuous.

Still another impact on religion has come from the migrants to these central cities. Lenski has noted in Detroit, for example, that Southern rural migrants have often found the central city churches uncomfortable. Here the migration experience must be responded to by the churches.

> . . . the transition from the semirural South to a modern metropolitan community is in many respects a change comparable to that experienced by a first-generation immigrant from abroad. The metropolis is a new world filled with unfamiliar

institutions. The established white Protestant churches seem strange and unfamiliar by rural southern standards, and hence not especially attractive. A few congregations have been organized which seek to recapture the spirit and flavor of the rural, southern congregations, but such efforts are, at best, only partially successful.[15]

These are examples of the response of the religious institutions to the changes in population composition and distribution brought about by migration. Individual religious groups may also be affected by demographic processes in special ways. The Church of Jesus Christ of Latter-Day Saints, or Mormon church, for example, has not allowed blacks to hold the priesthood in the church, a position held by all white men. More recently, growing numbers of blacks have migrated to the Western areas of the United States, where the Mormon church has most of its membership. These blacks have been putting pressure of various kinds on the church to change this policy. In Salt Lake City, the center of the church, a group of black Mormons called The Genesis Group has organized to ask for recognition as full members in the church.

These examples illustrate the fact that both international migration and residential mobility within countries, by changing population composition and distribution, have influenced the form and nature of religious institutions.

Population and Religious Doctrine

Religions, like other institutions in society, do change their doctrines, practices, and membership in response to social changes of other kinds. Since religion has traditionally been the institution which sets moral guidelines for societies, these changes become very important.

In the case of the Mormon church and blacks, mentioned above, if the church grants the priesthood to blacks, that will be a change in its traditional beliefs and teachings stimulated at least in part by changing population composition. Some have suggested that population processes have also played a role in encouraging the Roman Catholic church to re-evaluate its stand on the use of birth control devices. We will present this argument here briefly as an example of the more subtle ways in which population processes can be at least one influence on doctrinal changes of this kind.

In the 1960s two population-related factors were in evidence. First, in many countries that were predominantly Catholic, population growth rates and the pressure on resources generated by these rates became very great. Poverty in Latin American countries, for example, was acute. Second, the development of the birth control pill made effective contraception possible and provided a way of eliminating unwanted children and hence relieving some of the pressure generated by large families.

The stand of the Catholic church on the use of any means of birth regulation other than rhythm has been consistently negative. But in the 1960s some priests were taking it upon themselves to counsel their parishioners in the use of effective contraception. This was in direct opposition to church policy. Debate raged within the Catholic church over the exact interpretation of previous rules. In developed countries it became apparent that growing numbers of Catholic women had begun to use contraception, feeling that the issue was in doubt. Some statement on the part of the church seemed necessary. A papal encyclical was issued in 1968 which reiterated the church stand opposing the use of any method of birth control except rhythm.[16]

The reactions of Catholic women to the encyclical, at least in developed countries where they are documented, were overwhelmingly negative. Some women left the church entirely rather than give up the use of effective contraception; others curtailed their involvement in the church or simply disobeyed the church view. Even some priests continued to counsel their parishioners in the use of birth control when the consequences of additional births in families seemed negative. Currently, over 80 percent of Catholic women in the United States are using some form of contraception prohibited by their church. What ultimate effect this will have on the cohesiveness of the Catholic Church remains to be seen.

It is, of course, entirely possible to interpret this sequence of events as the result of technological developments in birth control, political processes within the church, or other events quite distinct from population processes. It is also possible to suggest that population processes and pressures, on the family as well as the society level, were at least partly responsible for a change in adherence to religious teaching, if not a change in religious doctrine.

While religion has exerted stronger effects on population processes than the reverse, the above examples suggest that religion as an institution is not free from the effects of population growth, size, composition, and distribution.

Population and the Family

We began discussing the influences of population processes on other institutions by looking at societal impacts on education, the economy, and the environment. In this chapter we have moved from societal and group political effects of population to a consideration of population influences on religion for both the society and particular religious groups. We come finally to the family, the site of many decisions relating to fertility, mortality, and residential mobility. It is within the context of the family that many of the educational, economic, environmental, political, and religious consequences we have discussed have their impact on individuals.

Here we will examine three examples of this process: (1) population effects on the societal structure and importance of families, (2) population effects on the formation and composition of families, and (3) population effects on children and parents within families.

Population and Family Structure

The family has long been an important unit in society. It has been the mechanism by which status and privilege in societies are defined and the most basic unit of social organization. As other changes in social structure occur, so changes in the importance and form of the family occur as well. Population processes can also contribute to these changes.

In countries or continents now beginning to experience a trend toward urbanization, a tendency has been noted for the social structure to become based on contracts and formal associational arrangements rather than on kinship. In Africa, for example, the family is becoming less important in defining social status and rights and privileges than was the case before high rates of mobility and urbanization began.[17]

On the Ivory Coast these same population processes have eroded ethnic differences in family customs.[18] Women who move to urban areas tend to have about the same rates of marriage and to engage in roughly the same child-rearing practices, thereby blurring distinctions in these phenomena that existed between ethnic groups before the population was concentrated in urban areas.

These are changes that occur in urbanizing societies as migration rates increase. A similar effect has been found for the United States by Fenelon.[19] He states that divorce rates are higher in states with high migration rates. Even though divorce is still regarded as somewhat negative by the general population, Fenelon's hypothesis is that the prohibition against divorce cannot be effectively enforced in places where there is a high turnover of residents, and thus more impersonal social relationships. More recent research has indicated that this effect, while plausible, is really not very strong.[20] Divorce laws have been liberalized during the last several years in various states, and this could influence these findings. Further, the age structure of the populations in these states and their average age at marriage differ, and this may also offer a partial explanation for these patterns.

One of the principal duties of the family has traditionally been child rearing. These practices too can be influenced by population processes. In a study of Basque society, Kasdan reports that land cannot be subdivided between children upon the death of the parents because there would then not be enough land to support the growing population of the region.[21] To cope with this problem, Basque custom specifies that family farms will be inherited by the oldest son or daughter only. Thus, other children born to the family are taught to be self-reliant and aggressive in finding other ways to support themselves. Kasdan goes on to speculate that this practice predisposes the migrating Basque children to success at entrepreneurial careers.

Ireland is another country where limited amounts of land and high birth rates have combined to lead to special family practices. Kennedy has argued that one of the traditional reasons for lowering fertility in Western countries has been the desire to raise "quality" children.[22] This means, among other things, being able to provide educational and occupational opportunities for children as they grow up. In Ireland, where all children but the eldest can be expected to emigrate, Kennedy suggests that parents are not likely to plan far into the future with regard to the welfare of these children. Relieved of this burden, motivation to limit fertility is not strong.

In each of the cases above, population pressure induced by a shortage of land has led to family inheritance or child-rearing practices that in turn influence demographic processes. In this way, population influences the family and the family influences population patterns.

The Formation and Composition of Families

Because the family is such an important unit for demographic processes, those interested in studying population have seen the description of family processes to be important, quite apart from the impact of population on the family per se. The rate at which families form and dissolve and the resultant composition of those families is both a cause and a consequence of demographic patterns. Because of the importance of these topics, we will describe family formation and composition in some detail, using the United States as an example. Then we will explore life-cycle approaches to the study of the family, and finally consider special demographic circumstances that can influence family formation and composition patterns.

Interesting trends with regard to the prevalence and form of the family in the United States are beginning to emerge.[23] First, as Table

Table 8.1   Household and family characteristics, 1940–1974,
United States

Year	Percent of households which are families	Average population per family	Average population per household
1940	92.0	3.76	3.67
1950	90.2	3.54	3.37
1955	87.6	3.59	3.33
1960	85.4	3.67	3.33
1965	83.5	3.70	3.29
1970	81.4	3.58	3.14
1974	78.8	3.44	2.97

Source: U. S. Bureau of the Census, "Households and Families by Type: March 1974," *Current Population Reports*, Series P-20, No. 266, Tables 1 and 5.

8.1 shows, while the number of households and families in the United States have been increasing, families constitute a smaller and smaller proportion of households. A *household* consists of all persons who occupy a housing unit, while *family* refers to two or more persons living together who are related by blood, marriage, or adoption. In 1940 families were 92.0 percent of households; in 1974 they were only 78.8 percent.

The average population per family, also shown in Table 8.1, declined from 1940 to 1950, then rose until 1965, when it again declined. This reflects rising and falling birth rates during this period. The average population of households has declined from 1940 to 1974, owing both to decreased fertility and to an increase in the number of adults living alone.

These trends in the formation and composition of families and households are further amplified by Figure 8.1. This figure shows the first marriage rate, the divorce rate, and the remarriage rate for the United States population from 1920 to 1971. The pattern of first mar-

Figure 8.1   First marriage rates per thousand single women, divorce rates per thousand married women, and remarriage rates per thousand widowed or divorced women, United States, three-year averages, 1921 to 1971

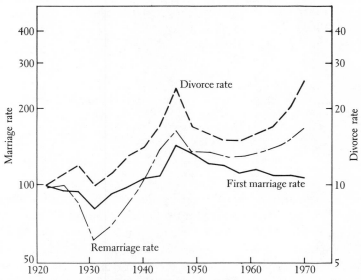

Source: Paul C. Glick and Arthur J. Norton, "Perspectives on the Recent Upturn in Divorce and Remarriage," *Demography*, Vol. 10, No. 3 (August 1973), 301–314, Figure 1.

riages looks much like the pattern of fertility during this time period. After declining in the Depression years, the rate of first marriages rose after World War II and has declined since that time.

Divorces and remarriages, on the other hand, show a similar pattern until after World War II, when instead of declining, these rates continue to rise. New data to 1974 indicate that while divorce rates are still climbing and rates of first marriages still declining, rates of remarriages are beginning to level off or decline somewhat.[24]

These trends mean that at present between 25 and 30 percent of

Table 8.2   Percentage of families with female heads, by color,
United States, 1955–1973

Year	Total	White	Negro
1955	10.1	9.0	20.7
1960	10.0	8.7	22.4
1965	10.5	9.0	23.7
1970	10.9	9.1	28.3
1973	12.2	9.6	34.6

Source: U. S. Bureau of the Census, "Female Family Heads," *Current Population Reports*, Series P-23, No. 50, July 1974, Table 1.

all women near thirty years old have ended or will end their first marriages in divorce.[25] If remarriage rates taper off, an additional increase in families headed by females will occur. Table 8.2 indicates that such families are already more numerous. Between 1955 and 1973, the number of families headed by females increased from 4.2 million to 6.6 million.[26] Among whites, females head 9.6 percent of families, while among Negroes, 34.6 percent of families are headed by females.

In Chapter 4 we speculated on the effect these changes may have on demographic processes. It is difficult to believe that childbearing and family-size patterns will not change at all. The important point here is to recognize that demographic patterns can change family patterns, which in turn change demographic patterns again.

Another way to look at the family is to use a life-cycle approach.[27] This approach emphasizes the interdependence of family and demographic characteristics by analyzing the ages at which families move from marriage to child rearing, children leaving home, and dissolution of the family. When these events are shown for cohorts of women born at different time periods, changes in the life-cycle patterns of the family can be seen.[28]

Figure 8.2 presents such data for women born from 1880 to 1939. This figure permits at least two kinds of comparisons: the trend in each of these events can be seen over time, and the relative space in years between each of these events can be examined for each birth cohort. In Chapter 4 attention was given to the first of these; we examined age patterns of marriage and childbearing over time. In Chapter 3 we examined trends and age patterns of mortality as well. We will concentrate here on the second of the comparisons mentioned.[29]

First, the interval between first marriage and birth of the first child has become somewhat longer. While the first child came almost immediately after marriage for women born in 1880–1889, the first child came two to three years after marriage for later cohorts. Since some of the lines in Figure 8.2 are based on projections, it is difficult to perceive any clear trend in the change in interval between first and last child for the younger cohorts. However, it seems clear that children are being spaced closer together by the later cohorts than by those born earlier.

The period of child rearing is rather prolonged for United States women, as can be seen by comparing ages at which the birth of the first child occurs with the ages at which the first marriage of the last child takes place. This latter event usually signals the beginning of the "empty nest" period. The period without children in the home until the dissolution of the marriage by death of one spouse is becoming longer and longer, owing primarily to the increase in life expectancy in combination with smaller family size and shorter birth intervals.

Using this life-cycle approach, then, we can see how changing demographic patterns of birth and death influence formation and composition of families. With this brief introduction to this approach, we can now look at these figures in another way in order to compare the life cycle of American families with the life cycle of Indian families.[30]

Table 8.3 shows the median age of husband and wife at stages of the family life cycle in the United States and in Banaras, India. If we compare the figures for 1950 in the United States with those for 1956

Figure 8.2   Stages of the family life cycle for women born from
1880 to 1939

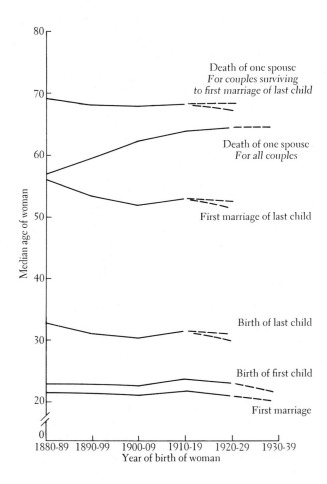

Source: Paul C. Glick and Robert Parke, Jr., "New Approaches in Studying the Life
Cycle of the Family," *Demography*, 2 (1965), 187–202, Figure 1.

in Banaras, several differences in the life-cycle pattern are apparent. We have noted that in American families, there is a short period before the birth of the first child, a relatively short interval between children, a prolonged period of child rearing, and then an extended period without children in the home. Collver has shown that in this area of India, these stages of the family life cycle were less distinct and overlapped to a greater degree. Childbearing began sooner, lasted longer, and overlapped with marriage of the children. Marriage of the last child typically post-

Table 8.3 Median ages of husband and wife at each stage of the family cycle, United States, and Banaras, India

Stage	Median age of husband				Median age of wife			
	Banaras	U.S.A.			Banaras	U.S.A.		
	1956	1890	1940	1950	1956	1890	1940	1950
First marriage								
Shadi[c]	13.6	—	—	—	10.9	—	—	—
Gauna[d]	17.3	26.1	24.3	22.8	14.6	22.0	21.6	20.1
Birth of first child	20.9	27.1	25.3	24.5	18.2	23.0	22.6	21.8
Birth of last child	39.7	36.0	29.9	28.8	37.0	31.9	27.2	26.1
Marriage of first child	36.9	51.1	48.3	46.0	34.2	47.0	45.6	43.3
Marriage of last child	55.7	59.4	52.8	50.3	53.0	55.3	50.1	47.6
Death of one spouse[a]	42.2	57.4	63.6	64.1	39.5	53.3	60.9	61.4
Death of one spouse[a]	47.2	a	a	a	44.5	a	a	a
Age at own death[b]	64.4	66.4	69.7	71.6	54.5	67.7	73.5	77.2

[a] The couple survives jointly to the age shown. The figures for Banaras and the United States are not exactly comparable, for Glick assumed that the deaths of husband and wife are independent events. The Banaras figures are computed on the assumption that they are correlated. If they were independent, the joint survival of a couple would be shortened by five years, to ages 42.2 and 39.5.

[b] Spouse survives separately from marriage.

[c] Shadi refers to the formal marriage ceremony.

[d] Gauna refers to the consummation of the marriage.

Source: Andrew Collver, "The Family Cycle in India and the United States," *American Sociological Review*, 28 No. 1 (February 1963), 86–96, Table 1.

dated the death of the parents. In short, in a society with high birth and death rates, the life-cycle patterns are quite different.

In any society, there are several demographic events which can interrupt or change the usual processes of family formation. One of these is called a marriage squeeze. In general, the term *marriage squeeze* refers to a shortage of potential marriage partners. This situation may arise because of age, sex, or racial-ethnic imbalances in the population.

For example, in countries like the United States it has been customary for females to marry males approximately two years older than themselves. But if in a two-year period the birth rate changes rather drastically, imbalances may occur. Suppose, for example, that men born in 1971 will be searching for potential brides among the women born in 1973. Since fertility was much lower in 1973 than in 1971, there are not enough females in the later cohort to provide brides for all these men. These men are then said to be in a marriage squeeze. Likewise, women born in the first year of the post-World War II baby boom have been looking for husbands in a cohort of men born before the baby boom began, and therefore experience a shortage of potential marriage partners.

The solutions to such age imbalance problems are to marry a person of the same age, to marry a person from an age cohort in which spouses are more plentiful, or to remain unmarried. Thus, fluctuations in the number of births affect the number of families formed and the societal definition of an acceptable marriage partner.

Likewise, racial or ethnic imbalances can cause redefinition of an acceptable marriage partner. Members of groups immigrating to countries where there are not enough potential spouses from their own group must remain single or marry those of races or religions ordinarily regarded as ineligible. In the United States, for example, the current sex ratio in the Filipino population is 122. This is an excess of 22 males for every 100 females. Conversely, the sex ratio for the Japanese population is 85, or fewer males than females.[31] Members of each of these populations may experience problems in finding marriage partners within their own ethnic group.

An interesting case of readjustment of marriage primarily owing to sex imbalances has been documented in the British Caribbean.[32] Because of heavy male emigration, the sex ratio in these islands does not permit the operation of a monogamous system of formal marriage. Marino has suggested that visiting sexual unions and common-law marriages have persisted on these islands because making legal, monogamous marriage the only legitimate setting for sexual relations would leave large numbers of women celibate. It is this adjustment of the family system that has enabled these islands to maintain high rates of fertility in spite of sexual imbalances, according to Marino.

These examples illustrate only some of the ways in which family formation and composition can be influenced by demographic processes.

Costs to Children and Parents

Still another way to view the impact of population processes on families is to examine the effect number of siblings has on the growth, development, and success of a child. Much research has been done on what happens to children who grow up in large or small families.[33]

Quite obviously, to sort out the direct influence of having many brothers and sisters, research must take into account the general economic status of the family. Since low-economic-status families have more children than high-economic-status families, differences in the developmental processes in large and small families may have more to do with this economic factor than with the sheer size of the family.

Many studies that have addressed the relationship of number of siblings to other characteristics of children have not controlled for economic status. Nevertheless, when economic status is controlled, impacts from large families still appear. Wray summarizes the results of this literature in this way:

> The effects associated with family size on the well-being
> of individuals — primarily the children — in a family are varied,
> but serious: increased illness, including malnutrition, serious

enough in younger children to increase mortality rates; less satisfactory growth and intellectual development. . . .[34]

In addition to economic explanations for this finding, some have postulated that the personal attention each child receives in large families is less. As Thomas notes, however, a great deal of personal care and attention may be given to children in large families by mothers and fathers motivated to do so.[35] The negative effects of having many brothers and sisters can thus be lessened, but it is not entirely clear that they can be eliminated.

Likewise, there are familial impacts from different patterns of child spacing. Maternal health may suffer from having children spaced close together. This is a rather obvious effect. But having children close together can produce negative consequences for the children as well:

> The evidence regarding the effects of birth interval is less extensive than that relating to family size but no less disconcerting. At first glance, the effects appear to be quite similar — increased mortality, increased morbidity, less satisfactory growth, and less adequate intellectual development. It appears, in fact, that excessive crowding of children — too many children too quickly — in a family with a young mother will produce the same effects quickly that excessive numbers of children will produce more slowly in larger families.[36]

The mention of the age of the mother is important here, since most of these studies have indicated that both these problems, large families and closely spaced children, are aggravated among young mothers.

Having additional children, or having children at all, of course influences the opportunities and lifestyles of parents as well. The United States Commission on Population Growth and the American Future estimates, for example, that the cost of having and raising the first child is $59,627.[37] This includes a college education and the money foregone by a wife who does not work so as to care for the child. Such figures are very difficult to calculate and will rise as costs of goods and services in the society rise. Nevertheless, the cost in dollars and cents has a real impact on families when children are added.

Finally, in an analysis of agrarian countries, Kingsley Davis has noted that population pressure tends to make it necessary that children be used as laborers and producers for families.[38] This factor not only lowers the overall productive capacity of the children later in life, but prevents the society from selecting those most able for given positions through a more prolonged education process.

In the sections above we have only touched on the myriad ways in which population processes can affect family formation, family structure, and members of families. Suffice it to say that while the family may be the institution that regulates the birth of children, and hence ultimately is the location of many population-relevant decisions, it in turn is influenced by these very processes.

Notes

1. Kingsley Davis, "Population and Power in the Free World," in *Population and World Politics*, ed. Philip M. Hauser, Free Press, Glencoe, Ill., 1958, pp. 193–213.
2. Gerry E. Hendershot, "Population Size, Military Power, and Antinatal Policy," *Demography*, 10, No. 4 (1973), 517–524.
3. A. F. K. Organski, Bruce Bueno de Mesquita, and Alan Lamborn, "The Effective Population in International Politics," in *Governance and Population: The Governmental Implications of Population Change*, Vol. IV of research reports of the U. S. Commission on Population Growth and the American Future, U. S. Government Printing Office, Washington, 1972, pp. 235–249.
4. Roger H. Davidson, "Population Change and Representation Government," in *Governance and Population*, pp. 58–82.

5. Daniel J. Elazar, "Population Growth and the Federal System," in *Governance and Population*, pp. 15–24.
6. John G. Grumm, "Population Change and State Government Policy," in *Governance and Population*, pp. 125–140.
7. Dov Friedlander and Eitan Sabatello, "Israel," *Country Profiles*, The Population Council (February 1972).
8. A historical and current analysis of this position can be found in Robert G. Weisbord, "Birth Control and the Black American: A Matter of Genocide?" *Demography*, 10 (November 1973), 571–590.
9. Quoted in Weisbord, p. 580.
10. Mary Treadwell, "Is Abortion Black Genocide?", *Family Planning Perspectives*, 4 (January 1972), 4.
11. Reynolds Farley, *Growth of the Black Population*, Markham, Chicago, 1970, p. 203.
12. Farley, p. 49.
13. Brian Silver, "The Impact of Urbanization and Geographical Dispersion on the Linguistic Russification of Soviet Nationalities," *Demography*, 2 (February 1974), 89–103.
14. For a fuller discussion of this process, see Gerhard Lenski, *The Religious Factor*, Anchor Books, Doubleday & Co., Inc., Garden City, N.Y., 1961, 1963, pp. 359–362.
15. Lenski, pp. 45–46.
16. A thorough discussion of events before and after the papal encyclical can be found in Leslie A. Westoff and Charles F. Westoff, *From Now to Zero*, Little, Brown, Boston, 1968, especially chap. 5.
17. Peter C. W. Gutkind, "African Urbanism, Mobility and the Social Network," *International Journal of Comparative Sociology*, 6 (March 1965), 48–60.
18. Remi Clignet, "Urbanization and Family Structure in the Ivory Coast," *Comparative Studies in Society and History*, 8 (July 1966), 385–401.
19. Bill Fenelon, "State Variations in United States Divorce Rates," *Journal of Marriage and the Family*, 33 (May 1971), 321–327.
20. James A. Weed, "Age at Marriage as a Factor in State Divorce Rate Differentials," *Demography*, 11 (August 1974), 361–375.

21. Leonard Kasdan, "Family Structure, Migration and the Entrepreneur," *Comparative Studies in Society and History*, 7 (July 1965), 345–367.
22. Robert E. Kennedy, Jr., *The Irish*, University of California Press, Berkeley, 1973, pp. 195–196.
23. Paul C. Glick and Arthur J. Norton, "Perspectives on the Recent Upturn in Divorce and Remarriage," *Demography*, 10 (August 1973), 301–314.
24. Personal conversation with Paul C. Glick, January 6, 1974.
25. Glick and Norton, p. 311.
26. U. S. Bureau of the Census, "Female Family Heads," *Current Population Reports*, Series P-23, No. 50, July 1974, p. 6.
27. Paul C. Glick and Robert Parke, Jr., "New Approaches in Studying the Life Cycle of the Family," *Demography*, 2 (1965), 187–202.
28. See also U. S. Bureau of the Census, "Marriage, Divorce, and Remarriage by Year of Birth: June 197i," *Current Population Reports*, Series P-20, No. 239, September 1972.
29. For a thorough discussion of these trends, see Glick and Parke.
30. Andrew Collver, "The Family Cycle in India and the United States," *American Sociological Review*, 28 (February 1963), 86–96.
31. Computed from U. S. Bureau of the Census, *U. S. Census of Population, 1970*, Vol. I, Part B.
32. Anthony Marino, "Family, Fertility, and Sex Ratios in the British Caribbean," *Population Studies*, 24 (July 1970), 159–172.
33. A summary of much of this research can be found in John A. Clausen and Suzanne R. Clausen, "The Effects of Family Size on Parents and Children," in *Psychological Perspectives on Population*, ed. James T. Fawcett, Basic Books, New York, 1973, pp. 185–208; and Joe D. Wray, "Population Pressure on Families: Family Size and Child Spacing," in *Rapid Population Growth Consequences and Policy Implications*, Johns Hopkins, Baltimore, 1971.
34. Wray, p. 454.
35. Darwin L. Thomas, "Family Size and Children's Characteristics," in *Population, Resources, and the Future: Non-Malthusian Perspectives*, ed. Howard M. Bahr, Bruce A. Chadwick and Darwin L.

Thomas, Brigham Young University Press, Provo, Utah, 1972, pp. 137–157.

36. Wray, p. 454.
37. The Commission on Population Growth and the American Future, *Population and the American Future*, Signet, New York, 1972, p. 128.
38. Kingsley Davis, "The Population Impact on Children in the World's Agrarian Countries," *Population Review* (Madras), 9 (January–July 1965), 17–31.

Suggested Additional Readings

For further reading on population consequences for the family, see:

Davis, Kingsley. "The American Family in Relation to Demographic Change." In *Demographic and Social Aspects of Population Growth*. Vol. I of research reports of the U. S. Commission on Population Growth and the American Future, U. S. Government Printing Office, Washington, 1972, pp. 237–265.

Espenshade, Thomas J. *The Cost of Children in Urban United States*. Population Monograph Series, No. 14, University of California, Berkeley, 1973.

Peck, Ellen, and Judith Senderowitz, eds. *Pronatalism: The Myth of Mom and Apple Pie*. Crowell, New York, 1974.

Wray, Joe D. "Population Pressure on Families: Family Size and Child Spacing." In Roger Revelle, ed. *Rapid Population Growth: Consequences and Policy Implications*. Johns Hopkins, Baltimore, 1971, pp. 403–461.

For a collection of readings on population and the polity see:

U. S. Commission on Population Growth and the American Future. *Governance and Population: The Governmental Implications of Popu-*

lation Change. Vol. IV of research reports, U. S. Government Printing Office, Washington, 1972.

Readings on population and religion include:

Nam, Charles B., ed. *Population and Society.* Houghton Mifflin, Boston, 1968, chap. 13.

Westoff, Charles F., and Larry Bumpass. "The Revolution in Birth Control Practices of U. S. Roman Catholics." *Science,* 179 (1973), 41–44.

Westoff, Leslie A., and Charles F. Westoff. *From Now to Zero.* Little, Brown, Boston, 1968, especially chap. 5.

"I ask you, what's wrong with the environment?"

Drawing by Alan Dunn; © 1972 The New Yorker Magazine, Inc.

9

Influencing Demographic Change

During the past few decades, as governments and the public have become more aware of population change, concerted efforts have been made to influence such change. In this final chapter, we shall be concerned with organized interventions in population processes. What have been some of the large-scale attempts to alter demographic conditions, and how successful have they been?

Strategies for Population Change

We have already indicated that population change is the result of myriad decisions by individuals, whose ideas are shaped by the groups to which they belong or aspire and whose behavior is facilitated or constrained by events in the world around them. The strategies for change that have been adopted from time to time have sought to provide bases for modifying these decisions of individuals. A strategy may be adopted to supplement, extend, or counteract another strategy. It may also serve to contend with a laissez-faire attitude on the part of groups or individuals, an attitude that suggests that one is powerless to change population conditions or that population events are predetermined.

The plans or methods for achieving certain goals within the population sphere take many forms, yet one can identify a few major approaches that characterize modern attempts to direct demographic change. Those discussed below include general economic and social development, fertility control, modifying social structures, educational approaches, and pluralistic approaches.

General Economic and Social Development

The theory of the demographic transition, as pointed out earlier, posits a relationship between social and economic change and demographic change. Basically, industrialization, urbanization, and other aspects of modernization are believed to be precipitating agents in, first, the decline of mortality and, later, the decline of fertility.

There is ample evidence that past reductions in the death rates of developing, as well as developed, nations can be ascribed in large part to economic and social improvements, some of which operated directly to raise the levels of living of families, and thereby improve their health and longevity, and some of which operated indirectly to improve life expectancy, such as medical advances. Nevertheless, it seems possible today to bring about substantial reductions in mortality without great economic and social changes. This has happened in some countries of Asia and Latin America, where the technology of mortality reduction has been borrowed from other countries. One might say, therefore, that substantial economic improvement may be a sufficient condition for a decline in mortality, but it is not today a necessary condition.[1]

Fertility seems to be less responsive to general economic and social improvements than mortality. In societies that have already completed the transition, the social changes that were associated with declines in death rates were also related to declines in birth rates, but only after a time lag. In many less-developed countries, even where economic and social changes were associated with mortality reductions, there has as yet been no substantial reduction in birth rates.

The notion of a "threshold" of economic development which must be exceeded if population growth rates are to be reduced was popular in the late 1950s and early 1960s and has gained favor in many quarters today. The argument is that demographic change can come about only if per capita income rises, but high fertility and declining mortality will produce a population growth rate that is too high, relative to normal economic development, for per capita income to go up.[2] The first major policy imperative with regard to reducing population growth thus was to make heavier economic investments in the development of low-income countries. The foreign aid programs of the United States and other developed nations incorporated sizable components which might help to break the threshold and thereby achieve reductions in birth rates.

The experiences of the late 1950s and early 1960s convinced many that general economic and social development could not by itself bring about changes in fertility. Improvements in per capita income were very modest and did not alter reproductive behavior. Much of the gain in per capita income contributed to countrywide changes that did not create meaningfully higher levels of living for individual families. Many thus argued that development must be accompanied by changes in attitudes and motivations toward fertility, as well as increased direct means for limiting family size, in order to be effective.

Fertility Control

Although fertility-control programs had existed before, it was not until the early 1960s that the family planning movement became widespread. The need to provide birth control to supplement economic and social development as means of limiting population growth became more apparent at that time. Knowledge-Attitude-Practice (KAP) studies of fertility were showing that people in many less-developed countries desired families that were considerably smaller than those they were having. Furthermore, they expressed interest in learning how to control their own fertility and asked for assistance in this respect.[3]

The family planning agencies which began to emerge throughout the world had several barriers to overcome — dealing with the erroneous ideas and misinformation about the reproductive process and its control that many people had, contending with some religious opposition to fertility control, and convincing national leaders that the activity was politically feasible.[4] By vast investments in reproductive technology, in educational and public relations activities, and in organization of support services, the family planning movement was given a great stimulus, and some of these barriers were overcome.

Programmatic goals for family planning programs were rarely elucidated as the movement developed, but the general assumption was that these programs were designed to enable couples to have the number of children they desired by facilitating access to contraceptive materials and educating people in their proper use. Newer means of contraception, such as the pill and the IUD, were heralded as important contributions to the arsenal of techniques that would enable the efficient control of births.

The value of the family planning approach has been debated vigorously for several years. Supporters of the approach have pointed to the countries where declines in the birth rate followed the implementation of fertility-control programs (e.g., Taiwan, Hong Kong, Singapore, Egypt, Chile, and South Korea). In addition, there have been substantial increases in attendance at birth control clinics, sharp rises in the sale and free distribution of contraceptives, and an elaboration of organizational structures to administer family planning programs, all of which are partial indicators of program success.

On the other hand, critics of the approach have pointed out that declines in fertility had begun long before family planning programs were instituted in the countries mentioned, that awareness and use of contraception does not guarantee subsequent birth rate declines, and that the approach itself might have some impact in the short run but would not provide the psychological and social bases for sustained fertility limitation.[5]

Writing in 1967, a staunch advocate of the family planning movement surveyed its performance and concluded:

> It is indeed too early to claim at this time in history that national family planning programs are sure to bring world population growth under control. But it is also entirely too early to make gloomy predictions as to the ultimate impact of

these programs which, after all, are still in their infancy. We must hope that family planning programs of five years from now will represent substantial improvement over those of today: better methods of contraception, more effective administration, more imaginative educational programs, and more sensitive methods of evaluation.[6]

A review of the situation in 1974 showed that some notable gains had been made in the areas of promise specified above. Between 1969 and 1974, the number of developing countries supporting the provision of family planning services increased from forty to sixty-three.[7] In about half of the sixty-three countries, including three-fourths of the people in the developing world, family planning was explicitly designed to decrease the rate of population growth. In the other countries, family planning was supported mainly on the grounds of health or human rights.

Contraceptive development programs have produced better products for currently used techniques as well as materials for innovative approaches in fertility control.[8] Family planning organizations have given greater consideration to administrative problems and to the need for evaluating program effectiveness. Yet the birth rate in many of the developing countries in 1974 was still high enough to maintain population growth rates of 2 percent a year or greater. Evidence that the family planning approach alone could produce desired changes was not yet available.

Modifying Social Structures

Despite its apparent partial success in controlling fertility, the family planning movement has suffered from a neglect of the behavioral bases of individuals' family limitation actions. A leading supporter of family planning efforts admitted:

It seems to me that birth control movements have shown a naïve preoccupation with methods. We experiment with one method, and when it does not work after half a trial, people get discouraged and say "My, my, we need a different method." With the next method the same thing happens, and the same thing happens on down the line. Always, we conclude that the method is wrong, when in fact the difficulty has been equally a weakness in motivation.

One cannot read the demographic record of Europe without realizing that the folk methods of birth control brought the birth rates down initially and are still of substantial importance. One could almost say that the decline of the birth rate caused the invention of modern contraception; this makes as much sense as saying that the invention of modern contraception caused the decline of the birth rate. The desire to limit fertility certainly stimulated the development of the various inventions.

That all populations have known effective means throughout history of controlling their fertility and that some have used them and some have not must suggest that there are problems of wider scope than those involving the gadgetry. The method is of course important as well, but I want to re-emphasize the proposition that the problem of altering people's behavior and giving adequate normative support to the altered form of behavior also lies at the core of our concern. . . .[9]

Davis has indicated that the neglect of motivation goes even deeper than is first supposed. The family planning movement does, indeed, concern itself with motivation of individuals insofar as it relates to acceptance of particular contraceptive methods, but there does not seem to be much concern about the motivation to restrict family size.[10] Moreover, if family planning is the first step in a sequence of population-control stages, and is viewed as a means of quickly reducing the birth rate until institutional supports for lower fertility are provided, then we lack the overall plan for specifying the next steps.

Berelson has responded to this criticism by cataloguing the approaches suggested by some that go beyond voluntary family planning. These include:[11]

A. Extensions of voluntary fertility control
    1. Institutionalization of maternal care in rural areas of developing countries as a means of offering family planning education and services
    2. Liberalization of induced abortion
B. Establishment of involuntary fertility control
    1. Mass use of fertility control agents by government to regulate births at an acceptable level
    2. Marketable licenses to have children, the number of which is controlled to produce a replacement level of fertility
    3. Temporary sterilization of all women via time-capsule contraceptives that would permit reversal by government approval
    4. Compulsory sterilization of men with three or more children, and induced abortion of all illegitimate pregnancies
C. Intensified educational campaigns
    1. Inclusion of population materials in school systems
    2. Promotion of national satellite television systems for information on population and family planning
D. Incentive programs
    1. Payment for the use of contraception and sterilization
    2. Payment for periods of nonpregnancy or nonbirth
E. Tax and welfare benefits and penalties
    1. Withdrawal of maternity benefits
    2. Withdrawal of child or family allowances
    3. Tax on births after a given number
    4. Limitation of government-supported social programs to families with few children
    5. Reversal of tax benefits to favor the unmarried and parents of few children
    6. Provision by the state of a limited total number of years of free

schooling to a family, to be allocated by the family among
their children
7. Pensions for poor parents with few children
F. Shifts in social and economic institutions
1. Increase in minimum age of marriage
2. Facilitation of female participation in the labor force
3. Direct manipulation of the family structure to reduce the non-economic utility of offspring
4. Promotion of two types of marriage — one childless and readily dissolved, and the other licensed for children and designed to be stable
5. Encouragement of long-range social trends leading toward lower fertility
6. Continued reductions in infant and child death rates
G. Approaches via political channels and organizations
1. Population control as a condition for economic aid
2. Reorganization of national and international agencies to deal with population problems
3. Promotion of a zero population growth rate
H. Augmented research efforts
1. Research on social means of achieving fertility goals
2. Research on practical methods of sex determination
3. Research on improved contraceptive technology

In terms of scientific, medical, and technological readiness; political
viability; administrative feasibility; economic capability; moral, ethical,
and philosophical acceptability; and presumed effectiveness, some of the
suggestions seem sound and others of dubious merit. Berelson has
suggested rating each proposal by these criteria (Table 9.1). While all
the proposals have some potential, several of them seem more likely to
be implemented than others.

Modification of the structures of societies requires profound alterations in values and norms and customary ways of behaving. It also
assumes a population with a more rationalistic belief system than is
found among many groups today. Yet, on the face of it, the above set

of alternative, non-family planning approaches to controlling population growth offers additional means of making economic development and fertility control more effective in directing demographic change.

Educational Approaches

Of all the potential non-family planning approaches mentioned, one that seems likely to be feasible and to have a lasting effect on population conditions is population education. The broadest definition of population education includes sex education, family-life education, population-awareness education, and provision of basic value orientations.[12] Each of these aspects has received some attention, both in schools and through the mass media and other forms of out-of-school education.

Those elements of the broader concept of population education which are most controversial tend to be in areas involving techniques of fertility control and human physiological processes. In the United States, opposition in some parts of the country to the introduction of sex education in the elementary and secondary grades led some state legislatures to withhold funds for such a purpose. Public information programs, such as that carried out by SIECUS (the Sex Information and Education Council of the United States), for example, have helped to change the climate of opinion about sex education in some places.

Some treatments of population education are designed to indoctrinate individuals into certain ways of thinking about population. These, too, are likely to be controversial and to engender resistance, especially on the part of parents whose children are being instructed to accept views contrary to their own.

Probably the fastest-growing approach to population education is one which stresses population awareness and which defines it as "the process by which the student investigates and explores the nature and meaning of population processes, characteristics, and changes for himself, his family, his society, and the world."[13] Population is viewed not as a problem to be solved, but as a phenomenon to be understood. Emphasis is on the causes and consequences of population patterns. The student learns about various alternative solutions to population

Table 9.1   Illustrative appraisal of proposals by criteria

	Scientific readiness	Political viability	Administrative feasibility
A. Extension of voluntary fertility control	High	High on maternal care, moderate to low on abortion	Uncertain in near future
B. Establishment of involuntary fertility control	Low	Low	Low
C. Intensified educational campaigns	High	Moderate to high	High
D. Incentive programs	High	Moderately low	Low
E. Tax and welfare benefits and penalties	High	Moderately low	Low
F. Shifts in social and economic institutions	High	Generally high, but low on some specifics	Low
G. Political channels and organizations	High	Low	Low
H. Augmented research efforts	Moderate	High	Moderate to high
Family planning programs	Generally high, but could use improved technology	Moderate to high	Moderate to high

Economic capability	Ethical acceptability	Presumed effectiveness
Maternal care too costly for local budget, abortion feasible	High for maternal care, low for abortion	Moderately high
High	Low	High
Probably high	Generally high	Moderate
Low to moderate	Low to high	Uncertain
Low to moderate	Low to moderate	Uncertain
Generally low	Generally high, but uneven	High over long run
Moderate	Moderately low	Uncertain
High	High	Uncertain
High	Generally high, but uneven on religious grounds	Moderately high

issues and the reasons different people have opted for different courses. In this manner, the techniques of rationalistic thinking are strengthened, and the "population actor" can arrive at a decision about behavior that follows from consideration of a number of possibilities and that is personally meaningful.[14] This educational process, which systematizes population learning, can be introduced to out-of-school youth, as well as to adults, through the mass media and community educational programs.[15]

The educational approach to population learning is the principal approach of the Population Reference Bureau; it is currently fostered mostly through university-based programs in the United States. The ministries of education in Sri Lanka, India, and the Philippines, for example, have developed pilot population-education projects for their schools, and other countries are moving in this direction.

It remains to be seen how effective this kind of movement will be in terms of population trends. Its impact on young people might be seen principally in the areas of knowledge and attitude change, and only secondarily in the area of behavior. Its impact on adult behavior could be more immediate; however, lifelong learning is regarded as a more substantial basis for education that involves the development of values and norms than is learning only at older ages, which might present the person with views that are at variance with those he or she was indoctrinated in earlier in life.

Pluralistic Approaches

That no single approach to population control is adequate is a conclusion that can be reached by studying the means that have brought down the population growth rate in developed countries. Davis showed that reduction in population increase in many societies was the result of a determined, *multiphasic demographic response* (the implementation of a variety of means of effecting population change).[16] Even in countries where the declines are traditionally linked to a single factor, a number of means can be identified.

In Japan, abortion programs were complemented by postponed marriage, widespread contraceptive use, the introduction of sterilization, and emigration. In Ireland, population decline may have been due principally to emigration, but late age at marriage, high rates of celibacy, and extensive birth control also took place there. Other countries of Europe likewise combined a variety of means to reduce population growth. Their multiphasic responses differed from those of Ireland and Japan only in the relative emphasis placed on the various means.

Rich has provided evidence that combining policies that give special attention to improving the well-being of the poor majority of the population with large-scale, well-executed family planning programs should make it possible to stabilize population in developing countries much faster than relying on either approach alone.[17] Those developing countries that have already brought down their birth rates to a significant extent have also spread social and economic benefits among a majority of the population, thereby contributing to the motivation to have small families.

Commissions and Conferences: Stimuli for Action?

The debate about population change, its determinants and consequences, has entered the public arena in a substantial way. The mass media (newspapers, journals, and radio and television programs, in particular) have enabled a wide audience to learn about many of the issues and the views taken by speakers from different segments of society. Scholars, politicians, and religious leaders, among others, have presented their opinions. It is probably the case, however, that little of the day-to-day debate about population issues reaches the masses of people who are affected by the course of demographic change. It is even questionable how much impact much of this material has had on key decision makers in different societies. Commissions and conferences designed to survey the demographic situation and make recommendations regarding population problems offer a means of focusing attention on key issues and arriving at a consensus for change. Do these efforts, in effect, produce consensus and the stimuli for action? A review of one national commission's work and developments at a world conference are informative in this regard.

The Commission on Population Growth and the American Future[18]

A number of countries have established national commissions concerned with population issues. In 1969, for the first time in the history of the United States, the President and the Congress set up a commission to examine the growth of the population and its impact on the American future. The commission was asked to examine the probable extent of population growth and internal migration in the United States until the end of the century. It was also asked to assess the impact that population change will have upon government services, the economy, and resources and the environment, and to make recommendations on how the nation can best cope with that impact.

The commission spent two years conducting an extensive inquiry, during which it solicited research reports, heard numerous witnesses testify in public hearings and in executive meetings, and prepared a series of reports surveying population conditions in the United States and giving numerous recommendations for influencing demographic change in the future.

The recommendations of the commission were by no means arrived at unanimously. The group was composed of individuals from different walks of life — including minorities, youths and the elderly, women and men, rich and poor, governmental leaders and social scientists — and it was often difficult to achieve consensus on specific matters. In fact, the commission began its main report by citing three distinct approaches to dealing with population issues, apparently a reflection of the diversity of opinions on the commission itself.

The first approach acknowledges the benefits to be gained by slowing growth, but regards the population problem today primarily as a result of large numbers of people being unable to control an important part of their lives — the number of children they have. In this view, freedom of choice and equality of access to the means of fertility control is seen as the desirable means of achieving desired family size. This approach depends on education, research, and national debate to illuminate population issues that transcend individual welfare. It assumes that in this way the best collective decisions about population issues, based on knowledge of the tradeoffs between demographic choices and the quality of life, would be achieved. It also assumes that the situation will be reconsidered from time to time, with the expectation that new decisions might be forthcoming.

A second approach acknowledges the need for education and knowledge but stresses that the population problem is but one facet of the more general problem of denial of equal opportunity. Discrimination against ethnic minorities, women, the economically deprived, and other groups makes it difficult for them to act freely in matters relating to population. Permitting fuller access to social opportunities, it is reasoned in this view, will also result in modification of behavior relative to population.

Still a third approach looks at population in an ecological framework and calls for a far more fundamental shift in the operative values of modern society. In this view, the need for more education and knowledge and the need to eliminate poverty and racism are important but not all-important. The population problem is felt to be a concrete symptom of the imbalance between people and nature occasioned by the destructive effects of mass urban industrialism. To remedy the situation, a new set of values concerning nature, the economy, and human identity is needed that will reject the growth ethic and promote realization of the highest potential of individual humanity.

Despite these disparities in basic positions, the commission endorsed, with occasional dissenting opinions, a series of recommendations covering forty-seven areas of significance to population development. These recommendations (presented in Appendix A) deal with population and sex education; child care, children born out of wedlock, and adoption; equal rights for women, racial minorities, and the poor; voluntary sterilization, abortion, other methods of fertility control, and fertility-related health services; the relation of contraception to the law and to minors; family planning and health training and services, for teenagers as well as adults; population stabilization; immigration, illegal aliens, population distribution, and migration policies; guiding urban expansion and assisting depressed rural areas; and a variety of research and government organizational steps that would facilitate the study of population trends and their consequences and permit government action, when and where needed.

Many of the recommendations involve actions that would be universally acceptable provided the funds to implement them could be generated. Several recommendations, however, caused controversy when they were reported and may have drawn attention away from the numerous other recommendations in the commission's report. The controversial areas included provision of birth control information and services for teenagers and the liberalization of abortion laws.

The negative reaction of former President Nixon to the controversial recommendations, and his failure to endorse the commission's work generally, muted the effect of the commission's labors. The crucial recommendation that the nation welcome and plan for a stabilized population was presented to the Congress and the public at a time when the country's birth rate had already declined sharply and appeared to be dropping to a level consistent with a stable population. It may not be surprising, therefore, that many of the actions anticipated by the commission following their report did not come to pass. But the commission had informed the public about population conditions in the United States to perhaps a greater extent than ever before, and, should population trends be altered, there is much in the commission's main report and research appendixes that can be instructive to lay people as well as to national and community leaders.

World Population Conference, 1974[19]

Conventions of experts to discuss world population trends and their consequences have been held at various points in time since 1927, but the World Population Conference of 1974 was held when greater attention was being given to population issues in the world than at any previous time. More and more nations were becoming aware of the role population growth was playing in the welfare of the society and its members, and they were prepared to discuss the issues and their resolution. Like the United States, more than fifty countries had set up population commissions that would establish national positions and present them at the conference.

The meeting, which took place in Bucharest, Rumania, in August 1974, actually consisted of two separate but related forums. The first was a conference of government delegates who were to consider and vote on a United Nations–sponsored World Population Plan of Action. The second was a Population Tribune involving nongovernmental organizations. The two-week meeting often included lively debates on critical population issues in which one party would favor the original Plan of Action that stressed the need for reducing population growth and suggested fertility control measures to bring that about, and another would argue that heavier investment by developed countries to advance the economic and social development of developing countries is necessary *before* population limitation can become a reality.[20] Some nations (especially in Africa and Latin America) took the position that further population growth would be beneficial, others preferred a laissez-faire attitude toward population change, and a great number of countries favored hastening the decline of population growth rates.

In the last analysis, the conference agreed upon a revised Plan of Action (with only the Vatican refraining from support) that incorporated some demographic recommendations and broader social and economic imperatives. Highlights of the accepted plan are presented on the following page.

A Look to the Future

From the foregoing discussion, one can get the impression that there is more interest in influencing demographic change today than ever before, even if there is not a consensus among countries, or among

Highlights of the World Population Plan of Action as agreed
by the World Population Conference at Bucharest

Population policies and programs are an integral part of economic and social
development and should be directed toward the ultimate goal of improving
the quality of life for all men, women, and children. To this end, the World
Population Conference recommends that:

1. Governments should develop national policies and programs relating to
    the growth and distribution of their populations, if they have not al-
    ready done so, and the rate of population change should be taken into
    account in development programs.
2. Countries should aim at a balance between low rather than high death
    rates and birth rates.
3. Highest priority should be given to the reduction of high death rates.
    Expectation of life should exceed sixty-two years in 1985 and seventy-
    four years in 2000. Where infant mortality continues high, it should
    be brought down to at least 120 per thousand live births by the year
    2000.
4. Because all couples and individuals have the basic human right to de-
    cide freely and responsibly the number and spacing of their children,
    countries should encourage appropriate education concerning respon-
    sible parenthood and make available to persons who so desire advice
    and means of achieving it.
5. Family planning and related services should aim at prevention of un-
    wanted pregnancies as well as elimination of involuntary sterility or sub-
    fecundity to enable couples to achieve their desired number of children.
6. Where family planning programs exist they should be coordinated with
    health and other services designed to raise the quality of life.
7. Countries which consider their birth rates detrimental to their national
    purposes are invited to set quantitative goals and implement policies to
    achieve them by 1985.
8. Developed countries should develop appropriate policies in population,
    consumption, and investment, bearing in mind the need for funda-
    mental improvement in international equity.
9. Because the family is the basic unit of society, governments should as-
    sist families as far as possible through appropriate legislation and ser-
    vices.
10. Governments should ensure full participation of women in the educa-
    tional, economic, social, and political life of their countries on an equal
    basis with men.
11. Countries that wish to increase their rate of population growth should

do so through low mortality rather than high fertility, and possibly immigration.

12. To achieve the projected declines in population growth and the projected increases in life expectancy, birth rates in the developing countries should decline from the present level of thirty-eight to thirty per thousand by 1985, which will require substantial national efforts and international assistance.

13. In addition to family planning, measures should be employed that affect such socioeconomic factors as reduction in infant and childhood mortality, increased education particularly for females, improvement in the status of women, land reform, and support in old age.

14. To assure needed information concerning population trends, population censuses should be taken at regular intervals and information concerning birth and deaths should be made available at least annually.

15. Policies should be developed to reduce the undesirable consequences of excessively rapid urbanization and to develop opportunities in rural areas and small towns, recognizing the right of individuals to move freely within their national boundaries.

16. International agreements should be concluded to regulate the migration of workers and to assure nondiscriminatory treatment and social services for these workers and their families.

17. National efforts should be intensified through expanded research programs to develop knowledge concerning the social, economic, and political interrelationships with population trends; effective means of reducing infant and childhood mortality; new and improved methods of fertility regulation to meet the varied requirement of individuals and communities, including methods requiring no medical supervision; the interrelations of health, nutrition, and reproductive biology; and methods for improving the administration, delivery, and utilization of social services, including family planning services.

18. International, intergovernmental, and nongovernmental agencies and national governments should increase their assistance in the population field on request.

19. In exercising their sovereign right to determine their population policies and programs, governments should do so consistent with human rights and the effects of their national policies on the interests of other nations and of mankind.

20. The Plan of Action should be closely coordinated with the International Development Strategy for the Second United Nations Development Decade, reviewed in depth at five-year intervals, and modified as appropriate.

Source: Population Crisis Committee Circular, September 26, 1974.

groups within countries, concerning the desirable direction of influence. A positive outlook might lead one to welcome this development on the grounds that greater population awareness will provide the basis for rational solutions to population problems in the future. And so long as the dialogue among countries and groups continues, there is some prospect that common solutions will be reached that will enable population developments to take place within a framework of maximum human welfare.

Notes

1. Ansley J. Coale and Edgar M. Hoover, *Population Growth and Economic Development in Low-Income Countries*, Princeton University Press, Princeton, N.J., 1958, p. 14.
2. A classic statement of this thesis is in Harvey Leibenstein, A *Theory of Economic-Demographic Development*, Princeton University Press, Princeton, N.J., 1954, chaps. 4–6.
3. Bernard Berelson, "KAP Studies on Fertility," in *Family Planning and Population Programs*, ed. Bernard Berelson et al., University of Chicago Press, Chicago, 1966, p. 660.
4. Leona Baumgartner, "Family Planning Around the World," in Berelson et al., pp. 277–294.
5. Philip M. Hauser, "Family Planning and Population Programs: A Book Review Article," *Demography*, 4, No. 1 (1967), 397–414.
6. Oscar Harkavy, "Impact of Family Planning Programs on the Birth Rate," paper prepared for the Eighth International Conference of the International Planned Parenthood Federation, Santiago, Chile, April 9–15, 1967 (also issued as a Ford Foundation Reprint).
7. Dorothy Nortman, "Population and Family Planning Programs: A Factbook," in *Reports on Population/Family Planning*, No. 2, 6th ed., December 1974 (a publication of The Population Council).
8. Bruce Schearer, "Tomorrow's Contraception," in *Toward the End of Growth*, ed. Charles F. Westoff, Prentice-Hall, Englewood Cliffs, N.J., 1973, pp. 47–56.

9. Frank W. Notestein, "Keynote Address," in *Population Dynamics: International Action and Training Programs,* ed. Minoru Muramatsu and Paul A. Harper, Johns Hopkins, Baltimore, 1965, pp. 5–6.

10. Kingsley Davis, "Population Policy: Will Current Programs Succeed?" *Science,* 158 (November 10, 1967), 733.

11. Reprinted with the permission of The Population Council from "Beyond Family Planning," by Bernard Berelson, Studies in Family Planning, No. 38 (February 1969), p. 1–3.

12. Ozzie G. Simmons, "Population Education: A Review of the Field," *Studies in Family Planning,* No. 52 (April 1970), 1–5.

13. Stephen Viederman, "Population Education in Elementary and Secondary Schools in the United States," in *Aspects of Population Growth Policy,* Vol. VI of research reports of the U. S. Commission on Population Growth and the American Future, U. S. Government Printing Office, Washington, 1972, p. 433.

14. Byron G. Massialas, "Population Education as Exploration of Alternatives," *Social Education,* 36 (April 1972), 347–356.

15. Thomas Poffenberger, "Population Learning and Out-of-School Youth in India," *Studies in Family Planning,* 2 (August 1971), 171–175.

16. Kingsley Davis, "The Theory of Change and Response in Modern Demographic History," *Population Index,* 29 (October 1963), 345–366.

17. William Rich, *Smaller Families Through Social and Economic Progress,* Overseas Development Council, Washington, 1973.

18. The discussion in this section is based on the Commission's principal report, *Population and the American Future,* The Report of the Commission on Population Growth and the American Future, U. S. Government Printing Office, Washington, 1972).

19. The summary which follows is based partly on United Nations Fund for Population Activities, *WPY Bulletin,* No. 16 (September–October 1974), and partly on the special conference issue of *People,* 1, No. 5 (1974), published by the International Planned Parenthood Federation.

20. For an enlightening presentation of typical views of the opposing

camps, see the exchanges between Pierre Pradervand and R. T. Ravenholt in *Equilibrium*, 2 (April 1974), 12–17.

Suggested Additional Readings

Piotrow, Phyllis Tilson. *World Population Crisis: The United States Response*. Praeger, New York, 1973. An informative review of the historical stance of the United States Government on population issues that reveals the restrained effort until very recently to influence world demographic change.

U. S. Commission on Population Growth and the American Future. *Commission Research Reports*. 7 vols. U. S. Government Printing Office, Washington, 1972. These reports provide substantial documentation for many of the Commission's recommendations, as well as research and opinion which suggest contrary positions.

Driver, Edwin D. *Essays on Population Policy*. Heath, Lexington, Mass., 1972, chaps. 3 and 4. A useful summary of the various types of direct and indirect population-related policies in the United States in recent years.

Organisation for Economic Co-operation and Development. *Population International Assistance and Research*. OECD, Paris, 1969. Discusses the population assistance programs of governmental and nongovernmental organizations throughout the world at the time of the report.

"A Report on Bucharest." *Studies in Family Planning*, 5 (December 1974). A complete report of the 1974 World Population Conference which presents the detailed World Population Plan of Action.

Glossary

The following terms used in the text are listed here with brief definitions and/or explanations as a ready reference for understanding the dimensions of population status and change.

Age.   A fundamental characteristic of population structure, usually expressed in years. For most demographic purposes, age is reckoned as of last birthday, but sometimes it refers to nearest birthday. According to the traditional Chinese method of counting age, a person is one year old at birth and becomes a year older at every Chinese New Year.

Age-sex pyramid.   A histogram, or vertical bar chart, that portrays the relative number of males and females in each age category of the population. Because of normal population processes the chart often assumes the general shape of a pyramid, but it can assume a variety of forms.

Cause of death.   The reported reason for death, such as a disease, condition, or misfortune. Frequently, multiple or joint causes of death are given, and a distinction may be made between immediate and underlying causes.

Census.   Typically a complete canvass of the population of a given area that lists the people and some of their characteristics.

Cohort fertility.   The number of births experienced over time by a group of women or men who were born at about the same time (a birth cohort) or married at about the same time (a marriage cohort). (See *Period fertility* for a contrasting measure.)

Components of population change.   The basic processes of mortality, fertility, and residential mobility, which account for all variations in population size over time.

Contraception.   The prevention of conception; it may involve mechanical, chemical, or surgical means, or the regulation of intercourse to avoid the ovulation stage of the menstrual cycle.

Crude rate.   A ratio of the number of events (births or deaths) reported in an area during a year to the total population of that area.

Demographic transition.   An historical transformation of birth and death rates from high to low levels; the decline in mortality precedes the decline in fertility, thus leading to substantial population increase.

Demography.   The scientific study of human populations, including their size, composition, distribution, and characteristics, and the causes and consequences of changes in these factors.

Dependency ratio.   The ratio of the older and/or younger segments of the population to those in the middle age groups. It assumes that the latter generally provide support for the former, and hence the measure is an approximation of the economic burden carried by those in prime working ages.

Desired family size.   The number of own children a woman would like to have, irrespective of other considerations. (Sometimes called *preferred family size.*)

Emigration.   The departure of persons from a country for other places outside the country's borders.

Employment status.   Whether or not an individual is working full-time or part-time (employed) or without a job but looking for work (unemployed) during a specific period of time.

Ethnic status.   Classification of an individual on the basis of race, color, nationality, religion, or other cultural background factors.

Expected family size.   The number of own children a woman anticipates having, with due consideration for possible inability to control childbearing in conformity with her desires.

Family.   Two or more persons living in the same housing unit who are related by blood, marriage, or adoption. (Related persons who live elsewhere are not part of a family, demographically speaking, although they are often reported in the social science literature as members of an extended family.) Family units may be further differentiated according to internal relationships (e.g., there may be two or more marital sets within one family).

Fecundity.   The physiological capacity of a woman, man, or couple to produce a living child. Lack of fecundity may be due to physical or biological impairments, to prolonged psychological inhibitions, or to surgical operation (sterilization). The term *subfecundity* is used to indicate that the capacity is below normal for any of the above reasons, but that this may not be a permanent condition.

Fertility.   Actual reproductive performance, or the bearing of a live child by a woman.

Fetal death.   A stillbirth, spontaneous abortion, miscarriage, or other development which terminates the life of a fetus (or pregnancy) before birth.

Gross reproduction rate.   The average number of live daughters that would be born to each member of a female birth cohort that completes the reproductive cycle, subject to current age-specific fertility rates (that is, those prevailing in the population at the time). The measure is thus a hypothetical one that illustrates the reproductive consequences of a given fertility schedule.

Household.   A group of persons who occupy a housing unit. A household may consist of one person living alone, two or more unrelated individuals, one or more families, or a combination of families and unrelated individuals. In addition to some household members who are not family members, there are some persons (such as military personnel in barracks or residents of homes for the aged) who are not (private) household members.

Ideal family size.   The number of children a person regards as most suitable for themselves or others to have.

Immigration.   The entry of people into a country from places outside the country's borders. While attempts are made to record all such movements, there are frequent illegal entries which go unrecorded.

In-migration.   Movement into a political unit (such as a county) from some place outside the unit.

Infant mortality rate.   The ratio of deaths of children under one year of age in a given year to the total number of live births registered in the same year. Often this rate is broken down into deaths during the first month of life (neonatal deaths) and deaths during the remainder of the year (post-neonatal deaths).

Labor force.   The total number of persons currently employed (at work) and unemployed (not at work but seeking a job). Persons in neither category (such as many housewives, students, and retired persons) are regarded as not in the labor force.

Life expectancy.   The average number of years of life remaining to each of a group of persons reaching a particular age. At age zero, this measure, which is derived from a life table, is heavily influenced by survival rates during infancy.

Life span.   The maximum possible number of years of life a person could expect to live.

Local movers.   Persons who change their permanent residence but do not move across a critical boundary (e.g., a county boundary in the United States).

Logistic curve.   A mathematical function which describes fairly well the long-term growth of world (and many national) populations. The curve first increases at an increasing rate, then continues to increase at a decreasing rate, and ultimately approaches an upper asymptote (or levels off).

Marital status.   Matrimonial condition, typically broken down into single (never married), currently married, divorced, separated, and widowed. Among the currently married, legal and consensual marriages are sometimes differentiated.

Metropolitan area.   A central city plus an adjacent area which is socially and economically integrated with the central city. In the United States, the standard metropolitan statistical area is composed of one or more contiguous counties, at least one of which has a city of 50,000 or more on which all the counties depend for economic activity.

Migrant.   A person who changes permanent residence and in the process crosses a critical boundary (e.g., a county boundary in the United States).

Migration.   Movement of people across a critical boundary (e.g., a county boundary in the United States) for the purpose of establishing a new permanent residence.

Mortality.   Death of members of a population.

Movers.   People who change their permanent residence, regardless of the distance or direction of the move; this includes both migrants and local movers.

Natural decrease.   An excess of deaths over births in a population during a given period of time.

Natural increase.   An excess of births over deaths in a population during a given period of time.

Neonatal deaths.   Deaths which occur during the first month (or four weeks) of life after birth.

Net reproduction rate.   The average number of live daughters that would be born to each member of a female birth cohort that completes the reproductive cycle, subject to current age-specific fertility and mortality rates. It differs from the gross reproduction rate in that allowance is made for mortality of some of the women before they complete the reproductive cycle.

Optimum population.   The number of people in an area that would best facilitate a balance of people and goods. The goods may be measured in terms of various resources or other economic or social criteria. Overpopulation exists when the population is considered too large for the allocation of goods, and underpopulation exists when the population is below what the optimum balance would be.

Out-migration.   Movement out of a political unit (such as a county in the United States) to some other place.

Period fertility.   The current reproductive performance of a group of women or men, or their fertility during a particular period of time. (See *Cohort fertility* for a contrasting measure.)

Population characteristics.   Items of information which distinguish certain people (such as their education, occupation, and religion).

Population composition.   Classification of people according to basic demographic attributes (e.g., age, race, sex).

Population density.   The total number of people in an area in relation to the size of the area (e.g., the number of persons per square kilometer).

Population distribution.   The geographical spread or arrangement of people over units of land area (e.g., between urban and rural areas or among places of different size).

Population education.   The teaching and learning of the dynamics of population change and its causes and consequences. Such education may occur at any level of formal schooling (from primary grades through the university) or in out-of-school situations (through adult education or the mass media).

Population equation.   The formula which indicates that population change in an area between two points in time equals births during the time interval minus deaths during the interval plus or minus the net movement into and out of the area. This formula is sometimes referred to as the *balancing equation of population.*

Population estimate.   An indirect determination of the size or other aspects of a population, usually when direct information is lacking. The calculated number may relate to past, present, or future status.

Population explosion.   A term used in the popular literature to refer to a period of rapid population increase. It is most often used to describe the stage of the demographic transition where the gap between birth and death rates is the greatest.

Population growth.   An increment to the size of a population resulting from the balance of births, deaths, and residential movements (the basic components of population change).

Population growth rate. A measure of the average annual increase in size of a population over a period of time. (For example, in recent years, the world's population growth rate was about 2 percent per year.)

Population policy. Stipulated and understood means by which a government (or other formal organization) intends to influence population change.

Population projections. Estimates of future numbers of people based on certain assumptions regarding fertility, mortality, and residential mobility.

Population redistribution. The geographical relocation of people over a period of time as a result of the basic population processes of fertility, mortality, and residential mobility.

Population register. A continuous registration system in which a card or listing on every member of the population is maintained and updated by local registration officers. A person's record is transferred when the person changes residence.

Race. A group of persons with certain common physical characteristics which are hereditarily transmissible.

Residential mobility. The process of movement of people for the purpose of establishing a new residence. It is one of the three basic components of population change.

Rural population. The number of people living in communities smaller than a given size (e.g., 2,500 in the United States) or in areas not classified as urban. It is often broken down into people living on farms and those living in rural nonfarm areas.

Sample household survey. A data-collection mechanism; information is collected from a sampling of households in an area through interviews or questionnaires. Such surveys may be taken periodically and used to provide data during the interval of time between censuses.

Sex ratio. The number of males per hundred females in a population.

Socioeconomic status. A classification of people or groups on the basis of such social and economic variables as their educational level, occupation, income, and housing status.

Stillbirth.   A type of fetal death in which the delivery of a child from its mother results in a dead birth rather than a live birth.

Unemployment.   The situation in which an individual does not have a job but is looking for work during a specified period of time.

Urban population.   The number of people living in communities larger than a given size (e.g., 2,500 or above in the United States) or in areas closely integrated with such places.

Urbanization.   Growth in the number of urban places and/or in the size of populations in such places.

Urbanized area.   A central city of 50,000 or more people and the contiguous densely settled area. It differs from a metropolitan area in that it is composed not of county units but of census enumeration districts. Hence, an urbanized area incorporates only urban population, while a metropolitan area may include rural population within the county boundary.

Vital registration.   A system of recording vital events in a population (typically births, deaths, marriages, and divorces).

Appendix A

U.S. Commission on Population Growth and the American Future:
Compilation of Recommendations

Population Education   In view of the important role that education can play in developing an understanding of the causes and consequences of population growth and distribution, the Commission recommends enactment of a Population Education Act to assist school systems in establishing well-planned population education programs so that present and future generations will be better prepared to meet the challenges arising from population change.

   To implement such a program, the Commission recommends that federal funds be appropriated for teacher training, for curriculum development and materials preparation, for research and evaluation, for the support of model programs, and for assisting state departments of education to develop competence and leadership in population education.

Sex Education   Recognizing the importance of human sexuality, the Commission recommends that sex education be available to all, and that it be presented in a responsible manner through community organizations, the media, and especially the schools.

Child Care   The Commission recommends that both public and private forces join together to assure that adequate child-care services, including health, nutritional, and educational components, are available to families who wish to make use of them.

Because child-care programs represent a major innovation in child-rearing in this country, we recommend that continuing research and evaluation be undertaken to determine the benefits and costs to children, parents, and the public of alternative child-care arrangements.

Children Born Out of Wedlock   The Commission recommends that all children, regardless of the circumstances of their birth, be accorded fair and equal status socially, morally, and legally.

The Commission urges research and study by the American Bar Association, the American Law Institute, and other interested groups leading to revision of those laws and practices which result in discrimination against out-of-wedlock children. Our end objective should be to accord fair and equal treatment to all children.

Adoption   The Commission recommends changes in attitudes and practices to encourage adoption thereby benefiting children, prospective parents, and society.

To implement this goal, the Commission recommends: (1) Further subsidization of families qualified to adopt, but unable to assume the full financial cost of a child's care. (2) A review of current laws, practices, procedures, and regulations which govern the adoptive process.

Equal Rights for Women   The Commission recommends that the Congress and the states approve the proposed Equal Rights Amendment and that federal, state, and local governments undertake positive programs to ensure freedom from discrimination based on sex.

Contraception and the Law   The Commission recommends that: (1) states eliminate existing legal inhibitions and restrictions on access to contraceptive information, procedures, and supplies; and (2) states develop statutes affirming the desirability that all persons have ready and practicable access to contraceptive information, procedures, and supplies.

Contraception and Minors   The Commission recommends that states adopt affirmative legislation which will permit minors to receive contraceptive and prophylactic information and services in appropriate settings sensitive to their needs and concerns.

To implement this policy, the Commission urges that organizations, such as the Council on State Governments, the American Law Institute, and the American Bar Association, formulate appropriate model statutes.

Voluntary Sterilization   In order to permit freedom of choice, the Commission recommends that all administrative restrictions on access to voluntary contraceptive sterilization be eliminated so that the decision be made solely by physician and patient.

To implement this policy, we recommend that national hospital and medical associations, and their state chapters, promote the removal of existing restrictions.

Abortion   With the admonition that abortion not be considered a primary means of fertility control, the Commission recommends that present state laws restricting abortion be liberalized along the lines of the New York statute, such abortion to be performed on request by duly licensed physicians under conditions of medical safety.

In carrying out this policy, the Commission recommends: That federal, state, and local governments make funds available to support abortion services in states with liberalized statutes. That abortion be specifically included in comprehensive health insurance benefits, both public and private.

Methods of Fertility Control   The Commission recommends that this nation give the highest priority to research in reproductive biology and to the search for improved methods by which individuals can control their own fertility.

In order to carry out this research, the Commission recommends that the full $93 million authorized for this purpose in fiscal year 1973 be appropriated and allocated; that federal expenditures for these purposes rise to a minimum of $150 million by 1975; and that private organizations continue and expand their work in this field.

Fertility-Related Health Services   The Commission recommends a national policy and voluntary program to reduce unwanted fertility, to improve the outcome of pregnancy, and to improve the health of children.

In order to carry out such a program, public and private health

financing mechanisms should begin paying the full cost of all health
services related to fertility, including contraceptive, prenatal, delivery, and postpartum services; pediatric care for the first year of life;
voluntary sterilization; safe termination of unwanted pregnancy; and
medical treatment of infertility.

Personnel Training and Delivery of Services   We recommend creation
of programs to (1) train doctors, nurses, and paraprofessionals, including indigenous personnel, in the provision of all fertility-related
health services; (2) develop new patterns for the utilization of professional and paraprofessional personnel; and (3) evaluate improved
methods of organizing the delivery of these services.

Family Planning Services   The Commission recommends: (1) new legislation extending the current family planning project grant program for five years beyond fiscal year 1973 and providing additional
authorizations to reach a federal funding level of $225 million in
fiscal year 1973, $275 million in fiscal year 1974, $325 million in
fiscal year 1975, and $400 million thereafter; (2) extension of the
family planning project grant authority of Title V of the Social Security Act beyond 1972, and maintenance of the level of funding at
approximately $30 million annually; and (3) maintenance of the
Title II OEO program at current levels of authorization.

Services for Teenagers   Toward the goal of reducing unwanted pregnancies and childbearing among the young, the Commission recommends that birth control information and services be made available
to teenagers in appropriate facilities sensitive to their needs and concerns.

The Commission recommends the development and implementation of an adequately financed program to develop appropriate
family planning materials, to conduct training courses for teachers
and school administrators, and to assist states and local communities
in integrating information about family planning into school courses
such as hygiene and sex education.

Population Stabilization   Recognizing that our population cannot grow
indefinitely, and appreciating the advantages of moving now toward

the stabilization of population, the Commission recommends that the nation welcome and plan for a stabilized population.

Illegal Aliens   The Commission recommends that Congress immediately consider the serious situation of illegal immigration and pass legislation which will impose civil and criminal sanctions on employers of illegal border-crossers or aliens in an immigration status in which employment is not authorized.

To implement this policy, the Commission recommends provision of increased and strengthened resources consistent with an effective enforcement program in appropriate agencies.

Immigration   The Commission recommends that immigration levels not be increased and that immigration policy be reviewed periodically to reflect demographic conditions and considerations.

To implement this policy, the Commission recommends that Congress require the Bureau of the Census, in coordination with the Immigration and Naturalization Service, to report biennially to the Congress on the impact of immigration on the nation's demographic situation.

National Distribution and Migration Policies   The Commission recommends that:

The federal government develop a set of national population distribution guidelines to serve as a framework for regional, state, and local plans and development.

Regional, state, and metropolitan-wide governmental authorities take the initiative, in cooperation with local governments, to conduct needed comprehensive planning and action programs to achieve a higher quality of urban development.

The process of population movement be eased and guided in order to improve access or opportunities now restricted by physical remoteness, immobility, and inadequate skills, information, and experience.

Action be taken to increase freedom in choice of residential location through the elimination of current patterns of racial and economic segregation and their attendant injustices.

Guiding Urban Expansion   To anticipate and guide future urban growth, the Commission recommends comprehensive land-use and public-facility planning on an overall metropolitan and regional scale.

The Commission recommends that governments exercise greater control over land-use planning and development.

Racial Minorities and the Poor   To help dissolve the territorial basis of racial polarization, the Commission recommends vigorous and concerted steps to promote free choice of housing within metropolitan areas.

To remove the occupational sources of racial polarization, the Commission recommends the development of more extensive human capital programs to equip black and other deprived minorities for fuller participation in economic life.

To reduce restrictions on the entry of low- and moderate-income people to the suburbs, the Commission recommends that federal and state governments ensure provision of more suburban housing for low- and moderate-income families.

To promote a more racially and economically integrated society, the Commission recommends that actions be taken to reduce the dependence of local jurisdictions on locally collected property taxes.

Depressed Rural Areas   To improve the quality and mobility potential of individuals, the Commission recommends that future programs for declining and chronically depressed rural areas emphasize human resource development.

To enhance the effectiveness of migration, the Commission recommends that programs be developed to provide worker-relocation counseling and assistance to enable an individual to relocate with a minimum of risk and disruption.

To promote the expansion of job opportunities in urban places located within or near declining areas and having a demonstrated potential for future growth, the Commission recommends the development of a growth center strategy.

Institutional Responses   The Commission recommends the establishment of state or regional development corporations which would have the responsibility and the necessary powers to implement comprehensive development plans either as a developer itself or as a catalyst for private development.

Population Statistics and Research   The Commission recommends that the federal government move promptly and boldly to strengthen the basic statistics and research upon which all sound demographic, social, and economic policy must ultimately depend, by implementing the following specific improvements in these programs.

Vital Statistics Data   The Commission recommends that the National Center for Health Statistics improve the timeliness and the quality of data collected with respect to birth, death, marriage, and divorce.

Enumeration of Special Groups   The Commission recommends that the federal government support, even more strongly, the Census Bureau's efforts to improve the completeness of our census enumeration, especially of minority groups, ghetto populations, and all unattached adults, especially males, who are the least well counted.

International Migration   The Commission recommends that a task force be designated under the leadership of the Office of Management and Budget to devise a program for the development of comprehensive immigration and emigration statistics, and to recommend ways in which the records of the periodic alien registrations should be processed to provide information on the distribution and characteristics of aliens in the United States.

The Current Population Survey   The Commission recommends that the government provide substantial additional support to the Current Population Survey to improve the area identification of those interviewed and to permit special studies, utilizing enlarged samples, of demographic trends in special groups of the population.

Statistical Reporting of Family Planning Services   The Commission recommends the rapid development of comprehensive statistics on family planning services.

National Survey of Family Growth   The Commission recommends program support and continued adequate financial support for the

Family Growth Survey as the first condition for evaluating the effectiveness of national population policies and programs.

Distribution of Government Data   The Commission recommends that the various statistical agencies seek to maximize the public usefulness of the basic data by making identity-free tapes available to responsible research agencies.

Mid-Decade Census   The Commission recommends that the decennial census be supplemented by a mid-decade census of the population.

Statistical Use of Administrative Records   The Commission recommends that the government give high priority to studying the ways in which federal administrative records, notably those of the Internal Revenue Service and Social Security Administration, could be made more useful for developing statistical estimates of local population and internal migration.

Intercensal Population Estimates   The Commission recommends that the government provide increased funding, higher priority, and accelerated development for all phases of the Census Bureau's program for developing improved intercensal population estimates for states and local areas.

Social and Behavioral Research   The Commission recommends that substantial increases in federal funds be made available for social and behavioral research related to population growth and distribution, and for the support of nongovernmental population research centers.

Research Program in Population Distribution   The Commission recommends that a research program in population distribution be established, preferably within the proposed Department of Community Development, funded by a small percentage assessment on funds appropriated for relevant federal programs.

Federal Government Population Research   The Commission recommends that the federal government foster the "in-house" research capabilities of its own agencies to provide a coherent institutional structure for improving population research.

Support for Professional Training   The Commission recommends that support for training in the social and behavioral aspects of population be exempted from the general freeze on training funds, permitting government agencies to support programs to train scientists specializing in this field.

Organizational Changes   The Commission recommends that organizational changes be undertaken to improve the federal government's capacity to develop and implement population-related programs; and to evaluate the interaction between public policies, programs, and population trends.

Office of Population Affairs, Department of Health, Education, and Welfare   The Commission recommends that the capacity of the Department of Health, Education, and Welfare in the population field be substantially increased by strengthening the Office of Population Affairs and expanding its staff in order to augment its role of leadership within the Department.

National Institute of Population Sciences   The Commission recommends the establishment, within the National Institutes of Health, of a National Institute of Population Sciences to provide an adequate institutional framework for implementing a greatly expanded program of population research.

Department of Community Development   The Commission recommends that Congress adopt legislation to establish a Department of Community Development and that this Department undertake a program of research on the interactions of population growth and distribution and the programs it administers.

Office of Population Growth and Distribution   The Commission recommends the creation of an Office of Population Growth and Distribution within the Executive Office of the President.

The Commission recommends the immediate addition of personnel with demographic expertise to the staffs of the Council of Economic Advisers, the Domestic Council, the Council on Environmental Quality, and the Office of Science and Technology.

Council of Social Advisers   The Commission recommends that Congress approve pending legislation establishing a Council of Social Advisers and that this Council have as one of its main functions the monitoring of demographic variables.

Joint Committee on Population   In order to provide improved legislative oversight of population issues, the Commission recommends that Congress assign to a joint committee responsibility for specific review of this area.

State Population Agencies and Commissions   The Commission recommends that state governments, either through existing planning agencies or through new agencies devoted to this purpose, give greater attention to problems of population growth and distribution.

Private Efforts and Population Policy   The Commission recommends that a substantially greater effort focusing on policy-oriented research and analysis of population in the United States be carried forward through appropriate private resources and agencies.

Source: U. S. Commission on Population Growth and the American Future, *Population and the American Future*, U. S. Government Printing Office, Washington, 1972, pp. 141–147.

Appendix B

1975 World Population Data Sheet
of the Population Reference Bureau, Inc.*

Prepared by Paul F. Myers, Former Chief, Foreign Demographic Analysis Division, U. S. Department of Commerce, in collaboration with Leon F. Bouvier, Research Director, PRB, and James R. Echols, Former President, PRB.

Except as noted, this *Data Sheet* is based primarily on unpublished United Nations (UN) figures. While expressing its deep gratitude to the UN's Population Division for these data, the PRB assumes all responsibility for the accuracy of the figures given in the *Data Sheet*.

The publication was prepared with support from the George Washington University Population Information Program.

The Population Reference Bureau gathers, interprets, and publishes information about population trends and their economic, environmental, and social effects. Founded in 1929, it is a private, nonprofit educational organization that is supported by foundation grants, individual and corporate contributions, memberships, and subscriptions. It consults with other groups in the United States and abroad and operates an information service, a library, and an international program.

Source: Population Reference Bureau, Inc., *1975 World Population Data Sheet*, Washington, D.C., March 1975.

* Nam/Gustavus note: Some of the data presented in the following table may not correspond to comparable figures for recent years presented in the chapter texts. This is because certain data are shown in the table as based on 1970–1975 averages, whereas the same kind of information in the text is reported for a single year (such as 1973). These data should, therefore, be regarded as illustrative rather than as precise indications of current demographic phenomena.

Region or Country[1]	Population Estimate Mid-1975 (millions)[2]	Birth Rate[2,3] (1970–75 avg.)	Death Rate[2] (1970–75 avg.)	Rate of Population Growth (annual, percent)[2,4] (1970–75 avg.)	Number of Years to Double Population[5]	Population Projection to 2000 (millions)[2]	Infant Mortality Rate[6]	Population under 15 Years (percent)[2] (mid-1975)	Median Age (years)[2]	Life Expectancy at Birth (years)[2] (1970–75 avg.)	Dietary Energy Supply (kilocalories per person per day)[7]	Per Capita Gross National Product (US$)[8]
WORLD	3,967	31.5	12.8	1.9	36	6,253	98	36	22.4	55	2,470	940
AFRICA	401	46.3	19.8	2.6	27	813	156	44	17.8	45	2,250	240
Northern Africa	98	43.3	15.2	2.7	26	192	126	44	17.7	52	2,240	300
Algeria	16.8	48.7	15.4	3.2	22	36.7	(128)	48	16.0	53	1,730	430
Egypt	37.5	37.8	14.0	2.4	29	64.6	103	41	19.4	52	2,500	240
Libya	2.3	45.0	14.8	3.0	23	4.7	(130)	44	17.8	53	2,570	1,830
Morocco	17.5	46.2	15.7	2.9	24	35.9	149	47	16.4	53	2,220	270
Sudan	18.3	47.8	17.5	3.0	23	39.0	(141)	45	17.2	49	2,160	120
Tunisia	5.7	40.0	13.8	2.2	32	10.9	(128)	44	17.4	54	2,250	380
Western Africa	115	48.7	23.0	2.6	27	238	178	45	17.6	41	2,200	150
Cape Verde Islands	0.3	32.8	13.7	1.9	36	0.4	91	44	17.7	50	—	180
Dahomey	3.1	49.9	23.0	2.7	26	5.9	(185)	45	17.3	41	2,260	110
Gambia	0.5	43.3	24.1	1.9	36	0.9	(165)	41	19.8	40	2,490	140
Ghana	9.9	48.8	21.9	2.7	26	21.2	156	48	16.2	44	2,320	300
Guinea	4.4	46.6	22.9	2.4	29	8.5	216	43	18.5	41	2,200	90
Guinea-Bissau	0.5	40.1	25.1	1.5	46	0.8	(208)	37	22.1	38	—	250

Ivory Coast	4.9	45.6	20.6	2.5	28	9.6	(164)	43	18.5	44	2,430	340
Liberia	1.7	43.6	20.7	2.3	30	3.2	159	41	19.4	44	2,170	250
Mali	5.7	50.1	25.9	2.4	29	11.3	(188)	44	18.0	38	2,060	70
Mauritania	1.3	44.8	24.9	2.0	35	2.3	189	42	19.0	38	1,970	180
Niger	4.6	52.2	25.5	2.7	26	9.6	200	46	17.2	38	2,080	90
Nigeria	62.9	49.3	22.7	2.7	26	134.9	(180)	45	17.4	41	2,270	130
Senegal	4.4	47.6	23.9	2.4	29	8.2	(159)	43	18.3	40	2,370	260
Sierra Leone	3.0	44.7	20.7	2.4	29	5.7	136	43	18.6	44	2,280	190
Togo	2.2	50.6	23.5	2.7	26	4.6	(179)	46	17.2	41	2,330	160
Upper Volta	6.0	48.5	25.8	2.3	30	11.0	182	43	18.3	38	1,710	70
Eastern Africa	114	48.1	20.7	2.7	26	240	160	45	17.5	44	2,240	160
Burundi	3.8	48.0	24.7	2.3	30	7.3	150	44	18.4	39	2,040	70
Comoro Islands	0.3	46.6	21.7	2.5	28	0.5	(160)	43	18.4	42	—	140
Ethiopia	28.0	49.4	25.8	2.4	29	53.7	(181)	44	18.2	38	2,160	80
Kenya	13.3	48.7	16.0	3.3	21	31.0	(135)	46	16.7	50	2,360	170
Malagasy Republic	8.0	50.2	21.1	2.9	24	17.8	(170)	45	17.3	44	2,530	140
Malawi	4.9	47.7	23.7	2.4	29	9.5	148	45	17.5	41	2,210	100
Mauritius	0.9	24.4	6.8	1.8	38	1.3	65	37	20.5	66	2,360	300
Mozambique	9.2	43.1	20.1	2.3	30	17.6	(165)	43	18.8	44	2,050	300
Reunion	0.5	31.2	8.5	2.3	30	0.7	—	43	18.6	63	—	950
Rhodesia	6.3	47.9	14.4	3.4	20	15.1	122	48	16.1	52	2,660	340
Rwanda	4.2	50.0	23.6	2.6	27	8.7	133	44	17.8	41	1,960	60
Somalia	3.2	47.2	21.7	2.6	27	6.5	(177)	45	17.2	41	1,830	80
Tanzania	15.4	50.2	20.1	3.0	23	34.0	162	47	16.6	44	2,260	120
Uganda	11.4	45.2	15.9	2.9	24	24.2	160	44	17.7	50	2,130	150
Zambia	5.0	51.5	20.5	3.1	22	11.6	(157)	48	16.2	44	2,590	380
Middle Africa	45	44.4	21.7	2.3	30	88	165	43	18.6	42	2,120	170

Region or Country[1]	Per Capita Gross National Product (US$)[8]	Dietary Energy Supply (kilocalories per person per day)[7]	Life Expectancy at Birth (years)[2] (1970–75 avg.)	Median Age (years)[2]	Population under 15 Years (percent)[2] (mid-1975)	Infant Mortality Rate[6]	Population Projection to 2000 (millions)[2]	Number of Years to Double Population[5]	Rate of Population Growth (annual, percent)[2,4] (1970–75 avg.)	Death Rate[2] (1970–75 avg.)	Birth Rate[2,3] (1970–75 avg.)	Population Estimate Mid-1975 (millions)[2]
Angola	390	2,000	38	18.8	42	(203)	12.5	30	2.3	24.5	47.3	6.4
Cameroon	200	2,410	41	19.6	40	137	11.6	38	1.8	22.0	40.4	6.4
Central Africa Republic	160	2,200	41	19.0	42	190	3.4	33	2.1	22.5	43.4	1.8
Chad	80	2,110	38	19.4	40	160	6.9	35	2.0	24.0	44.0	4.0
Congo (People's Rep. of)	290	2,260	44	18.8	42	180	2.7	29	2.4	20.8	45.1	1.3
Equatorial Guinea	—	—	44	23.3	37	(165)	0.5	41	1.7	19.7	36.8	0.3
Gabon	240	2,220	41	29.8	32	229	0.7	69	1.0	22.2	32.2	0.5
Zaire	880	2,060	44	17.8	44	(160)	49.4	28	2.5	20.5	45.2	24.5
Southern Africa	100	2,720	51	19.1	41	121	56	26	2.7	16.2	43.0	28
Botswana	790	2,040	44	16.7	46	(97)	1.4	30	2.3	23.0	45.6	0.7
Lesotho	240	—	46	21.1	38	181	2.0	36	1.9	19.7	39.0	1.1
Namibia	90	—	41	19.7	41	(177)	1.3	32	2.2	23.2	45.5	0.7
South Africa	850	2,740	52	19.2	41	(117)	50.0	26	2.7	15.5	42.9	24.7
Swaziland	260	—	44	16.7	46	(149)	0.9	26	2.7	21.8	49.0	0.5
ASIA	270	2,160	54	20.8	38	102	3,636	33	2.1	13.6	34.9	2,255
Southwest Asia	510	2,760	54	18.4	43	112	174	25	2.8	14.3	42.8	88

Bahrain	0.3	49.6	18.7	3.1	22	0.5	(138)	(45)	—	47	—	640
Cyprus	0.7	22.2	6.8	1.2	58	0.8	33	30	25.3	71	2,670	1,180
Gaza	0.6	49.6	18.7	3.4	20	1.3	—	(50)	—	—	—	—
Iraq	11.1	48.1	14.6	3.4	20	24.4	(99)	47	16.6	53	2,160	370
Israel	3.4	26.5	6.7	2.9	24	5.6	21	33	24.2	71	2,960	2,610
Jordan	2.7	47.6	14.7	3.3	21	5.9	(99)	46	16.8	53	2,430	270
Kuwait	1.1	47.1	5.3	7.1	10	3.2	44	47	16.6	67	—	4,090
Lebanon	2.9	39.8	9.9	3.0	23	6.1	(59)	43	18.1	63	2,280	700
Oman	0.8	49.6	18.7	3.1	22	1.6	(138)	(45)	—	(47)	—	530
Qatar	0.1	49.6	18.7	3.1	22	0.2	(138)	(45)	—	(47)	—	2,590
Saudi Arabia	9.0	49.5	20.2	2.9	24	18.6	(152)	45	17.6	45	2,270	520
Syria	7.3	45.4	15.4	3.0	23	15.8	(93)	45	17.2	54	2,650	310
Turkey	39.9	39.4	12.5	2.5	28	72.6	(119)	42	19.0	57	3,250	370
United Arab Emirates	0.2	49.6	18.7	3.1	22	0.5	(138)	(45)	—	(47)	—	3,220
Yemen Arab Republic	6.7	49.6	20.6	2.9	24	13.8	(152)	45	17.6	45	2,040	90
Yemen, People's Republic of	1.7	49.6	20.6	2.9	24	3.4	(152)	45	17.6	45	2,070	120
Middle South Asia	838	41.7	17.0	2.4	29	1,501	138	43	18.3	48	2,070	120
Afghanistan	19.3	49.2	23.8	2.5	28	36.7	(182)	44	17.9	40	1,970	80
Bangladesh	73.7	49.5	28.1	1.7	41	144.3	(132)	46	16.7	36	1,840	70
Bhutan	1.2	43.6	20.5	2.3	30	2.1	—	42	18.9	44	—	80
India	613.2	39.9	15.7	2.4	29	1,059.4	139	42	18.8	50	2,070	110
Iran	32.9	45.3	15.6	3.0	23	66.6	(139)	46	17.0	51	2,300	490
Maldive Islands	0.1	(46)	(23)	2.0	35	0.2	—	(44)	—	—	—	90
Nepal	12.6	42.9	20.3	2.2	32	23.2	(169)	42	18.8	44	2,080	80
Pakistan	70.6	47.4	16.5	3.1	22	146.9	(132)	46	16.6	50	2,160	130
Sikkim	0.2	(48)	(29)	2.0	35	0.4	208	(40)	—	—	—	80
Sri Lanka	14.0	28.6	6.4	2.2	32	21.3	45	39	19.9	68	2,170	110

Region or Country[1]	Population Estimate Mid-1975 (millions)[2]	Birth Rate[2,3] (1970–75 avg.)	Death Rate[2] (1970–75 avg.)	Rate of Population Growth (annual, percent)[2,4] (1970–75 avg.)	Number of Years to Double Population[5]	Population Projection to 2000 (millions)[2]	Infant Mortality Rate[6]	Population under 15 Years (percent)[2] (mid-1975)	Median Age (years)[2]	Life Expectancy at Birth (years)[2] (1970–75 avg.)	Dietary Energy Supply (kilocalories per person per day)[7]	Per Capita Gross National Product (US$)[8]
Southeast Asia	**324**	**42.4**	**15.4**	**2.7**	**26**	**592**	**106**	**44**	**18.0**	**51**	**2,070**	**150**
Burma	31.2	39.5	15.8	2.4	29	54.9	(126)	41	19.6	50	2,210	90
Indonesia	136.0	42.9	16.9	2.6	27	237.5	125	44	18.0	48	1,790	90
Khmer Republic	8.1	46.7	19.0	2.8	25	15.8	127	45	17.2	45	2,430	120
Laos	3.3	44.6	22.8	2.2	32	5.7	(123)	42	18.9	40	2,110	130
Malaysia	12.1	38.7	9.9	2.9	24	22.1	(75)	44	17.7	59	2,460	430
Philippines	44.4	43.8	10.5	3.3	21	89.7	(78)	46	17.0	58	1,940	220
Portuguese Timor	0.7	44.3	23.0	2.1	33	1.1	(184)	42	18.9	40	—	110
Singapore	2.2	21.2	5.2	1.6	43	3.1	20	33	22.1	70	—	1,300
Thailand	42.1	43.4	10.8	3.3	21	85.6	(65)	46	16.9	58	2,560	220
Vietnam (Dem. Republic of)	23.8	41.4	17.9	2.4	29	43.1	—	41	19.1	48	2,350	100
Vietnam (Republic of)	19.7	41.7	23.6	1.8	38	32.7	—	41	19.3	40	2,320	170
East Asia[9]	**1,006**	**26.2**	**9.8**	**1.6**	**43**	**1,369**	**50**	**33**	**24.0**	**62**	**2,220**	**420**
China (People's Republic of)	822.8	26.9	10.3	1.7	41	1,126.2	(55)	33	23.5	62	2,170	160
Hong Kong	4.2	19.4	5.5	1.4	50	5.6	17	32	23.2	70	—	980
Japan	111.1	19.2	6.6	1.3	53	132.9	12	24	30.4	73	2,510	2,320

338

Korea (Dem. People's Republic of)	15.9	35.7	9.4	2.6	27	27.5	—	42	18.6	61	2,240	310
Korea (Republic of)	33.9	28.7	8.8	2.0	35	52.0	(60)	37	20.4	61	2,520	310
Macau	0.3	(31)	(8)	1.7	41	0.4	(78)	(38)	—	(58)	—	150
Mongolia	1.4	38.8	9.4	3.0	23	2.7	—	44	18.1	61	2,380	380
Taiwan (Rep. of China)	16.0	(24)	(5)	1.9	36	21.8	(28)	(39)	—	(69)	—	490
NORTH AMERICA	**237**	**16.5**	**9.3**	**0.9**	**77**	**296**	**18**	**25**	**28.5**	**71**	**3,320**	**5,480**
Canada	22.8	18.6	7.7	1.3	53	31.6	17	27	27.2	72	3,180	4,440
United States[10]	213.9	16.2	9.4	0.9	77	264.4	18	25	28.6	71	3,330	5,590
LATIN AMERICA	**324**	**36.9**	**9.2**	**2.7**	**26**	**620**	**79**	**42**	**18.8**	**61**	**2,530**	**650**
Middle America	**79**	**42.2**	**9.4**	**3.2**	**22**	**173**	**66**	**46**	**17.0**	**62**	**2,490**	**670**
Costa Rica	2.0	33.4	5.9	2.8	25	3.7	54	42	18.2	68	2,610	630
El Salvador	4.1	42.2	11.1	3.1	22	8.8	58	46	16.6	58	1,930	340
Guatemala	6.1	42.8	13.7	2.9	24	12.4	79	44	17.6	53	2,130	420
Honduras	3.0	49.3	14.6	3.5	20	6.9	(115)	47	16.6	54	2,140	320
Mexico	59.2	42.0	8.6	3.2	22	132.2	61	46	16.9	63	2,580	740
Nicaragua	2.3	48.3	13.9	3.3	21	5.2	(123)	48	15.7	53	2,450	470
Panama	1.7	36.2	7.2	2.8	25	3.2	(47)	43	18.4	66	2,580	880
Caribbean	**27**	**32.8**	**9.2**	**1.9**	**36**	**45**	**69**	**41**	**19.4**	**63**	**2,320**	**680**
Bahamas	0.2	23.8	5.7	2.8	25	0.3	33	(44)	—	—	—	2,400
Barbados	0.2	21.6	8.9	0.5	139	0.3	31	34	22.3	69	—	930
Cuba	9.5	29.1	6.6	2.0	35	15.3	25	38	22.0	70	2,700	510
Dominican Republic	5.1	45.8	11.0	3.3	21	11.8	(98)	48	15.9	58	2,120	470
Granada	0.1	27.9	7.8	0.4	173	0.1	34	(47)	—	(69)	—	330
Guadeloupe	0.4	29.3	6.4	1.6	43	0.5	(46)	40	19.1	69	—	840
Haiti	4.6	35.8	16.5	1.4	50	7.0	(150)	40	19.3	50	1,730	130
Jamaica	2.0	33.2	7.1	1.5	46	2.7	26	46	16.7	70	2,360	810
Martinique	0.4	29.7	6.7	1.4	50	0.5	32	41	19.0	69	—	970

Region or Country[1]	Population Estimate Mid-1975 (millions)[2]	Birth Rate[2,3] (1970–75 avg.)	Death Rate[2] (1970–75 avg.)	Rate of Population Growth (annual, percent)[2,4] (1970–75 avg.)	Number of Years to Double Population[5]	Population Projection to 2000 (millions)[2]	Infant Mortality Rate[6]	Population under 15 Years (percent)[2] (mid-1975)	Median Age (years)[2]	Life Expectancy at Birth (years)[2] (1970–75 avg.)	Dietary Energy Supply (kilocalories per person per day)[7]	Per Capita Gross National Product (US$)[8]
Netherlands Antilles	0.2	19.7	4.7	1.7	41	0.4	(25)	(38)	—	(74)	—	1,440
Puerto Rico	2.9	22.6	6.8	1.1	63	3.7	27	34	22.6	72	—	2,050
Trinidad & Tobago	1.0	25.3	5.9	1.1	63	1.3	(35)	39	19.6	70	2,380	970
Tropical South America	**180**	**38.3**	**9.2**	**2.9**	**24**	**351**	**90**	**43**	**18.2**	**60**	**2,470**	**530**
Bolivia	5.4	43.7	18.0	2.5	28	10.3	(108)	43	18.4	47	1,900	200
Brazil	109.7	37.1	8.8	2.8	25	212.5	(94)	42	18.8	61	2,620	530
Colombia	25.9	40.6	8.8	3.2	22	51.5	(76)	46	16.9	61	2,200	400
Ecuador	7.1	41.8	9.5	3.2	22	14.8	78	46	16.8	60	2,010	360
Guyana	0.8	32.4	5.9	2.2	32	1.3	40	44	17.5	68	2,390	400
Paraguay	2.6	39.8	8.9	2.8	25	5.3	(84)	45	17.2	62	2,740	320
Peru	15.3	41.0	11.9	2.9	24	30.6	(110)	44	17.8	56	2,320	520
Surinam	0.4	41.6	7.5	2.6	27	0.9	30	50	15.1	66	2,450	810
Venezuela	12.2	36.1	7.1	2.9	24	23.6	50	44	17.4	65	2,430	1,240
Temperate South America	**39**	**23.3**	**8.9**	**1.4**	**50**	**52**	**62**	**30**	**26.2**	**66**	**2,940**	**1,120**
Argentina	25.4	21.8	8.8	1.3	53	32.9	60	28	27.9	68	3,060	1,290
Chile	10.3	27.9	9.2	1.8	38	15.4	71	36	21.9	63	2,670	800

Uruguay	3.1	20.4	9.3	1.0	69	3.9	40	28	29.1	70	2,880	760
EUROPE	**473**	**16.1**	**10.4**	**0.6**	**116**	**540**	**24**	**24**	**32.4**	**71**	**3,150**	**2,380**
Northern Europe	**82**	**15.8**	**11.2**	**0.4**	**173**	**91**	**16**	**24**	**33.1**	**72**	**3,140**	**2,870**
Denmark	5.0	14.0	10.1	0.4	173	5.4	14	22	33.2	74	3,240	3,670
Finland	4.7	13.2	9.3	0.2	347	4.7	10	22	31.0	70	3,050	2,810
Iceland	0.2	19.3	7.7	1.2	58	0.3	12	29	25.7	74	—	2,800
Ireland	3.1	22.1	10.4	1.2	58	4.0	18	30	26.5	72	3,410	1,580
Norway	4.0	16.7	10.1	0.7	99	4.5	13	24	32.4	74	2,960	3,340
Sweden	8.3	14.2	10.5	0.6	116	9.4	10	21	35.0	73	2,810	4,480
United Kingdom	56.4	16.1	11.7	0.3	231	62.8	18	24	33.4	72	3,190	2,600
Western Europe	**153**	**14.6**	**11.1**	**0.6**	**116**	**171**	**18**	**23**	**33.5**	**72**	**3,230**	**3,380**
Austria	7.5	14.7	12.2	0.2	347	8.1	24	24	33.9	71	3,310	2,410
Belgium	9.8	14.8	11.2	0.4	173	10.8	17	23	34.3	73	3,380	3,210
France	52.9	17.0	10.6	0.9	77	62.1	16	24	31.6	73	3,210	3,620
Germany (Federal Republic of)	61.9	12.0	12.1	0.3	231	66.2	20	22	35.5	71	3,220	3,390
Luxembourg	0.3	13.5	11.7	0.2	347	0.4	16	21	36.0	71	3,380	3,190
Netherlands	13.6	16.8	8.7	0.8	87	16.0	12	26	29.4	74	3,320	2,840
Switzerland	6.5	14.7	10.0	0.8	87	7.4	13	23	32.9	72	3,190	3,940
Eastern Europe	**106**	**16.6**	**10.2**	**0.6**	**116**	**122**	**29**	**23**	**31.6**	**70**	**3,240**	**1,410**
Bulgaria	8.8	16.2	9.2	0.7	99	10.0	26	22	33.7	72	3,290	820
Czechoslovakia	14.8	17.0	11.2	0.6	116	16.8	21	23	31.9	69	3,180	2,120
Germany (Dem. Republic of)	17.2	13.9	12.4	0.2	347	18.2	18	22	35.3	73	3,290	2,190
Hungary	10.5	15.3	11.5	0.4	173	11.1	34	20	34.4	70	3,280	1,200
Poland	33.8	16.8	8.6	0.8	87	39.8	28	24	28.8	70	3,280	1,350
Romania	21.2	19.3	10.3	0.9	77	25.8	40	25	30.8	67	3,140	740
Southern Europe	**132**	**17.7**	**9.2**	**0.7**	**99**	**156**	**29**	**26**	**31.4**	**71**	**2,990**	**1,440**
Albania	2.5	33.4	6.5	2.7	26	4.3	87	41	19.2	69	2,390	480

341

Region or Country[1]	Population Estimate Mid-1975 (millions)[2]	Birth Rate[2,3] (1970–75 avg.)	Death Rate[2] (1970–75 avg.)	Rate of Population Growth (annual, percent)[2,4] (1970–75 avg.)	Number of Years to Double Population[5]	Population Projection to 2000 (millions)[2]	Infant Mortality Rate[6]	Population under 15 Years (percent)[2] (mid-1975)	Median Age (years)[2]	Life Expectancy at Birth (years)[2] (1970–75 avg.)	Dietary Energy Supply (kilocalories per person per day)[7]	Per Capita Gross National Product (US$)[8]
Greece	8.9	15.4	9.4	0.3	231	9.6	27	23	34.5	72	3,190	1,460
Italy	55.0	16.0	9.8	0.5	139	60.9	26	24	33.4	72	3,180	1,960
Malta	0.3	17.5	9.0	0.2	347	0.3	24	25	28.2	71	2,820	950
Portugal	8.8	18.4	10.1	0.3	231	9.9	44	27	30.0	68	2,900	780
Spain	35.4	19.5	8.3	1.0	69	44.9	15	27	30.3	72	2,600	1,210
Yugoslavia	21.3	18.2	9.2	0.9	77	25.7	43	26	29.0	68	3,190	810
USSR	255	17.8	7.9	1.0	69	315	26	36	22.3	70	3,280	1,400
OCEANIA	21	24.8	9.3	2.0	35	33	50	31	25.4	66	3,270	2,480
Australia	13.8	21.0	8.1	1.9	36	20.2	17	28	27.6	72	3,280	2,980
Fiji	0.6	25.0	4.3	2.1	33	0.8	26	38	19.8	70	—	500
New Zealand	3.0	22.3	8.3	1.4	50	4.3	16	30	25.9	72	3,200	2,560
Papua-New Guinea	2.7	40.6	17.1	2.4	29	5.0	(159)	42	18.9	48	—	290

General Notes

World Population Data Sheets of various years should not be used as a time series. Because every attempt is made to use the most accurate information, data sources vary and radical changes in numbers and rates from year to year may reflect improved source material, revised data, or a later base year for computation, rather than yearly changes. The only exception to this general caution is that population totals for mid-1975 along with those for mid-1974 presented in the supplement to this *Data Sheet* may be used as a time series.

Birth and death rates: Annual number of births or deaths per 1,000 population.

Population growth rate: Annual rate of natural increase (birth rate minus the death rate in a given year) combined with the plus or minus factor of net immigration or net emigration.

Infant mortality rate: Annual number of deaths to infants under one year of age per 1,000 live births.

Median age: That age which divides the population into two equal-size groups, one of which is older and the other which is younger than the median.

Figures in parentheses are from U. S. Bureau of the Census, *World Population: 1973 — Recent Demographic Estimates for the Countries and Regions of the World,* May 1974. The figures from this source generally were presented here if no equivalent figures are available from the UN or its publications.

Figures for the regions and the world: Population totals take into account small areas not listed on the *Data Sheet.* Totals may also not equal the sums of their parts because of independent rounding. Infant mortality, dietary energy supply, and per capita gross national product are weighted averages of the figures shown.

Dashes indicate data are unavailable.

Footnotes

1 The *Data Sheet* lists all UN members and all geopolitical entities with a population larger than 200,000.

2 Unpublished materials from the Population Division of the UN. These data are from the recently completed "medium variant" set of projections and are to be published in a series of working papers under the general title *World Population Prospects, 1970–2000, As Assessed in 1973.* Birth and death rates, annual rate of population growth, and life expectancy at birth refer to the average of the 1970–75 period; the percentage of the population under 15 years and median age refer to mid-1975.

3 Presumably because of recent fertility declines, current birth rates for many countries, and especially those for Canada, the United States, Finland, Norway, the United Kingdom, Austria, Belgium, the two Germanies, Luxembourg, the Netherlands, Switzerland, Australia, and New Zealand are appreciably lower than those given here for the average of the 1970–75 period.

4 Differences between the values in this column and those for natural increase represent the assumptions made by the UN regarding net immigration or net emigration for the 1970–75 period. The countries assumed to have the highest rates of net immigration are Kuwait, Israel, Australia, the Federal Republic of Germany, and Switzerland. Those assumed to have the highest rates of net emigration are Puerto Rico, Jamaica, Martinique, Trinidad and Tobago, and Surinam.

5 Assuming no change in the growth rate.

6 Latest available year as given in UN, *Population and Vital Statistics Report,* Series A, V. 26, No. 4, 1974. Because of deficient registration in some countries, rates estimated by the UN were used where the registered rates were unrealistically low.

7 UN World Food Conference, *Assessment of the World Food Situation Present and Future,* Rome, Italy, November 5–16, 1974.

8 International Bank for Reconstruction and Development, 1971 or 1972 data.

9 The United Nations does not show figures for Taiwan. These figures were separately estimated. The population of Taiwan was assumed to increase during the next 25 years at the same rates as for the People's Republic of China. The infant mortality rate was estimated by the International Statistical Programs Center of the U. S. Bureau of the Census and will appear in its forthcoming publication *World Population: 1974 — Recent Demographic Estimates for the Countries and Regions of the World.*

10 UN figures are the same as those given for the Series E projection in the U. S. Bureau of the Census, "Projections of the Population of the United States, by Age and Sex: 1972 to 2020, *Current Population Reports,* Series P-25, No. 493, December 1972.

World Population Estimates Mid-1974 (millions) for
160 Countries of the Population Reference Bureau
(A Supplement to 1975 World Population Data Sheet)

WORLD	**3,893**	Comoro Islands	0.3
		Ethiopia	27.3
		Kenya	12.8
AFRICA	**391**	Malagasy Republic	7.8
		Malawi	4.8
Northern Africa	**96**	Mauritius	0.9
Algeria	16.3	Mozambique	9.0
Egypt	36.7	Reunion	0.5
Libya	2.2	Rhodesia	6.1
Morocco	17.0	Rwanda	4.1
Sudan	17.7	Somalia	3.1
Tunisia	5.6	Tanzania	15.0
		Uganda	11.0
Western Africa	**113**	Zambia	4.9
Cape Verde Islands	0.3		
Dahomey	3.0		
Gambia	0.5	**Middle Africa**	**44**
Ghana	9.6	Angola	6.2
Guinea	4.3	Cameroon	6.3
Guinea-Bissau	0.5	Central African Republic	1.8
Ivory Coast	4.8	Chad	3.9
Liberia	1.7	Congo (People's Rep. of)	1.3
Mali	5.6	Equatorial Guinea	0.3
Mauritania	1.3	Gabon	0.5
Niger	4.5	Zaire	23.9
Nigeria	61.3		
Senegal	4.3		
Sierra Leone	2.9	**Southern Africa**	**27**
Togo	2.2	Botswana	0.7
Upper Volta	5.9	Lesotho	1.1
		Namibia	0.7
Eastern Africa	**111**	South Africa	24.0
Burundi	3.7	Swaziland	0.5

ASIA   2,208

Southwest Asia   86
Bahrain   0.2
Cyprus   0.7
Gaza   0.6
Iraq   10.7
Israel   3.3
Jordan   2.6
Kuwait   1.0
Lebanon   2.8
Oman   0.7
Qatar   0.1
Saudi Arabia   8.7
Syria   7.0
Turkey   38.9
United Arab Emirates   0.2
Yemen Arab Republic   6.5
Yemen, Peoples Rep. of   1.6

Middle South Asia   818
Afghanistan   18.8
Bangladesh   72.5
Bhutan   1.1
India   598.7
Iran   32.0
Maldive Islands   0.1
Nepal   12.3
Pakistan   68.4
Sikkim   0.2
Sri Lanka   13.7

Southeast Asia   315
Burma   30.5
Indonesia   132.6

Khmer Republic   7.9
Laos   3.2
Malaysia   11.8
Philippines   43.0
Portuguese Timor   0.7
Singapore   2.2
Thailand   40.8
Vietnam (Dem. Rep. of)   23.2
Vietnam (Republic of)   19.3

East Asia   989
China (People's Rep. of)   809.4
Hong Kong   4.2
Japan   109.7
Korea (Dem. P'ple's Rep. of)   15.4
Korea (Republic of)   33.3
Macao   0.3
Mongolia   1.4
Taiwan (Rep. of China)   15.7

NORTH AMERICA   235

Canada   22.5
United States   211.9

LATIN AMERICA   316

Middle America   76
Costa Rica   1.9
El Salvador   4.0
Guatemala   6.0
Honduras   2.9
Mexico   57.3
Nicaragua   2.2
Panama   1.6

LATIN AMERICA (*cont.*)

Caribbean   27
Bahamas   0.2
Barbados   0.2
Cuba   9.3
Dominican Republic   5.0
Granada   0.1
Guadeloupe   0.3
Haiti   4.5
Jamaica   2.0
Martinique   0.4
Netherlands Antilles   0.2
Puerto Rico   2.9
Trinidad & Tobago   1.0

Tropical South America   175
Bolivia   5.3
Brazil   106.7
Colombia   25.1
Ecuador   6.9
Guyana   0.8
Paraguay   2.6
Peru   14.9
Surinam   0.4
Venezuela   11.9

Temperate South America   38
Argentina   25.1
Chile   10.1
Uruguay   3.1

EUROPE   469

Northern Europe   81
Denmark   5.0

Finland   4.6
Iceland   0.2
Ireland   3.1
Norway   4.0
Sweden   8.2
United Kingdom   56.2

Western Europe   152
Austria   7.5
Belgium   9.8
France   52.5
Germany (Federal Rep. of) 61.5
Luxembourg   0.3
Netherlands   13.5
Switzerland   6.5

Eastern Europe   106
Bulgaria   8.7
Czechoslovakia   14.7
Germany (Dem. Rep. of)   17.2
Hungary   10.5
Poland   33.6
Rumania   21.0

Southern Europe   131
Albania   2.4
Greece   8.9
Italy   54.7
Malta   0.3
Portugal   8.7
Spain   35.1
Yugoslavia   21.1

USSR   253

OCEANIA 21

Australia	13.6	New Zealand	3.0
Fiji	0.6	Papua-New Guinea	2.7

Based on interpolation of the mid-1970 population estimate and the mid-1975 "medium variant" projection by the United Nations using the projected rate of growths for the 1970–75 period. These UN figures are to be published under the general title *World Popula-* *tion Prospects, 1970–2000, As Assessed in 1973.*

Population totals for the regions and the world take into account small areas not listed. They may not equal the sum of their parts because of independent rounding.

Index